BOOKS BY

ALEXANDER CAMPBELL

THE HEART OF JAPAN
(1961)

THE HEART OF INDIA
(1958)

THE HEART OF AFRICA
(1954)

These are BORZOI BOOKS,
published in New York by ALFRED A. KNOPF

THE HEART OF JAPAN

THE
Heart
OF
JAPAN

Alexander Campbell

1 9 6 1

ALFRED · A · KNOPF : New York

L. C. catalog card number: 61–15041

THIS IS A BORZOI BOOK,

PUBLISHED BY ALFRED A. KNOPF, INC.

FIRST EDITION

CONTENTS

THE HEART OF JAPAN

I

TOKYO:

THE BIGGEST CITY IN THE WORLD

*Here is an over-populated island, full of
well-washed poetic inhabitants*
STEPHEN SPENDER

NEAR WHERE we lived in Hata-Yuguri there was a "hotel for
couples." Everyone said it was a crying scandal that such a place
should exist in a respectable residential district. But nobody
did anything about it.

The "hotel for couples" had opened up right after the Anti-
Prostitution Law shut down the licensed brothels of Yoshiwara, on the other side of town. The night the brothels closed,
the Yoshiwara girls rose from their floor cushions at the stroke
of midnight and, holding hands with customers who were
weeping unashamedly, softly sang "Auld Lang Syne." The
Japanese have adopted this Scottish air—it is played by ships
leaving harbor, and by department stores at closing time—but
have put their own words to it:

*Snow on the window sill
Quickly follows the firefly's summer light;
Time passes before we know it—
Today we open our hearts to bid one another farewell.*

Those present that night say solemnly that to hear those words
sung in the ancient whorehouses of Yoshiwara was an unfor-
gettable experience.

In Hata-Yuguri the day began when in the temple compound
behind our house, at sunrise, an athletic Buddhist priest in a

3

yellow robe briskly swung a heavy wooden beam, hanging in chains, against a great bronze bell. Soon after, the public-address system of the neighborhood elementary school started playing loud music that could be heard several blocks away.

Stopping only to bow to passing schoolchildren, the shop-keepers in the narrow lanes scrubbed earnestly at their wooden floors and counters. Then they sat cross-legged on their straw mats, behind mounds of fresh peaches and giant strawberries and amid wooden barrels and buckets overflowing with fresh and pickled fish, to sip green tea and watch television.

All day there was a constant brisk coming and going of messenger boys on bicycles who magically balanced trays of food, and of loudly hooting trucks and motorcars that seemed determined to run them down. At night it was usually quiet enough. After everyone trooped home from the neighborhood bath-house with towel and soap bowl, and went to bed, the clack-clack of the night watchmen's sticks only emphasized the peace. Seldom more than thrice a week were we awakened by the wail of a fire truck speeding towards a group of wooden houses burning down.

Hata-Yuguri is only a drop in the ocean, one cell in the body of Tokyo, the largest city in the world. The twenty-three city wards, equivalent to New York's eight boroughs, have over 9,000,000 inhabitants; the population of Tokyo has for some years been growing by over 300,000 every year. The giant city sprawls over flats crisscrossed by scores of muddy canals. Its low skyline is pricked by television towers, and overhung by captive balloons dangling advertisements.

The metropolitan area of Tokyo extends far beyond the confines of the twenty-three wards. It stretches over several counties, and includes five islands far out in the bay. When you are in the countryside, amid the flashing silver mirrors of flooded rice paddies where white cranes stand on long legs darting their beaks at tiny fish, and where the steeply conical, shaggy hills are copied by the steeply sloping, hairy roofs of farmhouses

4

and the huge conical straw hats of the farmers, you are administratively speaking still in Tokyo, and liable to city fines for speeding. The immense city has sturdy rural roots.

The Japanese are a remarkable people. They copied China for twelve centuries, then retired into total isolation for two hundred years, at the end of which they learned to their chagrin that the world was dominated not by Chinese culture and aesthetics, but by European ships and firearms. They emerged an armed industrial state, and fatefully influenced world history, for it can be plausibly argued that first Russia and then China became Communist after being weakened by Japanese blows.

Then Japan was crushed by a new bomb invented in the West. She lost her empire and was again a crescent of beautiful volcanic islands, overcrowded and with a third of her factories in ruins and eight out of ten of her ships at the bottom of the sea.

Fifteen years later, her rebuilt cities blaze with neon, she has displaced France as the fifth largest steel producer, and is the world's biggest shipbuilder. Her living standards are far above the rest of Asia, because the diligent Japanese not only are producing more goods but apparently have reached a collective decision to produce fewer babies. Between the cherry-blossom season of 1947 and the cherry-blossom season of 1948, 2,500,-000 babies were born: one every twelve seconds. But since then, the birth rate has been halved and ranks with Britain's among the lowest in the world.

A tenth of this busy nation of 93,000,000 people live in Tokyo, which is run by gray-skinned investment bankers but occasionally commandeered in the name of *demokurasu* by rioting sloe-eyed teen-agers.

Of the foreigner in Japan, Lafcadio Hearn gloomily noted that he "must remain in the state of the Antarctic explorer, seeking month after month, to no purpose, some inlet through endless cliffs of everlasting ice." That was many years ago. The Japanese are still not at ease with foreigners, all of whom in

5

Japanese eyes behave with a uniform strangeness. But they are nevertheless determined, as a nation, to try to comprehend foreigners. To this end they have embarked on a mass onslaught on the English tongue: an undertaking at least as formidable for them as the successful halving of the birth rate.

Only in Japan will the foreigner be approached by a pretty school girl, English phrase book in hand, who will haltingly but resolutely read from it: "Sir, are you a kind gentleman?"

The ice has melted.

(2)

When American forces landed in Japan immediately after the surrender, to occupy the vanquished islands and hang the Japanese military leaders, including, possibly, the Emperor, they expected to encounter a good deal of public hostility. Instead, they found their routes through the war-shattered towns lined with crowds who smiled and bowed.

The smiles and bows were anxiously placatory, for the Japanese had been told that the Americans would kill most of the men, and rape all the women. Each side, therefore, was surprised and pleased by the other's behavior. Literally in a matter of hours, the Americans were busy buying souvenirs and dating girls. The good personal relations that were then established between Americans and Japanese have continued.

The American bases never seriously disturbed those personal relations, but did over the years act like political gallstones, irritating the Japanese into accusing America of almost everything, from having a "colonial attitude" to being cruel to clams. The fishermen of Aomori demanded $20,000 compensation, because, they said, "American target practice at Yokkawame beach scares the clams, so that they chop themselves in half by clamming up so fast, and thus are unmarketable."

The American military in Japan on the whole went out of their way to soothe Japanese susceptibilities. Some went very far indeed.

Near us in Hata-Yuguri there lived an American Army major and his family. The surrounding Japanese houses boomed in the evening with lively radio and television music, sung or played by the Dark Ducks or the Three Samurai, for the Japanese have taken enthusiastically to jazz. But weirder and more melancholy sounds came from the major's home, where he and his entire family were learning to play tenth-century Japanese classical music on quaint old Japanese instruments, like the *koto*, or Japanese harp, and the *shakuhachi*, or bamboo flute.

The major was a mild-mannered, middle-aged man, with wide blue eyes in a round, fair-freckled face. His only expletives were "By golly!" and, in moments of extreme tension and stress, "Holy cat!" He and his pretty wife were determined, as they said, to be "part of Japan." To this end, they had remodeled their rented home. Its Japanese owner had built it Western style in order to rent it to foreigners, but the major and his wife laid straw matting on their living-room floor, and all their doors were sliding doors, of paper instead of wood. In their bedroom they slept on the floor, Japanese style, instead of in a Western bed; and as much as possible they ate Japanese food, rice and fish and pickles, professing considerable aversion for such American dishes as steaks and hamburgers and hot dogs.

They sent their two small daughters, aged eight and ten, to the neighborhood Japanese school, instead of to the Tokyo American School, so the little girls would speak Japanese; and the major and his wife made it a rule to spend at least two hours a day speaking only Japanese to each other. Wearing kimonos, they practiced Japanese dances, so that at *o-bon* time, in midsummer, they could take part with their Japanese neighbors in traditional dancing at the neighborhood Shinto shrine. There, to the music of drums and flutes, they would slowly gyrate, moving arms and legs in stylized gestures, to indicate that they were fishermen hauling in the catch, or farmers cutting the first of the season's rice.

One day when I called on the major, his two little girls, wearing bright kimonos and looking like fair-haired butterflies, were being shrill in Japanese. Their mother looked harassed. "We're going home to the States in the fall," said the major, downcast. "Holy cat! We just have to get those kids to speak English again. They've forgotten how to talk anything but Japanese."

Unfortunately, incidents at or around the bases from time to time threw a wrench into such cultural exchanges. The most memorable was the so-called Girard case.

American bases, especially those where GIs went on practice maneuvers with live ammunition, were surrounded by notices warning Japanese civilians not to enter. This did not deter farmers, their children, and their wives, from swarming over the firing grounds to collect spent cartridges to sell to Japanese scrap merchants. This was called "scrounging brass," and the shell pickers were called "hot gloves," because they wore thick gloves so as to be able to snatch up the shells even if they were still hot. The "hot gloves" were so daring that they dug foxholes to crouch in while the firing was going on, then darted to get the shells the instant the shooting ceased. All attempts by the American military to shoo the shell pickers away had failed. It was an old Japanese custom; there had been "hot gloves" in the days when the same ranges were used by the Japanese Imperial Army.

One day, Mrs. Naka Sakai, the forty-six-year-old wife of a poor farmer and the mother of six children, was shot dead on a firing range, and an American soldier named William Sylvester Girard was blamed. It seemed that he had fired towards some shell pickers, meaning, as he said later, to scare them off, but had killed Mrs. Sakai. Nobody denied that Mrs. Sakai and the others had no right to be on the range. On the other hand, nobody had ordered Girard to shoot at them. Therefore, since

8

Girard had not been carrying out a military order, it was decided to hand him over to a Japanese civilian court for trial.

To ensure that an American boy was not martyred by the scoundrely Japanese, the trial was attended by, among others, Brigadier-General Charles L. Decker, United States Army Assistant Judge-Advocate; Mr. Charles Slayman, Chief Counsel to the American Sub-Committee on Constitutional Rights; Mr. Bernard Fensterwald, administrative assistant to Senator Thomas Hennings; Judge William Clark; Colonel Alvin M. Owsley, representing the American Legion; and the First Secretary of the United States Embassy in Tokyo. "The question is," Colonel Owsley said, "will this boy get a fair and just trial, as we in America understand it?" Judge Clark confidently predicted: "They can only find him guilty of negligence, and fine him three dollars."

Pending his trial, Girard enjoyed a fair degree of liberty, and endured a vast amount of publicity, on an American Army base north of Tokyo. He gave press interviews; and he also decided to get married, to a Japanese girl called Candy. The Army, sensitive to the charge that it had "thrown Girard to the wolves," leaned over backwards to ensure his comfort and peace of mind, and kindly arranged his wedding for him. The press besieging the base were handed a circular. "Private Girard," it said, "has laid down the following ground rules for representatives of mass media who wish to 'cover' his wedding. I: No photographers will be permitted inside the chapel. . . ." There were about ten ground rules. The thing had the flavor of royalty.

The trial was held 70 miles from Tokyo, at Maebashi, a town that is famous for its silkworms and its trout, and where during the day pretty girls stroll languidly under red and green parasols, and in the evenings, behind bamboo shutters, geishas sing plaintive songs as they pluck the strings of the lutes that the Japanese call samisens. The town is overlooked by forested hills, and enclosed by fields of bright green rice. Cypresses and weeping willows grow along the banks of swift cool streams, and on one of the hillsides there is a huge stone *Kannon*, or Goddess of Mercy, 130 feet tall.

Colonel Owsley went to Camp Drew, before the trial began, to talk with Girard. "There is something sweet about this youth," he declared. "He does not stand alone. He is part of America." Judge Clark's mood was darker. Colonel Owsley had got a spectator's ticket for the courthouse, but Clark was told he had applied too late. "Insolence!" he cried, and wondered aloud: "Is it because the Japanese courts are unwilling to have an experienced American judge witness their proceedings?"

Not to be outdone in chauvinism, young Japanese men paraded outside the courthouse, carrying wordy placards: "Uphold the pride of the Japanese race and protect the judicial system of Japan!" "Show the world the fairness of our trials and, for the sake of the murdered Mrs. Sakai, do not fall under the authority of America!"

About five hundred people, mostly elderly rice farmers, lined up, with wet towels tied round their heads to keep them cool in the hot sun. They clamored to get inside the tiny courthouse, which, however, had room for only thirty-five spectators. The problem was solved by drawing lots, and thirty-two men and three women won seats.

There was much talk about how to punish the young American who had shot a Japanese woman. "He should get about ten years," a seventeen-year-old student decided. "If he gets a suspended sentence and is allowed to return to America, I shall be very dissatisfied." A man selling oranges said cheerfully: "It can't, of course, be helped if he gets the death sentence, but in that case I would feel a bit sorry for him: he ought perhaps to get life imprisonment." A prim housewife remarked that if Girard got a suspended sentence, it would be very regrettable. "I think he should be kept in jail five years. As a Japanese woman, my feelings towards him cannot be good."

Girard, a fair-haired young man with a receding chin and a

generally adenoidal look, arrived in the custody of the provost marshal. He was followed into the courthouse by four Negro soldiers carrying water coolers and American-style lunches. There were three black-robed judges, but no jury. The court orderlies carried paper fans in their pockets. A chiming pendulum clock in a brown wooden case stood against one wall.

"I fired over their heads to scare the people," said Girard, looking up at the three seated judges. "It was a pure accident as far as I am concerned, and I am sorry about it."

There were sparrows and swallows on the courthouse lawn, and in the cherry trees. Inside, the clock chimed tinnily. Its shining round pendulum was busy behind its little glass window. The fluttering paper fans of the spectators displayed mountain peaks and seas, flowers and birds and trees, painted on rice paper.

The first day's proceedings were exceedingly dull. They were taken up with routine questioning, ballistics details, and the coroner's report. But this humdrum quality wrought a remarkable transformation in the visiting Americans. "Girard is guilty," decided Judge Clark. "If the Americans don't admit this, they are fools. Girard should plead guilty to negligence. The trial should not be prolonged." Colonel Owsley declared: "I was terribly impressed with that Japanese court. I stood in awe. Japan has rightful jurisdiction in the case. Girard is having a fair trial. That boy is in serious trouble."

The chief judge, Yuzo Kawachi, preserved complete calm. "After all," he explained, "it is not a very difficult case. No intricate issues are involved. The hearings will be simple."

The trial, with lengthy adjournments, went on for eighty-six days. Altogether, some hundred thirty American Army officers and men were taken up with what came to be known as "Girard duty." The affair cost the United States about $100,000— and a lot of face.

In the end, Girard was given a suspended sentence—meaning that he was free to leave Japan with his bride—and was ordered to pay the Japanese witnesses' expenses: $20. Judge Kawachi, with humiliating kindliness, called him "a simple soldier with an immature mind who gave way to a childish whim."

(3)

I never met a Japanese who could tell me why the Parliament or Diet building in Tokyo looked like a huge square bank vault, with a stone pyramid squatting on top of it. There was nothing Far Eastern, or despite the pyramid even Near Eastern, about this architectural horror.

Some *gaijins*, which is what the Japanese call foreigners, argued that the Diet building looked weird on purpose, because, though the Japanese had adopted democracy, it was alien to them, so they erected an alien-type building to practice it in.

When election time draws near, Japanese Dietmen of all parties set about wooing the voters. First, they send their constituents postcards (which the Diet post office obligingly handles free of charge) containing *dozo yoroshiku* or "best regards" messages. These are followed by personal visits. In his local district, the Dietman throws *nenkai*, or "forget past cares" parties, at which everyone drinks green tea, eats sweet bean paste, and (the Dietman hopes) praises the new bridge, road, or schoolhouse that he talked tight-fisted authority into financing.

Bribing the voters is an offense in Japan. Still, if a Dietman's motorcar should skid into a farmer's rice field, there is no law to prevent him from generously rewarding those who help haul it out. Also, the great Japanese ritual of gift-giving, at *o-bon* (midyear) and *o-sei* (year end), comes in especially handy. Politicians' gifts to constituents then range from scented soap, and hand towels inscribed with the names of the Dietmen, to lacquer boxes and hanging scrolls.

Conservative Japanese politicians are divided into eight

groups, which, however, in order to combat the Socialists have uneasily combined as the Liberal-Democratic party. Under this hyphenated umbrella, the eight factions continue to jostle one another, for power and money. The factions form fleeting alliances, and the alliance with a temporary majority in the caucus is called the "main current." Its opponents, in the temporarily outnumbered factions, are the "anti-main current."

Just as all Dietmen of whatever party or faction woo the voters, so the *zaibatsu*, or big Japanese businesses, woo the factions: particularly the factions of the Liberal-Democratic party, but without entirely ignoring the Socialists. Each of the eight factions among the conservative politicians can count on receiving from big business, *each month*, around $30,000. What the factions are expected to do in return, is discussed and decided at meetings held in such choice surroundings as expensive country inns at hot-spring spas, or still more expensive geisha restaurants in Tokyo. But nothing is decided in a hurry. First, patrons and politicians indulge in steaming baths, lying side by side like ancient Romans. Then, wearing colorful kimonos, they sit around low lacquer tables, eating, drinking, and conniving.

I once waited patiently for one of those sessions to conclude, in order to talk to a Dietman, who when he finally emerged led me to another room and explained to me: "What Japan needs is a great, spiritual regeneration; this is the only way to defeat Communism."

The leader of each faction must, of course, distribute among the members of his faction most of the money he receives from the *zaibatsu*—otherwise, he would rapidly cease to have a following. The Socialists also have factions, and their factions, too, expect to be paid. The money they get is called *mochi dai*, or rice money, and parallels the sums that a *daimyo*, or feudal lord, formerly distributed to his samurai retainers.

Once, a Socialist Dietman received a summons to call on the

Prime Minister, a conservative. He had been heckling the Prime Minister severely in the Diet, and it was thought the Prime Minister meant to try to bully him into silence. All his comrades urged him to stand up for himself like a man, and refuse to be browbeaten.

When he stepped into the Prime Minister's office, a smiling secretary took from a desk one of a large number of fat envelopes bearing the names of Dietmen, and handed it to him with a low bow. "Here is your *mochi dai*," he said affably. A terrible error had occurred. There were two Dietmen with the same name, the other being a conservative.

Gleefully, the Socialist Dietman opened the envelope and counted the contents: 300,000 yen, or over $800. Then he indignantly returned the money, delivered a lecture on the corruption of the conservatives, and stalked out. Back at the Socialist headquarters, he asked for and received his own *mochi dai*: $400. Socialists are poorer than conservatives.

Conservatives and Socialists differ over foreign policy, meaning American bases in Japan. But this difference has been exaggerated.

"We don't want to take over the American bases," my tubby friend Colonel Ashida, of the Japanese ground self-defense force, explained to me. "If the Russians or Chinese bomb an American base, that's the Americans' responsibility. If the Japanese had the base and the Communists bombed it, then Japan would be in trouble."

Colonel Ashida was, I think, a conservative in politics. Mrs. Shizuo Kato was a Socialist, but held what really amounted to the same views. Mrs. Kato, formerly the Baroness Ishimoto, had won an election with three quarters of a million votes—the most ever recorded in the history of the Diet. She got them by passionately advocating birth control instead of rearmament: fewer babies instead of more soldiers. Indeed, she wanted fewer soldiers as well as fewer babies. Japan had a volunteer army

14

(called a ground self-defense force in deference to the Mac-Arthur Constitution) of 160,000. Mrs. Kato wanted it reduced to 75,000. But the Americans, she said sadly, wanted the number increased instead of reduced. "It is not that we Socialists are anti-American," said Mrs. Kato. "It's the Americans who don't understand Japanese psychology."

Japan's leading Socialist, Mr. Inejiro Asanuma, wanted to have no army at all. He was, however, prepared to tolerate a small one, until capitalism was abolished, because under capitalism the only alternative to soldiering was unemployment. Bases he vigorously opposed, as constituting "American control of Japan." Mr. Asanuma was a burly man with a small mustache and a rasping voice. He looked like a *sumo* wrestling champion. He was a voluble, shirt-sleeves-and-galluses politician, much admired by Tokyo workingmen. Like Mrs. Kato, he insisted he was not anti-American. But he thought that if the Americans closed down their bases, the cold war would give place quicker to peaceful co-existence. When the bases stubbornly refused to disappear, Mr. Asanuma went on a visit to Peking, where his hosts encouraged his natural gas to catch fire. "American imperialism is the common enemy of China and Japan," Mr. Asanuma declared.

In Japanese elections, some 23,000,000 voters regularly supported the conservative Liberal-Democrats; 13,000,000 voted for Mr. Asanuma's Socialists; and about 1,000,000, for the Japanese Communist party. But a lot of young Japanese clearly tended to side with Asanuma about the American bases. This was not lost on the Liberal-Democratic leader, Mr. Nobusuke Kishi, who admitted: "A fairly large section of the younger generation thinks that we Liberal-Democrats are out-and-out American stooges."

Mr. Kishi's and Mr. Asanuma's attempts, in their different ways, to rectify the situation brought about Mr. Kishi's political ruin and Mr. Asanuma's murder: the American bases in Japan were the undoing of both.

(4)

Hata-Yuguri was a maze of little twisting lanes, and little wooden houses. But things were changing. Near the elementary school and within convenient distance of the neighborhood bathhouse, an enterprising contractor had erected a four-story building of tiny apartments for white-collar workers, whom the Japanese call "salarymen." The balconies on each floor blossomed daily with bright *futons*, Japanese bed quilts, spread out to air.

Some very interesting people lived in our lane. The most important was Mr. Tanaka, who was chairman of the neighborhood association. It was the association's business to see that the night watchmen carried out their patrol duties, and to cajole the shopkeepers into keeping the lanes tidy and putting up pretty neon lights. This made Mr. Tanaka an influential man, but he had other claims to significance. He had many friends among the politicians in the Japanese Diet and in other high places.

"He has a broad face," explained Sano-san, my driver, referring to Mr. Tanaka's wealth of useful contacts. We all benefited from Mr. Tanaka's broad face. Other lanes might be full of potholes, but ours was always kept in excellent repair, just because he lived in it. It was said that Mr. Tanaka could get you a telephone, an import license, a bank loan—even a seat in the Diet, if he was moved to befriend you. The most popular of Japanese fortunetelling cards promises the lucky drawer: "A powerful backer will come to your aid, and thus assure you of a favorable outcome." Mr. Tanaka personified this father figure.

There was, of course, another side to the business. As chairman of the neighborhood association, Mr. Tanaka was in control of the district's volunteer fire brigade: brawny men who spent their spare time practicing astonishing gymnastic feats at the tops of long ladders. Cynics claimed that the homes of Socialists and other foes of Mr. Tanaka's friends always seemed to burn down before help came.

A word from Mr. Tanaka would probably have sufficed to close down the "hotel for couples." But the word was never spoken, and the police also went out of their way to ignore the existence in our lane of the district headquarters of a notorious gang called the Matsubakai, which means "Pine Leaf Club," who did certain little jobs for Mr. Tanaka.

One day not long after our arrival in Hata-Yuguri, Mr. Tanaka paid us a call. He was a burly man, with a teak-hard face which much rice wine had permanently reddened. But his large hands were soft as a woman's, and he wore a black silk kimono. The eyes in the harsh face were like black pearls.

He arrived in a chauffeur-driven car and was accompanied by a young man who bowed deeply whenever anyone spoke, but who never said anything himself except to repeat in English what Mr. Tanaka said in Japanese.

When everyone had bowed to everyone else, we all sat down and my wife Jane had tea brought. Mr. Tanaka leaned forward, his black eyes fixed on us, and spoke lengthily in Japanese. When he had done, he picked up his cup and sucked.

"Mr. Tanaka say," the young man explained above the noise, "he is very happy you have come to live in his district. He wants to know if there—are anythings?—no; *is any thing*"—the young man smiled triumphantly—"he can do for you. He will be most happy to be at your service. He would like to know where you are from. He would like to know how long you will stay in Japan. He would like to know what is your occupation."

I told him, and the young man spoke in Japanese to Mr. Tanaka.

"But," I said, "we don't need anything done. It is very good of him to offer. We are very grateful."

The young man translated. Mr. Tanaka spoke in Japanese.

"Mr. Tanaka say, please call on him at any time, for anything you wish."

17

"We are most grateful," I repeated.

Mr. Tanaka rose, bowed, and spoke some parting words.

"Mr. Tanaka say," the young man translated, "no need for you to thank him. He help you; you perhaps help him. Nobody is living in this world by himself."

Mrs. Hayama, another of our neighbors in Hata-Yuguri, was an excellent if melancholy example of the Japanese fetish of "face." She was a tiny woman with faded brown eyes, who habitually wore faded brown kimonos. "She looks sad, because she does not like having an *on*," Sano-san said.

Mrs. Hayama had an *on* because of Japan's biennial ritual of gift-giving. Each household carefully notes every gift received, and its value. By accepting a gift you assume an *on*, or an obligation, usually satisfied by giving a gift in exchange. Whatever you give must have the same value as what you got. To accept a costly gift and give a trifle in return is what the Japanese scathingly call "repaying a sea bream with a minnow."

Mr. Hayama owned a trucking business, so that in the gift-exchange system the Hayamas were graded by their friends and neighbors as belonging in the Scotch-whisky and pearls category. But for months the trucking establishment had been at a standstill, because Mr. Hayama's workers were on a strike. They squatted patiently outside his yard, behind a thicket of red flags, and neither side it seemed was prepared to give an inch.

Mr. Hayama had bought his trucks on borrowed money at exorbitant interest. Now he was deeply in debt and simply couldn't afford to return Scotch for Scotch, or to match pearls with pearls. Cheap hand towels and humble cakes of soap were about all the Hayamas could manage.

In vain did Mrs. Hayama strive to save face. She got up at meetings of the neighborhood association, when everyone was voting in favor of providing the night watchmen with bowls of *soba*, Japanese noodle soup, to keep them awake and of decorating the police box with new paper lanterns, and urged abolition of unnecessary, wasteful gift-giving. "Let us abolish waste!" cried Mrs. Hayama. But nobody was deceived.

Like the English, the Japanese are terrible snobs. I felt sorry for Mrs. Hayama.

Every neighborhood has its black sheep: ours was Mr. Katama. Just as Mr. Shima, the court chamberlain who came to our house several days a week to brush up his English, represented exalted aristocratic circles, so did the Katamas symbolize the proletariat, Communism, and the powers of darkness. For Mrs. Katama was even more notorious than her husband. What made her case worse than his was that she was a traitor to her class.

She was a dowdy, dumpy woman well covered with warts, and had graying stringy hair. No one seeing her waddle along the lane to buy vegetables would guess that she was the illegitimate daughter of the husband of a great-aunt of the Emperor of Japan. Her mother had been a court lady, who succeeded in arranging a marriage between her illegitimate daughter, then sixteen, and a peer of the realm.

But, after six years, the exasperated peer divorced her by the then traditional Japanese letter of dismissal. A Japanese husband could get rid of an unwanted wife merely by informing her in writing: "This is to certify that I have divorced you of my own accord and, therefore, you have my permission to remarry." The peer, it seems, was driven to this desperate act by the discovery that his pretty young wife as well as being from the wrong side of the blanket was as wanton as her mother and was having affairs with all his friends. Four years later, the undaunted divorcee married a man who had the disadvantage of being a commoner, but the virtue of being a millionaire. She was twenty-six; he was sixty-two. He called her his White Lotus.

She was thirty-five when she fell in love with a left-wing poet, not yet thirty and tubercular; this was Katama. They belatedly eloped. She broke the news of her desertion to her husband in a letter, and thoughtfully sent a copy to a popular magazine that was urging equal rights for women. Unfortunately, the magazine received and published its copy before her husband had got his. This caused an immense scandal.

In her letter, she wrote: "I have lived the past nine years in tears and misery. Our marriage was feudalistic. I often thought of suicide, but poetry consoled my heart, until the gods sent me a poet for a lover. If things are left as they are now, I may commit a sin—though I hardly think it would be a sin when I recall your past conduct. You ignored a woman, and thought only of your wealth. I bid you farewell, and thank you for your past trouble. PS: I have returned you your jewels, under separate cover." A few months later, she bore the poet a child.

Ever since, as far as I could gather, it was she who had maintained her husband and her child, by her writing. She wrote anything and everything: novels, articles, short stories, and, nowadays, film and television scripts as well. She was Japan's George Sand and George Eliot rolled into one.

After spending years on the brink of death, Mr. Katama suddenly recovered. But permitting his wife to earn a living for both of them had become a fixed habit. She continued to write; he continued the political activities he had hitherto conducted from his sickbed, or, from time to time, from his prison cell. Both he and his wife were always heartily welcomed in Moscow and Peking.

Mr. Katama was a friendly little gnome. He had a bald head and big spectacles and looked like a little yellow Pickwick. He adored his wife and tirelessly denounced capitalists. "Before the war," he told me, "I was arrested a hundred sixty times. Each time I was released, they re-arrested me for 'further questioning.'" Meanwhile, his wife was jailed several times for clandestinely publishing "left-wing propaganda," in which category the authorities included her lectures on women's rights and birth control.

Mr. Katama had early in his career helped found the first

Japanese labor union, called the Yuaikai, or Friendly Love Society. This had been suppressed under the quaintly titled Peace Preservation Law.

"During the Pacific war," said Mr. Katama, who spoke excellent English, "I was imprisoned for opposing the war. When the war ended, I was released on General MacArthur's orders. In gratitude to him and the United States, I supported the MacArthur Constitution for Japan, which forbids Japan to rearm. Now, I am denounced by Americans for supporting this Constitution, because the Americans have changed their minds and insist that Japan should re-arm."

Hata-Yuguri is not a working-class, but a middle-class, neighborhood, and Mr. Katama was feared and disliked by most of the shopkeepers, small businessmen, and "salarymen" of the district. His own *bête noir* was Mr. Tanaka.

"Hayama is only a fool," he said, contemptuously. "He is a workingman who has managed to borrow some money and to exploit a few of his fellows. When the big capitalists are tired of him, they will foreclose and take his business away from him. Meanwhile, he is useful to them. He does the dirty job of grinding down the workers for them, and they have their goods transported cheaply by him.

"But Tanaka-san, though he, too, is only a tool of the real capitalists, is much more dangerous. He has close contact with the 'Pine Leaves,' who not only are racketeers who prey on little shopkeepers, but also are for hire as strikebreakers. Tanaka arranges all that sort of thing. He is not quite in the assassin class, but he would like to be. When he is old, and retired, he will boast when he has had too much sake that he ordered the killing of Socialists."

Our most glamorous neighbor was Yumiko Showa, the movie actress. Once, driving home from seeing someone off on a midnight plane, we came on a scene of tragedy. Grim-faced men were searching a little lake in a wood for a lovely girl who had threatened to drown herself to escape a loveless marriage arranged for her by her rich, ruthless father. The wood was full of men shouting directions and moving up cameras, and the little lake shimmered under glaring hot lights. A slender dripping figure was brought ashore; in a few broken words, just before expiring she forgave her distraught father for his cruelty. It was Yumiko Showa, enacting a romantic suicide.

Yumiko was an extremely pretty, hard-working girl, who spent her time posing for Japanese picture magazines, and being rushed frantically from one movie plot to another. Sometimes she would be making three different movies at once. Although extraordinarily cheerful by nature, Yumiko had a sad, beautiful face. She committed suicide in most of her films, usually by drowning. She was once taken forty miles south from Tokyo to Sagami Bay, and there thrown into a freezing sea, for a winter sunset effect.

This kind of life enabled her to enjoy such luxuries as a tiny cream-colored sports car, and a stereophonic phonograph on which she played avant-garde jazz. When not dressed up for the movies, she liked wearing black sweaters and tight tartan trousers. She also liked to cook.

Before getting into films, she had worked in a Tokyo department store, bowing to customers and throatily murmuring in Japanese, all day long: "Welcome to our store," and "A thousand thanks." With her first earnings as a film actress, she brought her mother to Hata-Yuguri, and installed them both in a little neat house, with a swimming pool, and a garden adorned with a stone lantern. The living room had proper chairs, and couches of strange modern design; but the bedroom had a straw floor, and sliding cupboards in the walls for stowing away rolled mattresses and futons, because Yumiko's mother preferred sleeping Japanese style, on the floor, to being in a Western bed.

Yumiko was not yet twenty. She was three when Emperor Hirohito broadcast the news of Japan's surrender, when the fire-bombs ceased falling on Tokyo, and when a score of Tokyoites who felt they had lost face proceeded to the Imperial Plaza, and committed ceremonial suicide with hara-kiri knives. Yumiko's father was killed in the war. She and her mother lived at first in a hole in the ground where their house had stood; later, with other refugees in a warren of makeshift shelters under the elevated railway.

Mr. Tanaka had a son called Yoshio who was studying law at Tokyo University. By an irony painfully familiar to parents, Yoshio Tanaka was a fiery torch of the left-wing Japanese students' federation, Zengakuren. He regularly cut classes to attend political rallies, and spent most of his nights talking politics in coffee shops. He believed the Americans should have hanged the Emperor of Japan as a war criminal, but also thought that America was plotting a third world war. He despised his father, of course, but with ruthless youthful logic he also scorned the Katamas for their worship of Russia. For, in his view, the Russian Communists were as great exploiters of the common man as the hated capitalists. "Khrushchev," said Yoshio gustily, "is a strikebreaker and an international blackleg." Though he smoked and talked too much, and rarely smiled, he had brooding good looks, flashing black eyes, and hair that waved like a revolutionary banner.

One day, Yumiko Showa's tiny cream sports car purred past and Yumiko was not driving. Instead, she sat in the passenger's red bucket seat, a silk scarf wound demurely around her head, and her gaze fixed on Yoshio Tanaka's handsome profile. Yoshio was evidently about to find out that there were other things in life besides politics and that, as his father would say, nobody lives in this world by himself.

(5)

A police box not much bigger than a telephone booth stood at the corner of our lane. Squeezed into it were two policemen who wore black revolvers in brown leather holsters, and drank green tea all day while admiring chrysanthemums in a blue vase. One had a daughter aged eight, who early each morning tottered along the lane to school on wooden shoes, clutching a small yellow umbrella, and carrying a bulging schoolbag strapped on her back. It bulged because it held a pillow for her afternoon nap. As she passed the police box, the tiny girl would bow gravely to her father, who would bow back.

We had been in Japan only long enough to learn such elementary things as that hospital rooms are never numbered 4 or 42, because both numbers signify death, and that you can easily tell a ghost from a real person, since a ghost has no feet. But we were acquiring fresh knowledge fast from Mr. Shima.

Mr. Shima was a thin man, with thin black hair and large brown eyes behind very round spectacles. His smile was broad but shy, climbing constantly from craggy gold-filled teeth to high, ledged cheekbones. I do not think we ever saw Mr. Shima when he was not smiling. He looked like a helpful floorwalker, a resemblance heightened by the black cutaway and striped trousers he often wore: for Mr. Shima was a court chamberlain.

He lived near us in Hata-Yuguri, and wanted to improve his English, so three times a week he sat poker-stiff on the edge of an easy chair in our living room, cautiously biting on phrases like a man with a bad tooth sampling chocolates. Mr. Shima also tried to teach us some Japanese, but in this he was hampered not only by our obtuseness but by his own peculiar difficulties in pronunciation.

"To say 'Thank you' in Japanese is easy," Mr. Shima would instruct, smiling broadly. "Easy to say, easy to lemember. Because, same as Amelican for 'clocodile.'"

"The same as *crocodile?*"

"Yes: a-li-ga-to. Spelt: a r i g a t o."

In time, this "l" and "r" confusion ceased to matter, so that when Mr. Shima referred to his new blown tie we knew instantly what he meant. But none of us became proficient in

Japanese, a language that possesses twenty non-interchangeable equivalents of the English pronoun "I," each one employed only in certain circumstances, and with a special one for use by men and another by women. Moreover, each different "I" conditions all pronouns and many of the other words in the sentence in which it appears.

So much for speaking Japanese. To write it, one has to memorize several thousand characters, and also remember that a Japanese sound may have two or more entirely different meanings, depending on the character used in writing it.

One morning when Mr. Shima came for his hour of conversation, we had news for him. "We've had a burglar!" Jane cried, and Mr. Shima's brown eyes behind his large round spectacles adequately registered alarm, even though, out of habit, he went on politely smiling.

"He didn't take anything," I said.

The house we had rented in Hata-Yuguri was in all respects admirable, save that its innumerable, unlockable sliding doors and paper screens made it peculiarly vulnerable. I woke to find the light of a torch shining straight in my face and, behind the torch, a dimly seen, short figure.

Before I had sleepily groped my way to the conclusion that this short figure was not one of us and must therefore be an intruder, there was a sharp in-hiss of breath and the torch was switched off. By the time I had fumbled on a bedside light, the intruder had departed by way of the upstairs veranda and the top of the garden fence.

One of the policemen from the nearby police box, he with the eight-year-old daughter, was summoned to make a search. "This guy thought you were lying right down on the floor, like a Japanese would," explained the policeman, who had worked several years for the Occupation and spoke fluent American. "When he flashed on his torch, he expected to be flashing it around the wall, above your head, not right in your face. Holy cow, what a shock for that poor guy."

Personally, I felt we were the poor guys who had been shocked.

Mr. Shima smiled in alarm when I said that the burglar hadn't had time to take anything.

"You are sure?" he said sorrowfully. "Nothing? Not even cuff links, perhaps? Some insignificant small coin, easily overlooked?"

"Nothing," I insisted.

"In Japan, burglary is a profession," Mr. Shima said. "It is often hereditary. Some men take great pride in being good burglars." I had a feeling he was trying to tell us something.

Two nights later Jane woke me, saying she thought she heard something, and we found that someone had tried to force a downstairs window. Summoned once more from his police box, the father of the small girl with the yellow umbrella worked his thin jaws in hideous silent laughter, meaning he was acutely embarrassed.

"I do not think this guy is a depraved bad character," he said. "He is only a burglar. But it is very unfortunate he did not manage to steal anything, the first time. It means he will persist in trying to crack your joint, because he has lost face."

When I told this to Mr. Shima, he gloomily nodded agreement. "Now he has failed twice," he pointed out. "He will become still more desperate. He may try to kill you. On the other hand," Mr. Shima added, more hopefully, "he may decide to kill himeslf, out of chagrin."

I said I desired neither to be killed by a persistent burglar, nor to have his suicide on my conscience. "How would it be," I suggested, "if I left something out for him to steal? Would he take it and not return?"

Mr. Shima shook his head. "He would guess you wanted him to do that," he said. "So it would not get him back his face."

There were times when Mr. Shima seemed to have a very negative approach to things.

(6)

Mr. Hayama, the trucker who had long been plagued with a strike of his drivers, at length appealed for help to the chairman of the neighborhood association, Mr. Tanaka, who agreed to use his broad face on Mr. Hayama's behalf, and picked the Hata-Yuguri festival as an ideal time.

Somewhere in Tokyo there is always a neighborhood festival in progress. One night, the road leading to the big Shinto shrine in Hata-Yuguri softly gleamed with pink and white paper lanterns. On a tall wooden platform, male drummers stripped to the waist whacked a huge drum, and round the base of the platform women danced in kimonos, with paper fans tucked in the backs of their brocaded waistbands.

The shrine was an open-face wooden structure, blooming with lanterns of all shapes and sizes, and smoky with incense. Nearby, a conjurer performed in a curtained booth, and fireworks flared in a field behind it. All around were stalls and barrows, selling sweet bean paste, goldfish, and bamboo flutes; pink celluloid dolls, and pink balloons; toy monkeys jerkily climbing wooden sticks; and flowers that grew magically in a glass of water.

On the steps of the shrine, an immense, good-humored crowd jostled eagerly for a chance to pull the god-bell that hung from a thick rope with white tassels. You rang the bell, in order to rouse the god; for good measure, you sharply clapped your hands. Then you bowed your head and prayed before ringing the bell once more, to send the god back, so you could get on with the real business of the evening, which was eating, drinking, and dancing; buying toys, souvenirs, and lucky charms; and watching the fireworks and the conjurer.

There are about two hundred Buddhist sects in Japan, and as many Shinto sects. Most Japanese are both Buddhists *and*

Shintoists, and there has in the past decade been a vast pro-
liferation of "new religions." One new sect worships the Pole
Star. Another, after earnest research, decided that an ideal object of worship would be Rutherford Alcock, the first British
ambassador to Japan; but this the British Embassy successfully
discouraged. During the Pacific war, some Japanese Christians
thought the way to reconcile their faith with Japan's pro-
claimed destiny of ruling the world "under one roof" would
be for the Holy Trinity to become a Quaternity, with the Emperor as its fourth Member.

Fourteen centuries ago, a Japanese Emperor was persuaded
by the head of the Soga clan to adopt Buddhism on the ground
that among civilized nations this religion had become the rage.
But Shinto was not superseded; it was announced that the
Shinto gods were really Buddhist gods with Japanese names,
and that Japan had been Buddhist all along.

This amiable flexibility suggests, at any rate to the no doubt
overrigid Western mind, that the Japanese tolerate all religions,
because they are not really religious. Both Japanese Buddhism
and Shinto operate on the principle of the Japanese fortunetelling card: they promise the worshipper a powerful backer.
The people we watched as they pulled the god-bell and clapped
their hands were not praying to be freed from sin, or for a
happy hereafter—few Japanese believe either in sin or in an
afterlife—but for health and wealth, *now*.

In various corners of their homes, people place little god-
tokens, to ward off such misfortunes as theft, fire, sickness: particularly in the northeast corner, which is the *kimon*, or devil
door, through which evil traditionally tries to enter. But, after
Japan's defeat in war and the ravaging of Tokyo and other
great cities with fire-bombs and of Hiroshima and Nagasaki
with atomic bombs, many Japanese quietly gave up keeping a
kamidana and a *butsudan*, a Shinto god-shelf and a miniature
Buddhist altar. It was apparently felt that the gods and Buddha
had let Japan down.

The half-naked drummers whacked away; the women in kimonos took two steps forward and one back, stiffly swinging their arms and wielding invisible picks, in a coal miners' dance. Everyone in Hata-Yuguri had come to watch, including Mr. Hayama's striking workers. The colorful spectacle had lured them away at last from their weary months of picketing. They stood looking on, their red flags furled. Still tied round their foreheads were the white towels emblazoned with defiant crimson Japanese characters that Japanese strikers wear to symbolize their readiness to sweat and strive for victory; the message printed in red on the head towels was the Japanese equivalent of "Hayama Trucking Co. Unfair to Drivers." But they were plainly off-duty, and relaxing; a huge jar of sake, the Japanese rice wine, was being fraternally passed around.

Not only off-duty, but also off-guard. The sake had been contributed by Mr. Tanaka, who never did anything without a purpose. As we watched, an excited messenger from the labor-union office rushed up and called the strikers to order. Hastily, uttering hoarse cries of anger and bafflement, they gathered up their red flags and ran, shouting "*Washo! Washo!*," the traditional—and untranslateable—war cry of all Japanese demonstrators.

Mr. Hayama's establishment was on the road that led to the shrine, so they did not have far to go. All the same, they were too late. They were brought to a halt by a locked and barred gate; over it, unfriendly faces glowered at them. By a clever bit of strategy, the prolonged strike had been transformed in a jiffy into a lockout.

The men holding the gate, explained Sano-san, my driver, were members of the Matsubakai, the notorious "Pine Leaves," who were always happy to play the role of strikebreakers. Driven desperate at last by the unending strike, but still determined not to give in to the strikers, Mr. Hayama had, through Mr. Tanaka, enlisted the Matsubakai against his workers.

The strikers sent for a top union man. Meanwhile, they

formed themselves in a column four abreast, the front rank gripping a thick bamboo pole held lengthwise, and marked time by jumping up and down, shouting "*Washo! Washo!*," as if they were about to charge the gate at any minute. The tough-looking men behind the gate jeered at them. From up the road came the beat of the shrine drum, and the bright soft glow of the colored paper lanterns.

The union official, when he came, was accompanied by Mr. Katama, who, as a leading left-wing influence in Hata-Yuguri, knew all about the strike. The union man talked briefly with the strikers, then walked to the gate and began shouting questions. Answers were shouted back.

"He asked them what they were doing in there," Sano-san reported. "They say they are working for Hayama-san."

Mr. Katama was shaking his fist at the closed gate, and at the men behind it.

"Katama-san says they are not workers, they are gangsters."

The union man shouted something at the gate.

"He says they can't drive trucks unless they belong to the truck drivers' union."

The defenders of the gate yelled back.

"They say Hayama-san hired them to protect drivers who are ready to work. Men who return to work can have their jobs back. Others are fired."

One of the men inside Hayama's yard climbed on the gatepost and made a speech.

"He says they should come back. Hayama-san is a good boss. They have been fooled by their union leaders, who are all Communists."

Mr. Katama and the union official each made a speech.

"They say anyone who crosses the picket line will be put out of the union."

The man standing on the gatepost spoke again.

"He says the ones who return to work can form a number two truck drivers' union that won't be run by Communists."

But the solidarity of the workers was not to be broken as easily as all that. Mr. Katama and the union man talked earnestly with the strikers, who began working up steam by prancing behind their bamboo pole and shouting "*Washo!*" with what seemed to be new vigor. Then in a solid mass they made for the gate.

The mass did not stay solid for long. A shower of stones and bottles thrown from behind the gate descended on it, and the mass staggered and shredded. The gate suddenly opened and men charged out, armed with thick poles that bristled with nails.

After the "Pine Leaves" had returned triumphant to the yard and shut the gate, and white ambulances had removed the more seriously injured strikers, policemen came and stood on guard outside Mr. Hayama's premises. This, however, was not the end of the night's activities. Indeed, that year's shrine festival is remembered in Hata-Yuguri not so much for the Hayama strike, but because of Mrs. Hayama's awful behavior some hours later.

Mrs. Hayama, as I have told, had recently and painfully lost face, and no doubt suffered in other ways as well, for Mr. Hayama was an overbearing little man. She may have been ripe for rebellion, but it is doubtful that she would have acted had the Katamas not taken a hand.

Mr. Katama was furious that the strikers had been outwitted. He rushed home to put his head together with his wife, and presently that vast warty woman, who had once had so many ardent lovers, waddled off to call on both Mrs. Hayama and Mrs. Tanaka.

She knew she would find them both alone, because she knew where their husbands were. Mrs. Katama always knew things like that.

First she called on Mrs. Tanaka, but there she failed in her purpose. The wife of the neighborhood association chairman was what the people of Hata-Yuguri called, approvingly, "a modest Japanese woman." They meant that she dressed in sex-less kimonos, and always had a wifely "low posture" in her husband's presence. She listened sadly to what Mrs. Katama had to say, but shrank in horror from any idea of doing something about it.

Hoping grimly that she had at any rate planted a seed for the future, Mrs. Katama waddled on to see Mrs. Hayama. Here she had better luck.

To celebrate the night's coup, Mr. Tanaka and Mr. Hayama had gone off at the end of the festival, at which they both drank deeply, to the "hotel for couples."

When hours later they had with difficulty put on their shoes again, and giggling girls had bowed them over the threshold into a still, moonlit night, Mr. Tanaka generously offered Mr. Hayama a lift home in his American motorcar. The distance was only a few hundred yards, but they sat in the back and sang to the impassive chauffeur all the way.

Mr. Hayama got out unsteadily, and made a wavering low bow.

"*Dom' arigato!*" he began, but got no further.

Above their heads a window slid open, and Mrs. Hayama's vengeful, clearly carrying voice began a tirade that lasted all the time Mr. Hayama was attempting with trembling fingers to open his front door. At intervals, unidentified objects were thrown out the window at Mr. Tanaka's gleaming motorcar.

Lights went on in all the surrounding houses. People came out into their gardens, to listen and watch, and hold both hands over their mouths to silence their laughter.

The Hayama strike was over within a week. In spite of the best efforts of Mr. Katama and the union man, most of Hayama's workers slunk back to their jobs. The union was split in two, and the "number two" union, which had Mr. Hayama's blessing and, more important, the protection of Mr. Tanaka and the Matsubakai, prevailed. But Mr. Hayama was never again undisputed master in his own home. And Mr. Tanaka's broad face was considerably less broad than before.

(7)

For some time we had been on Mr. Shima's conscience. Regularly each week he came to us for "conversation," and sat stiff-backed on the edge of his chair, clutching a teacup, while his round spectacles shone with concentration. But though he lived just around the corner from us in Hata-Yuguri, he didn't want to invite us to his home, fearing to lose face.

Mr. Shima, being an Imperial court chamberlain, went to a lot of parties in an official-looking long black limousine. Every day he was driven through the guarded Ohte Gate to the Imperial Household building inside the Imperial Palace grounds, which are in the center of Tokyo but are sealed off from the rest of the city by tall watchtowers and an ancient moat. At the parties and on days when he might meet Their Imperial Majesties, Mr. Shima wore a black cutaway coat and striped trousers.

But his home was a tiny wooden house that had more people in it than furniture, for the court chamberlains were poorly paid. Like Japan itself, Mr. Shima lived in a split-level world and the two halves of his existence were completely divorced.

The Americans had failed to hang the Emperor, as desired by Yoshio Tanaka and other left-wing students, but this did not mean that Japan's Imperial family and the nobles had come through the holocaust untouched. All, including the Emperor, had lost their vast estates, and most were as poor as palace mice. At least one ex-princess kept a flower shop, and the Emperor and Empress had been living for over fifteen years in a cottage in the palace grounds, the palace itself having burned down in a fire-bomb raid.

The Imperial Household building was where the Emperor

and his chamberlains did their work, and Emperor Hirohito walked to it from his cottage each morning, and walked back each noon to lunch with the Empress.

It was said that his daily walks gave him much pleasure, since he was considerably more interested in plant life than in pomp and palaces, and he often arrived at his office with muddy knees, having strayed off the path to kneel beside a scummy pond and examine fungi. Also, the Japanese Imperial family are fairly inured to poverty and hardship. They have had many ups and downs through the centuries, and hard times are nothing new. A sixteenth-century Emperor, for instance, could not be buried for lack of cash, and his body lay at the palace gates forty days. Another kept himself from starvation only by selling specimens of his signature and other souvenirs.

One day Mr. Shima sent us an invitation. We were asked to lunch, and then to the Imperial Palace grounds, to witness ancient polo and eighth-century dances. We accepted gratefully.

The lunch was at a geisha restaurant on the Sumida River. As we walked up the flagged footpath that meandered through a mossy garden with dwarf shrubs and little waterfalls, geishas bowed low to us from the doorway we were approaching. We removed our shoes, which were whipped into a cupboard, and stepped up one step on to a highly polished, velvet-smooth wooden floor, where the geishas gave us red leather slippers. In these, we shuffled along a polished wood passage, then up two flights of steeply twisting, polished stairs.

Mr. Shima's other expense-account guests included Colonel Ashida, of the Japanese self-defense ground forces; a former Japanese baron; a distinguished Japanese poet; and another court chamberlain who had been brought along to give Mr. Shima moral support.

The room where we were to have lunch was long and narrow, and built on wooden piles out over the river. We sat on cushions on the floor, spaced out on both sides of a long table, six inches high. Between each two guests kneeled a geisha, to pour rice wine and change plates. Beside the table was a low wooden counter, and behind it knelt a chef in a white cap, busily frying prawns and shrimp. We were to have a simple fried-fish lunch, which the Japanese call *tempura*.

From the start, it was clear that Mr. Shima had erred in his choice of guests. I think he had picked them mainly for their ability to speak English, in order to put us more at ease. But the baron had become corrupted by contact with American businessmen who thought kings and emperors were the bunk. The poet had just got back from Peking, and was full of revolutionary zeal. And the other chamberlain was so shy of foreigners that he had nerved himself for the ordeal with several stiff drinks. He now looked hopelessly glassy-eyed, and had a telltale red flush in his gaunt cheeks. Only the colonel, a short tubby man who preserved his inscrutability behind dark glasses, seemed completely self-possessed.

The poet smoked throughout the meal, dropping half-finished cigarettes into a china ash box and immediately lighting another. He was a middle-aged, swarthy man, with many gold teeth, and a sceptical brown eye that he lost no time in turning on Mr. Shima.

"Aha, there, Shima-san!" he exclaimed. "So you Imperial chamberlains are up to your old tricks again, eh?"

Mr. Shima smiled nervously. "I don't know what you mean."

"Oh, yes, you do." The poet turned briefly to me. "When Japan surrendered, these chamberlains were so terrified of being fired, or perhaps even hanged, that they tried hard to 'democratize' the Emperor. Hirohito came out from behind the moat, and mingled with the people."

"Who really and truly didn't know what to make of him," the baron murmured, in Jane's ear. "Until then, they hadn't even been allowed to look at him. When he passed by, they all had to bow down their heads. Now he went about raising his hat to them, stiffly, as if he was standing on tiptoe and trying to hang it on a high peg." The baron laughed. "Some people cheered and shouted 'banzai!'; some shook their fists and yelled that he should be hanged. These were the ones who had lost children in the air raids. But most of them just put their hands over their mouths, they were so embarrassed and afraid."

"But anyhow these days are over," declared the poet. "The chamberlains have put the Emperor back behind the moat. Once more he is 'living above the clouds,' as we say. Poor fellow! He has only been out of Japan once in his life, when he was a young man; and now they won't let him travel abroad. They allow him to go to watch *sumo* only once a year; the rest of the time, he must be content to see it on the palace television screen. He has never been to a horse race, and only once to a baseball game."

"The Emperor is a very reserved man," said Mr. Shima. "He would not go to horse races anyway. He likes a quiet, rural life."

"But still the chamberlains are not satisfied," said the poet, ignoring him. "They are stealthily restoring all the bad old feudal customs. When the Emperor pays a visit to some district, and has to stay at an inn, he is not allowed to read the newspapers until they have been especially ironed, in case the hand of some common man has touched the pages. And worse things happen! A week before he arrives at an inn, all the people who will serve him are forced to have medical examinations. This is undignified! This is feudal!"

"The one time that happened," said Mr. Shima, a trifle sulkily, "the Socialists raised such an outcry, the Grand Chamberlain publicly apologized. We chamberlains are as anxious as anyone to 'democratize' the Emperor. But it cannot be done in a day. We have trained Crown Prince Akihito to be a modern, constitutional monarch. When he becomes Emperor, with pretty Michiko as his common-born Empress, all will be different."

The baron, after whispering a while to Jane, had amused himself by pretending to pinch a geisha, who responded by giggling silently behind her hand, and occasionally slapping his. Now, however, the baron re-entered the discussion.

He looked exactly as I imagined an Oriental baron should. He was a short man with broad shoulders and a barrel-shaped chest. He had a square, reddish face, and his hair was cut short so that it stood up on his scalp. He looked as if he ought to have saber cuts on his cheeks; and he did wear a silver-rimmed monocle.

"Akihito," said the baron, "will be lucky if he is still around to ascend the throne, when Hirohito leaves it; if he does, he will certainly be its last occupant."

"You are a republican," said the poet, well pleased and laughing.

"Certainly I am a republican," said the baron. "The throne is finished in Japan."

While they all talked, my attention gradually turned to the odd antics of the kneeling chef. He busily refilled the plates handed him by the geishas with delicious fried fish, which we ate with wooden chopsticks, first dipping the fish in a little bowl of dark-brown soy sauce. But from time to time, he uttered a "tut!" of vexation, and made a sort of sideways swipe at something on the floor, which was hidden from me by the wooden counter. Several times I craned my neck, but in vain. Finally, on pretext of shifting my position on my cushion, I half-raised myself and snatched a peek.

The prawns, shrimp, and other fish the chef was popping in his frying pan came from a large wooden bucket of water at his side. They were not only still alive, but very lively, and repeatedly escaped from the bucket to squirm or hop over the floor. Then the chef would lean over sideways to grab them back, but instead of returning escapees to the bucket he dropped them straight into the pan, as it were to settle their hash.

I had been eating with gusto, but suddenly I found I had little appetite.

The glassy-eyed chamberlain, hitherto silent, addressed me in confidential tones.

"Did you ever hear of the great globefish heresy?" he asked.

When I said I hadn't, he continued: "Before the war, a man was put on trial here in Tokyo for preaching that the Emperor was not descended, as the Imperial family claims, from the Sun Goddess. To deny it was lese majesty, you know. But, when this man was brought into court, he declared that he hadn't been trying to belittle the Emperor. Far from it. He said that if only they gave him the chance, he would convince them the Emperor was actually descended from a globefish, which is the fish the Japanese like best of all."

"And did they give him his chance?"

"No; they gave him eight years."

The glassy-eyed chamberlain ruminated. Then he decided to confide in me again, and leaned closer.

"I'll tell you a secret. The Emperor wherever he goes is always accompanied by a red jewel box. It contains the Sacred Jewel, one of the three symbols of Imperial Majesty. The other two are the Sacred Mirror, and the Sacred Sword. The Mirror and the Sword are kept at two Shinto shrines, but the Emperor himself keeps the Jewel.

"The Jewel is supposed to be 'the essence of the moon,' but nobody knows what it really is, not even the Emperor. Some think it's jade, but others say it's a giant pearl. Now, ask me a question."

"Why doesn't he open the box, and find out?"

The glassy-eyed chamberlain nodded. "Exactly. But, do you know, he doesn't dare? You see, there is a theory the Jewel was stolen ages ago, and there is nothing in the box at all. If the Emperor opened the box and there was nothing in it, he would lose face."

The sake jars were all empty, and it was time to go. As I shook hands with the tubby Colonel Ashida, he hissed softly: "You

38

are a very wise man. You listen, and say nothing." I smiled feebly, unable to explain I had been made speechless.

(8)

Big-winged black butterflies fluttered prettily over the tea-green waters of the Imperial moat, as we approached the Ohte Gate. Just to see those pine-clad green slopes, the hoary gray masonry and the white-faced black-roofed watchtowers, a hundred sight-seeing buses draw up daily in the Imperial Plaza. From them descend people from all over Japan, showing gold teeth in anticipatory smiles, and clutching children and cameras. Led by a bus conductress holding aloft a bright yellow flag with their bus's number on it, so they will not get lost, they march with military precision towards the padlocked gates of the double bridge. Through the bars, they snap what they can of the enclosed 250 acres.

We were more privileged. Mr. Shima was saluted by guards who wore black tunics with bright gold chrysanthemum buttons. We passed through the massive gateway, and rounded a curving, high stone wall, 15 feet thick and topped by one of the watchtowers. Presently we came on a large lawn, where rows of wooden chairs faced towards a stage. Behind the stage, on a piece of lawn fenced off by strips of blue and white cloth, big refreshment tents had been put up. To the left of the stage there was another enclosure that looked like a football field. The people who had come to watch the polo and the dancing were strolling about, under trees that were heavy with white and pink blossom. The men wore morning coats and top hats. The ladies were dressed in Parisian dresses, or in kimonos, and twirled parasols.

Polo was invented by horse-riding tribesmen of Central Asia, and reached Japan thirteen hundred years ago in the form we were to watch, called *dakyu*. Eight horsemen rode on to the football field. Four wore salmon-colored coats over white shirts; the other four had scarlet coats and purple shirts. Each player was armed with a 3-foot bamboo pole with a scoop net attached.

At one end of the 60-yard field, there was an upright wooden board, with a hole in it, called the goal hole. Scattered about the field were red balls and white balls. The white-shirt team played only the white balls; the scarlet-coated players, the red balls. Each side had to get all its balls through the goal hole, plus an extra "game ball" marked with a cross. The team that did so first was the winner.

For some minutes the players were content to ride up and down the field, showing off their horses' paces. Then a fanfare of gongs and drums signaled the commencement of the game. There was a melee of wheeling horses in the center of the field, and a scarlet-coated rider broke for the goal hole, a red ball caught in his scoop net. A salmon-coated rider flew after him, but too late: scarlet coat lifted himself in his saddle as he passed the upright wooden board, and threw the red ball through the goal hole. A drum roll indicated a red goal.

The game continued in this fashion, with a drum sounded for a red goal and a gong for a white goal. Often, two opposing horses were reared on their hind legs, long necks straining, as one rider sought to throw a goal and the other rider strove to stop him. Many times, a thrown ball struck the wooden board and rebounded on to the field; it took a cunning wrist and a good eye to put the ball through the goal hole from the midst of one of the melees. The spectators lining both sides of the field applauded goals by either team. At the end of the game, both the drum and the gong were sounded, to indicate that the result was a draw.

The people who had been watching the *dakyu* immediately moved towards the rows of chairs facing the stage, to see the *bugaku*, or ancient court dances. The front row of chairs was reserved for the Imperial family; and the two chairs in the center of the row were different from the others. Each had a little triangle-shaped "roof," and a back of plaited straw. These were for the Emperor and Empress of Japan.

Abruptly, the Emperor came round the side of one of the tents, followed closely by the Empress, and at an interval by the Crown Prince and Crown Princess. Hirohito and his son wore morning coats. The Empress was in pink, and Princess Michiko wore a kimono the color of pale blossom.

The Emperor's hair was gray, and thinning, and he looked older than in his photographs, though still handsome and distinguished. Everyone stood up, until he and his family were seated. The Empress was plump-faced, smiling and at ease. But Hirohito seemed to be sulking, in a royal and dignified way.

"He does not like stage performances," Mr. Shima whispered in my ear. "He feels they are a waste of time. He would rather be in his laboratory, studying specimens."

The passion of the Emperor of Japan is marine biology. He has written several books about clams and crabs, and has an enormous collection of specimens from Sugami Bay. He used to go out in a small boat to look for them, while Shinto priests stood on the volcanic beach beating gongs and praying aloud for his safety. There is a distinct trace of eccentricity in the family. His father, the Emperor Taisho, abruptly retired from public life after an extraordinary scene in the Diet. Taisho was handed a rolled-up scroll, containing the speech from the throne. Instead of unrolling and reading it, he delightedly used it to peer at each bowing Dietman as through a telescope. Perhaps he was as profoundly bored by politics and Dietmen as is Hirohito by ancient court dances.

The music for the dances was provided by fourteen musicians playing drums and flutes. In addition to several smaller drums, there was an enormous court drum, painted with flames. One of the flutes was 18 inches long, and had not one but several reeds, like an organ. The dances were of two kinds, called *Samai* and *Umai*, or left-dancing and right-dancing. Left-dancing came from China, right-dancing from Korea. Both kinds date back to the eighth century.

The first dance was a languid affair, meant to call to mind the sight of court ladies' robes fluttering in a breeze. The flutes tooted mournfully; the drums beat slow and sad; and the male dancers, dressed in heavy, gorgeous costumes, with faces painted like kabuki actors, put one foot before another as if they were advancing through thick sand. The next dance was livelier: the dancers whirled lances and shields, and occasionally stamped heavily, for they were supposed to be warriors attacking a fortress. The gentlemen in morning coats and top hats, and the ladies in Parisian dresses or kimonos, applauded gently after each item. Prince Akihito, a good-looking young man with glossy black hair, sneaked an occasional yawn; his pretty peaches-and-cream wife, in her pale-blossom kimono, sat upright with her hands folded, plainly on her best behavior and determinedly exhibiting intelligent interest of an intensely absorbed and concentrated sort.

We thanked Mr. Shima for the lunch, and for the Imperial entertainment. He said the lunch had been uneatable and the entertainment flat and stale. But we could see that he was well pleased. He no longer had an *on* towards us. He had had his face restored.

That night, I was awakened by a noise I felt sure had not been just the clack-clack the watchmen make when they rap their two short sticks together to assure the neighborhood they are on their rounds. It seemed to come from the upstairs guest room, though we had no guest. I easily resisted any impulse to leap out of bed, and instead lay and slowly counted to a hundred, before switching on the bedside light with a very audible click. It seemed to me I heard an in-hiss of breath. Then there was a quick patter of bare feet down the stairs, and someone hastily unbolted the front door.

Jane and the children slept on. Leisurely, I went downstairs and closed and put the bolt back on the front door, which I found standing wide open. Then I went up to inspect the guest room.

I was glad I had taken Mr. Shima's advice and not tried to help out by leaving a window open or a small sum of money lying in sight. The guest-room window had been very expertly forced, with a minimum of damage, in a manner that must have given every satisfaction to a professional man. As for the silvery-looking cigarette box he had taken, it ought to keep him bemused about foreigners for the rest of his life. It had been presented to us by an indefatigable practical joker, who had it made just a millimeter shorter than an ordinary cigarette.

The main thing, however, was that the persistent burglar had also finally got back his face. I was quite sure he would not trouble us again. He never did.

(9)

Goto-san, which means Honorable Highwayman or Mr. Magnanimity, depending on which character is used to write it down, had been a mailman for over thirty years, and in all that time had never delivered mail except in Hata-Yuguri. A Japanese mailman starts his career in one neighborhood, or *cho*, and never leaves it. The reason is that it takes several years to get to know where everyone lives. And this has to be memorized, because all the little wooden houses look alike, and they are not numbered in a fashion calculated to aid a mailman. Next to number 1225 may be 75; and on the other side, 9.

Once a Japanese home has been tracked down, its doorpost will be found to contain a wealth of information about the householder in the form of little round tin badges carefully nailed to it. A century or so ago, every family had to post on its door its hereditary status and class position. Nowadays, the little plaques reveal the householder's name and his telephone number, and that he is in good standing with the gas and electricity companies and has paid his radio and television license fee; also, that he has made his annual donation to the Red Cross, is a duly registered voter, and a member of the "Let's prevent noise" committee of the neighborhood association.

In addition to having our name painted in large letters on our gate, we had it printed on a board that we had affixed to a telegraph pole at the entry of our lane, opposite the police box. But the lane itself had no name, so we had a little map printed, along with written directions in both English and Japanese, to give to our friends. In spite of this, we estimated that we lost about ten per cent of those who set out to find us.

Tokyo is a clueless maze for most foreigners. One man we knew always told cab drivers when he was lost to take him to the Imperial Hotel: then at least he knew where he was. Another, the day his driver phoned to say he was sick, asked a friend for a lift home from the office. When the friend said he did not pass his way, and suggested he take a cab, the man replied dismally: "I can't: I've just realized I don't know where I live!"

The Japanese do not attempt to find out where their friends live, beyond asking in which *cho* they are. Then they go to a *cho* police box and give the name, and a policeman will direct them to the house. This, however, is not practicable for foreigners who do not speak Japanese. The next best thing is to have a printed card of directions in Japanese, and a map, and show these to a cab driver; but this procedure does not necessarily work either, since many Tokyo cab drivers do not know their way about the city. Jane once hired a cab whose driver said cheerfully she would have to guide him, since he had just arrived from Osaka, having driven the 300 miles in his cab. He explained he was a fourth-grade judoist, wanted to get his fifth grade, and could get it only in Tokyo.

Japanese cab drivers also incline to be suicidal, and are called *kamikaze*, after the Japanese suicide pilots of wartime. It rains a lot in Japan, and the streets are often a wet blur of chaotically driven automobiles. The harder it rains, the more furious the driving. This is why main intersections have huge boards with numbers on them: for instance, 9–188. Many strangers innocently mistake these for winning lottery numbers, or for the score in some peculiar Japanese game. Neither guess is correct, though the latter comes nearer the truth. The numbers refer respectively to the dead and injured in traffic accidents the day before. The figure for deaths does not include those who reach hospital alive but die thereafter.

The only thing a Tokyo automobile will stop for is a red light. But even traffic lights can cause confusion. In one Tokyo district where traffic is especially heavy—an elevated train dashes through a tunnel in the side of a department store every few minutes, and on the ground whole armies of pedestrians surge solidly across intersections—a child was killed where three roads meet. The neighborhood association out of its own pocket paid for and erected a fourth set of traffic lights, which, however, work independently of the municipality's lights. Where the three streets meet is now bedlam.

The most devilish drivers are the cab men, partly because they are ruthlessly exploited by cab companies that pay starvation wages for long hours but offer bonuses to the drivers who make the most trips. A wise move before hiring a Tokyo cab is to look in the back for footmarks. If the previous passenger had to brace himself by planting both feet against the driving seat, take another cab. It is also wise to memorize the Japanese for "go slow," which is *yukkuri*.

A tall Texan climbed shakily out of a tiny Tokyo cab in front of the Imperial Hotel, made straight for the bar, and gulped down a double bourbon. He told his friends: "When my cab driver began to speed up and miss other cars by inches, I leaned forward and said the Japanese word for 'slow' in his ear. Didn't make a bit of difference. Darned if the little s.o.b. didn't feed his engine more gas.

"I reached over his shoulder and grabbed out the ignition key. Then I gave him a real tongue-whipping. I said, 'Listen, son, when I say I want to go slow, I mean real *slow*. Now, let's try her again.'

"He seemed terrified of me, but still it was no use. We passed everything else on the road, including two police cars and a fire truck, and all the way he was jabbing a finger at his speedometer, and jabbering at me, as if he thought I ought to be congratulating him instead of wanting to wring his neck."

Someone asked the Texan what word he had used for "slow" and he replied "*hayaku*," which means "go faster."

Another man who had only five minutes to catch a train used *hayaku* to a Tokyo cab driver, and meant it, but swore he would never do it again. He said they drove most of the way on the wrong side of the road, and sometimes were partly on the sidewalk. Every sixty seconds, the driver took his eyes off the road to turn round and make a countdown, holding up one hand with a finger over—*five four three two one*—and screeching to a halt at the station as he folded down the fifth finger.

Ed Seidensticker, a man with an iron nerve, claimed he found Tokyo cab drivers pleasantly talkative rather than suicidally fast. They talked to him, he declared, about the respective chances of the Taiyo Whales and the Kokutetsu Swallows, these being baseball teams; knew fascinating, intimate details about the lives of Japanese movie stars; and could discuss knowledgeably and with compassion the plight of the girls thrown out of work by the Anti-Prostitution Law. Ed also took a charitable view of their chronic inability to find a Tokyo address. "In Tokyo," he said, "even the fire department can't find the right house before it's too late." He added that he had once met a cab driver who tried in vain to extricate himself from a Setagaya blind alley. "In the end, he had to hail another cab to take him home; a most humiliating experience, like a telephone operator giving himself a wrong number."

46

If the cab drivers go like the wind, so do all other Tokyo vehicles, including hearses. The Japanese hearse is an enormous, elaborately carved wooden structure shaped like a house, with a regular roof in an inverted V. It used to be drawn by horses, but nowadays has been motorized. It is not uncommon in Tokyo to see this awe-inspiring vehicle take a corner on two wheels, with a red-lit traffic indicator sticking out at a rakish angle.

What makes Tokyo's vast, roaring Niagaras of traffic especially sinister on a pouring wet day is that many of the drivers then put on face masks: pads of white cotton over the nose and mouth, held in place by tapes tied behind the ears. This is to prevent the spread of cold and influenza germs, but the effect on the already petrified pedestrian is to make him feel that he is being hunted down remorselessly by murderous-looking bandits bent on his destruction.

Walking in Tokyo has other dangers. "The logic of necessity," wrote Nishi Amane last century, "requires people to plant both feet firmly, and expand the elbows into any opening that may occur." This still holds, with the additional warning that a determined Tokyo pedestrian will employ, as well as his elbow, his knee, his foot, and his umbrella; and if necessary will use his mother-in-law or wife as a battering-ram. Also, he is apt to come to an abrupt halt in the middle of the sidewalk, in order to exchange deep bows with an acquaintance.

The Japanese bow stiffly, from the hips, their arms rigid at their sides. The heads of the two bowers go down to about diaphragm level, and hover there in an exploratory sort of way, while each quickly tries to work out the exact degree of deference due to himself and to the other. This calls for a considerable knowledge of their respective incomes, future business prospects, and blood and marriage ties past, present, and expectable. If accuracy is unattainable, and it usually is, one will raise his head an experimental inch or so. If the other follows suit, they both have to duck down again, and this may go on for some time, until they simply become tired, or until other users of the sidewalk become impatient and shove them both out of the way.

Girls employed in Tokyo department stores are taught to bow superbly. Indeed, the ones who stand beside the escalator at each floor have nothing else to do. They wear trim lavender uniforms and lavender-colored gloves, and as each customer passes them on the escalator they bow low and murmur "welcome." In English, this does not sound very special. But in Japanese it can sound like the throatiest, sexiest, soulfulest four syllables ever spoken by feminine tongue. And the girls are taught to utter it just that way.

But Yumiko Showa, who lived in Hata-Yuguri and was a movie actress, explained to us that there was another side to life in a department store. Before she went in for movies and modeling, Miss Showa had worked for a time as a department-store girl. She was paid $20 a month, and, on a busy day, might have to bow and throatily murmur *"Irasshaimas!"* twenty thousand times, or about once every one and one third second. Other girls, she said, were even worse off, as their job was to repeat over the store loud-speakers, again and again and again: "Buy with care; careful buying brings happiness."

The girls had to attend classes in flower arranging and the tea ceremony. The attitude of the personnel manageress to the girls—and Miss Showa quoted—was: "Most of you are stray bitches without manners or etiquette, but I will make ladies of you." The girls were forbidden to have romances with the store's male clerks, and were fired if they married. Employees of the department store were instructed to watch for people carrying parcels done up in the store's special wrapping paper. They were supposed to offer to help carry such parcels, and also to give up their seats on subways, buses, and streetcars to store customers.

Japan was the first country in the world to have department stores. First in the field was Matsuzakaya, in 1611, the year Shakespeare wrote *The Tempest*. But it was Mitsukoshi which invented price tags, free deliveries, and *okyakusama daiichi-shugi*—"the customer is always right." Mitsukoshi also gave away paper umbrellas on wet days.

Japanese economists devote serious attention to the sales figures of department stores, which they regard as the best possible index of business trends. The ten largest stores, with their branches, account for six per cent of total Japanese retail trade. The important months are July, when Japanese workers receive their midsummer bonuses, and December, when they get their year-end bonuses. The bonuses range between one month's and six months' pay, and they are never saved, but splurged on the grand national pastime, gift-giving. Most of the gifts are purchased in the department stores.

In the seventeenth century the stores chiefly sold kimonos, and still do sell them, but have added such lines as food, furniture, television sets, washing machines, and refrigerators. Most of the big ones also offer their 100,000 daily customers such sidelines as beauty salons; cocktail bars; concert halls; movie theaters; wedding halls, with Buddhist and Shinto priests in attendance and bridal wigs for hire; constant organ music; and on the roof a playground where customers may park their children while they shop; and even a zoo and a planetarium. Mitsukoshi, because of its rigorous precautions against fire and theft, is the only place in Japan outside the state museums where national treasures may be publicly exhibited.

(1 0)

I once ate *soba*, Japanese noodle soup, in a Tokyo restaurant with a Chinese philosopher. He was bursting with excitement. For years he had wandered through his own vast country, through Tibet, and all over India, seeking rare Buddhist books. And he had just made his best find in a Tokyo bookstore, in Kanda.

A whole street in Tokyo is given over to bookstores, most of them specializing in Oriental literature. Here any evening you will find rows of absorbed readers, standing entranced, with volumes open in their hands, while the booksellers benevolently look on. Any purchase, however trivial—for a few copper coins you may buy an entire sketchbook full of beautiful brush strokes of trees and flowers—is very carefully wrapped in pretty paper; an elastic band is slipped round it, and your change is politely handed you on a tiny tray.

Another street is lined solidly with god-shops, their windows filled with miniature Shinto shrines made of polished wood, bright with brass, and topped by phoenixes; and also with praying golden Buddhas, which tempt the passer-by to step inside and inquire: "How much is that Buddha in the window?"

In the Ginza, which is the heart of Tokyo, there is a vast gallery of restaurants and food shops. At their entrances, the restaurants have glass display cases whose shelves are laden with colored plastic replicas of the dishes available within. All you have to do is point. In all Tokyo there are 32,500 restaurants (New York has only 17,000), serving such delicacies as shrimp and prawns, lobsters and eels, trout and globefish, thinly sliced raw fish and rice balls, lily bulbs and lotus roots. This, of course, is in addition to side bowls of rice, noodles, and noodle soup.

One restaurant specializes in mudfish which are boiled *alive* in bean curd; another offers only pigs' wombs and testicles. One friend of ours who went on a culinary prowl found himself dipping a big spoon in a bowl of tiny wriggling fish that he was expected to swallow whole and alive. Another unwisely praised a paper-thin slice of raw fish that was placed before him. The chef at once produced the fish itself, still swimming in its glass tank, to prove his delicate surgical touch.

Tokyo's subway system is part privately owned, therefore cut into as many segments as a chopped-up worm. Even using it at random, a person always comes to the surface to find giant bouquets of paper flowers on giant wooden stilts standing outside a building to indicate that the premises are brand new and have just opened. The vast city clangs and snorts with bulldozers and steam cranes busily clearing the way for new eleven-story buildings that, like the ever-rising television towers of spidery steel, defy Tokyo's tradition of severe earthquakes.

To have done with dull facts and figures, Tokyo has twice as many movie theaters as New York, and more neon lights than any city in the world. It has 78 universities and over 300,000 students; 2:200 bathhouses and 11,000 cemeteries; 13,000 taxicabs and 35,000 bars; 5,500 beauty parlors and 15,000 bright-red public telephones. There are 1,455 Shinto shrines in the city, and 2,753 Buddhist temples. And there are 1,600 publishing companies, and 100 monthly *poetry* magazines.

But there are only 500,000 flush toilets, for 2,500,000 households.

The affairs of Tokyo, and of Japan, are mostly conducted from the city's business and banking district, called Marunouchi. Here the *zaibatsu*, or heads of the great Japanese banking, trading, and shipping combines, have their offices, in heavy gray anonymous-looking blocks of drab buildings. The little black-clad gray-skinned men come to work in Cadillacs whose doors are held open by low-bowing doormen with war-scarred faces. The *zaibatsu* pull the strings that work the politicians, who squabble like parrots in the pyramidal granite Diet building, and scheme in the geisha restaurants of Akasaka and along the Sumida River.

A hundred years ago, the same class of merchants and bankers held the great court nobles and landowners as well as the peasant masses in a tight vise of debts. Nevertheless, they had to walk warily, for officially they ranked below the meanest samurai, who could chop off their heads with his terrible two swords if they imperiled his "face." Today they have to pay at least lip

51

service to Japan's new *demokurasu*. Now as then, their profitable diversion is to provide the other classes of the community with plenty of amusement.

Throughout the six *sumo* seasons, all Japan breathlessly watches the traditional wrestling matches on television. The fluctuating fortunes of every would-be *yokozuna*, or grand champion, are suspensefully followed on millions of bright little screens, in homes, bars, and barbershops; schoolboys sometimes commit suicide in bitter disappointment if their favorite fails to make the grade.

Sumo claims to be fourteen or fifteen hundred years old. There are eleven grades of wrestlers, with the *yokozuna* at the top. Only one wrestler in five hundred ever gets as far as the first, or *ozeki*, grade, and this usually takes fifteen years. The top wrestlers, therefore, are men who are no longer young; and they have as a rule monumental bellies, because each day they consume vast quantities of a dish called *chankonabe*, which consists of beef, pork, fish, and vegetables all cooked together in an enormous pot. This they eat with five bowls of rice as side dishes.

The actual wrestling is highly stylized, yet each bout lasts only a few seconds. The wrestlers approach each other in a ring, or *dohyo*, 15 feet in diameter. The ring is decorated with four big tassels, representing the four seasons, and colored black, red, blue, and white. Each wrestler wears only a loincloth, and has his long hair in a topknot, whose function is to pad his skull against either blows or falls. In the ring there is also a referee, in a fancy kimono, who however is watched by twelve retired champions wearing black kimonos. They sit outside the ring like inquisitors, ready to challenge his judgment.

The wrestlers ritually toss handfuls of salt while they balefully eye each other, then retire to their corners, only to come out again. This time, however, they merely limber up, stamping the ground and grunting heavily, go down almost on all fours and glare into each other's face, then rise and retire once more.

This can go on for as long as four minutes, after which they must grapple. To win, a man must upset his opponent or at least force him to put a foot outside the ring.

To watch this spectacle, 15,000 people in Tokyo gather in a large hall. They are usually prepared to sit all day, through bout after bout, squatting in little square enclosures that look like orange boxes, and drinking sake, eating raw fish and seaweed, and brewing tea over little braziers specially provided for the purpose.

One American in Tokyo whom we knew had devised his own method of watching *sumo*, on television, in his favorite bar. He entirely ignored the screen while the wrestlers tossed salt, limbered up, crouched, and glared. But as they grappled, he would spin round on his bar stool just in time to catch the result. He had with practice developed a rhythm that matched the wrestlers' movements.

The other great show in Tokyo is the kabuki theatrical performances, which are a sort of Oriental opera, with chorus and orchestra but nonsinging principals. In the Kabukiza, in the Ginza, from morning to evening, gorgeously dressed warriors, emperors, princesses, concubines, clowns, witches, and monsters strut the boards in glittering pantomime, to the music of hand drums, bells, gongs, flutes, and fiddles. The faces of the heroes are painted white, to show how virtuous and genteelly handsome they are; the villains' faces are painted red, for evil. At climactic moments, the actors hold up the action while they put themselves in set poses. Such high spots are preceded usually by a loud clapping together of wooden sticks, called *hyoshigi*, to warn the audience of what is coming, so they won't miss a single thrill.

Most Japanese over the age of thirty know the kabuki plays by heart. It is as if English-speaking people could quote Shakespeare. The plays are so well known that just before a dull patch the audience streams out, to gossip in the lobby or eat fried shrimp in the theater restaurant. To make this easier, there are frequent intermissions. But some prefer to stay in their comfortable plush seats, and eat a simple meal out of a little wooden box. Women bare their breasts to feed their infants. The plays are very lengthy. The most famous of all, *Chushingura*, or the story of the forty-seven *Ronin*, lasts six hours; but nowadays only half of the full version is played.

One of the oddities of kabuki is that there are no women players. All the parts, including those of women, are played by men. The men who play the women's parts are called *onnagata*, and a hundred years ago they were compelled by law to wear women's clothing off-stage as well as on, and to enter the public bath through the women's entrance. One of Japan's greatest *onnagato* successfully played a seventeen-year-old girl when he was seventy.

If women did appear in kabuki, they would need to be tough. Any one of the gorgeous costumes may weigh as much as 40 pounds, and is worn with a huge headdress weighing the same. Kabuki acting is a hereditary profession, like burglary; one well-known player is seventeenth in direct line of descent from the first member of his family to play the same roles. Kabuki actors, even the humblest, take their art seriously. I knew one who had been playing the same part for over forty years, but still practiced sedulously, several hours a day. He was the front part of a kabuki horse.

The kabuki play is usually a tragedy. For instance, all of the forty-seven *Ronin* die. The Kabukiza is generally filled with people having a good cry, as are the Tokyo movie theaters, with their films of suicides and unrequited love. The Japanese prize sorrow and sacrifice above happiness and fulfillment; key words in Japanese popular songs are weep and part, not moon and June; in popular novels, the wind is always biting, the rain nearly always dismal as well as damp.

Nevertheless, young Japanese now show little interest in kabuki, and profess indifference to geishas. Theirs is the bright new gimcrack world of roaring motorcycles and all-night coffee shops, rockabilly singers and jazz combos. Over the city's bright-red public telephones, the black-haired teen-agers eagerly date one another—a thing unheard of in the stern days before *demo-kurasu* and the MacArthur Constitution.

As dusk falls on Tokyo, the city blooms with thousand-splendored neon lights. The Ginza, and the "amusement centers" of Asakusa, Shinjuku, and Shibuya, become brighter than Broadway.

We started off one night prowl of Tokyo in a café called the Julien Sorel. It offered Puerto Rico Specials to drink, Dizzy Gillespie records, and reproductions of Chagall on the walls. We went from there to a teahouse five stories tall; the band wore red hunting coats and moved between floors in a gilded elevator as they played. The walls were covered with purple velvet drapes decorated with white plaster doves. The third place we visited had bright tropical birds in cages, tropical fish in glass tanks, and several fountains that changed colors.

Then we drove to Ueno Park, whose lake has huge red water lilies floating on its surface. All around the lake, from stalls lit by paper lanterns, men were busily selling chrysanthemums, dwarf orange trees, and singing crickets imprisoned in tiny bamboo cages shaped like gondolas.

In Asakusa, close by the great Buddhist temple to *Kannon*, the Goddess of Mercy, we wandered through the seven-story Shinsekai. In addition to colored fountains, it had hot baths in the basement and a planetarium on the roof; the world's longest *sushi* "bar" (*sushi* consists of small balls of rice and raw fish); a Latin Quarter; a Venetian tea park; a Hawaiian room, serving fruit punch; an amusement gallery with trick mirrors and a tunnel of love; and a cabaret with one thousand hostesses.

The hostesses were numbered. A customer pointed out the girl he wanted, and a waiter called into a microphone for "687-san." Formerly, Japan's 132,000 prostitutes, known as *kiken na dokubana*, or "Dangerous Poison Flowers," had their own labor union, called the "National Federation of Special Restaurant

Workers," and Japan's 35,000 brothel owners were legally registered as the "National Venereal Diseases Prevention Auton-
omy Council."

When, under the Anti-Prostitution Law, the brothel keepers
were given a year's grace to find new occupations for themselves and the girls, some of them built "amusement centers."
One man, who turned his place into a playing-card factory, described how his girls gradually tapered off prostitution, as they
switched, as he put it, "from one special skill to another."

From the Shinsekai we went on to a much smaller and considerably more uninhibited place, where a handful of men who
were drunk on sake were tossing cherry bombs at a couple of
dancing girls wearing only colored ribbons, who seemed wholly
unperturbed and merely giggled.

Though it was barely eleven o'clock, life and gaiety were already ebbing from the "amusement centers" like spilt wine.
Only the *pachinko* parlors were still chinking in their dull me-
tallic fashion as we walked along the street. The truth is that the
average adult Japanese worker cannot on a wage of $40 a month
—$50 for white-collar "salarymen"—afford much more than *pa-
chinko*, which is a pinball game costing only a few cents. We
stepped into a *pachinko* parlor. A metal tag on one of the machines read, in English: "Have patience: please do not get angry." The dull-faced players looked patient to the point of total apathy. They were married men who did not want to go
home but could not afford drinking in a bar. Yet the cafés and
tea halls had been crowded—with teen-agers, boys and girls. In
Japan, as in other countries, the people with money to splurge
are the top people and the teen-agers.

For foreigners, the Japanese have devised amusements that
have given Tokyo a gaudy reputation. The Japanese themselves
have few inhibitions about sex, and have gained the notion that
foreigners like their sex hot and strong. At Yokosuka, where
there are a great many American sailors, there is an establish-

56

ment which calls itself, with a sort of grand simplicity, "Big Tits Bar." It has a girl lounging in the doorway, wearing a beckoning smile and sheer black silk pajamas.

The Ginza in Tokyo has a place where girls, wearing canary-yellow panties and bras, rock-and-roll while serving beer to the customers; and another that offers "high-stepping atomic girls," and explains on its specially printed card, in English: "Our girls are selected on the basis of a good figure and sex appeal. There are however limitations and please do take same into consideration when you comment on those very daring girls."

That night, back on the Ginza from Asakusa, we were eating fried chickens on wooden skewers, at a sidewalk *yakitori* stall, when a piece of paper was slipped furtively into my hand. It read: "Acrobat nude girls, pin-up models for photographers, we can do one day processing of color film, 2 hour service on B & W. Please make use of our newly opened bar. No cover, minimum, or hostess charges. Our girl Models await your patronage." On the back, there was a neatly drawn map, and directions in English and also in Japanese "for your taxi driver."

In really important matters, the Japanese evidently are determined to allow neither the language barrier nor the lack of street names in their capital nor the ignorance of taxi drivers to impede international relations.

(1 1)

Sano-san had been, among other things, a fishmonger's assistant and a law student. He was currently my driver, but this was only so that he could save more money, to have another whack at his studies. There are some 300,000 university students in Tokyo. To pay for a higher education, they act as human shoehorns, squeezing people into the overcrowded subway trains at rush hours; or parade outside dubious nightclubs, wearing grotesque costumes and carrying advertising placards; or sell their blood to blood banks, even though many of them are tubercular.

Sano-san was an alert young man, with black, upstanding hair, thin cheeks, and a constant cheerful grin. As we drove around Tokyo, speeding in and out of the Niagaras of traffic, he instructed me in many things, including how to avoid having to write a letter of apology.

Every *gaijin*, or foreigner, in Japan sooner or later writes a letter of apology. If a *gaijin* breaks a traffic rule, he usually gets off—but only if he is prepared to apologize, in writing. A *gaijin* who forgets to pay a tax or some other official levy by the due date will not be fined, provided he pens an apologetic note. Every resident *gaijin* must carry around with him an alien registration card. A *gaijin* who cannot produce his card when challenged has to write an apology.

The abjectness of the apology demanded depends entirely on the attitude adopted by the *gaijin*. If he blusters, or fumes, or indeed shows any trace of annoyance whatever, he may find that the only alternative to appearing in court is to admit in writing that because of his incredible stupidity the authorities have been put to an unparalleled degree of trouble, for which he humbly begs their forgiveness. Since a case can drag through the Japanese courts for years, most *gaijins* will abase themselves rather than risk it.

I knew one *gaijin* who was accused of not registering correctly the advent of his one-month-old daughter in Japan. "You did not write down how she entered the country," said an official. "But she was born in Japan!" the *gaijin* cried. "You did not state the port of entry," said the inexorable official, and made him write out three letters of apology, one for each department involved.

"The thing to do," advised Sano-san, "is always adopt a low posture. If you break a regulation, the official whose job is to enforce it loses face. To get his face back, he must persuade you to humble yourself to him. *Gaijins* who bluster and shout make him lose still more face. Then he *has* to punish them, even if they are *gaijins* who have a lot of pull, and he knows they can cost him his job.

"However, if a *gaijin* adopts a low posture, he can get away with almost anything," Sano-san added.

I tried out a low posture, and it worked. For several weeks I parked wrongly, went about without my alien registration certificate, ignored two demands for the ward tax, drove through traffic lights when I was satisfied there was no danger. Each time that I was caught, I did not try to defend my behavior, I simply admitted that I was completely in the wrong, and cried that no punishment could be harsh enough for such as I. Never was I charged with anything, or even asked to put my apology in writing. Instead, the officers who caught me at once set me free, for they were bursting with friendliness and doubled face.

I felt a bit two-faced myself. But I had proved Sano-san right.

As we drove about Tokyo, I noticed more and more red flags paraded outside more and more public buildings, as increasing numbers of civil servants staged strikes. It seemed impossible to turn a corner without finding traffic stalled by prancing crowds wearing head towels and chanting "*Washo! Washo!*"

Twice a year in Japan, in the spring and in the fall, the Sohyo, or Japanese labor-union federation, launches "offensives," for more wages. Railway workers ostentatiously walk away from their trains, teleprinters cease to chatter, and miners stop digging coal. But this time, said Sano-san, the schoolteachers and other Government workers parading outside the Ministries were not demanding higher pay, but protesting against rearmament and bases. Also, a big part was being played by the Zengakuren, the federation of student unions.

Sano-san was able to tell me much about the Zengakuren, being himself a member, who it was true had ceased paying his dues, but only temporarily.

The Zengakuren leadership was split in two, but the split was not of a sort calculated to bring cheer to Japanese or any other conservatives; half the student leaders professed Communism, and the other half sneered at Communists as sissies who had lost their revolutionary zeal and were letting the international black-leg, Khrushchev, take them back to false bourgeois standards.

I recognized the political faith of young Yoshio Tanaka, and when I mentioned his name, Sano-san nodded. "Tanaka-san is a leader in Zengakuren," he said. Evidently Yoshio's interest in our neighborhood's movie actress, pretty Yumiko Showa, had not, as yet, diluted his politics.

"Tomorrow," said Sano-san, "there will be a big demonstration at Tachikawa."

Tachikawa was an American air base, not far from Tokyo. The demonstrators proposed marching on the base, after tearing up the fence surrounding it. To prevent them from doing so, Japanese policemen took up stations inside the fence.

When I arrived that morning, both sides were adopting a low posture. The demonstrators had come in buses equipped with loud-speakers, which, however, were dispensing light music. Planted in the soft soil, beside the buses, were tall bamboo poles, with red flags fluttering at their tops.

"Sakura, sakura," sang the musical buses. " 'Cherry blossom, cherry blossom.' " While the record was being changed by a pretty girl who looked charming in a head towel, the demonstrators shouted, "Go home, Yankees," but good-humoredly.

The police also were on their best behavior. They stood in a long row, their hands peaceably behind their backs, facing the demonstrators, and wearing somewhat apologetic grins. Even when a few youthful demonstrators tossed little firecrackers at them, they were not particularly put out. Like the girl strippers in Asakusa, they just giggled.

But presently the buses stopped singing about cherry blossoms, and the demonstrators surged forward and laid hands on the fence stakes. Crying "Washo! Washo!," they tugged at the poles until they were loose, then pulled them right out of the ground. This done, they began to advance, stepping over the fallen fence on to the soil of the base.

While the demonstrators were uprooting the fence stakes, the policemen had been putting on white cotton gloves that they took from their pockets. Once gloved, they moved forward to meet the demonstrators, protecting themselves from firecrackers by holding little square wooden shields over their heads.

The clash, when it came, was not thunderous. Policemen and demonstrators just leaned against one another. Each side pushed. For what seemed minutes, nothing at all happened. Then the demonstrators slowly yielded.

The policemen continued to shove until the last demonstrator was back outside the fallen fence. The police then retreated a pace, though warily. Most of the demonstrators sat down on the grass, presumably to get their breath back. The policemen carefully replanted the fence, and straightened out the twisted barbed wire—I guessed this was why they had put on gloves.

An impasse having been reached, the two parties produced lunchboxes and began to eat, the police seated on their side of the fence, inside the base, and the demonstrators still outside. With fine impartiality, the buses provided canned music for both.

Lunch was followed by a lengthy siesta, which looked indeed as if it might go on indefinitely. Finally, the demonstrators got up, linked arms, and advanced once more, roaring "Washo! Washo!," while in their rear a big drum, like a festival drum, went "bong! bong!" But the replanted fence was too strong for them. Their arms folded, the policemen smiled sardonically. The sun was beginning to set, and a keen little wind had sprung up. The disgruntled demonstrators clambered aboard their buses, which one by one turned and bumped away towards the high road.

In most of the demonstrations the Zengakuren played an increasingly active part. When Mr. Inejiro Asanuma, the Socialist leader, marched up to the Diet at the head of several labor unions, the Zengakuren took over the show. Mr. Asanuma was trying to dissuade the Diet from passing a revised security treaty between Japan and the United States. But the more fiery members among the Zengakuren wished in addition to express their contempt and detestation of parliamentary politics, which they said were just bourgeois tricks. They did so by gleefully urinating *en masse* on the Diet steps and against the closed Diet door.

The police did not do much to restrain the students, because they were afraid that, if they did, everyone would say they were fascists, and just like the police in the bad old days, before *demokurasu*. But this consideration hardly weighed with actual fascists, of whom there were still quite a few left in Tokyo. They decided, or were commanded, to take a hand.

The Japanese Prime Minister and leader of the ruling conservative party, Mr. Nobusuke Kishi, was to fly to Washington to sign the new security treaty—though the Diet would still have to pass it, after that. The Zengakuren announced that they would attempt to prevent Mr. Kishi from reaching the Tokyo airport. Mr. Kishi fixed four in the morning as the discouraging hour of his departure, but thousands of undeterred students thronged the streets.

Most of them never even caught a glimpse of the Prime Minister's motorcar. Suddenly, instead of confronting patient police, they found themselves set upon by powerful adult thugs armed with thick clubs forested with sharp nails. The Zengakuren for all their blood and thunder talk had come unarmed to the fray.

I watched the astounded students being swept helplessly back by this onslaught. Some were seized by the throat, and thrown right across the street. Others were hammered down into the gutters under a rain of blows. Most just ran. It seemed to me that several of the clubbing men looked remarkably like "Pine Leaves."

Mr. Kishi got clear away, but a number of students reached the airport, where they were arrested after a free-for-all in the terminal restaurant which was witnessed by dazed Australians who had just stepped off a Qantas plane and had no idea what it was all about. One of the students who were arrested was a girl called Michiko Kamba, whose father was professor of sociology at Chuo University.

The perplexed professor sat down and wrote an indignant article entitled: "My Daughter Was Captured by Zengakuren." "She is my only daughter and my favorite child," he wrote. "She has been brought up in a free atmosphere, with few restrictions. She is bright, honest, and active, and has many friends. She was a good pupil at school, and a model child at home.

"When she began attending Tokyo University, she talked freely with her mother and myself about her ideas. She is progressive in her ideology, and critical of social conditions. Nevertheless, I can only think she has been drawn into these demonstrations by her loyalty to her Zengakuren friends.

"I cannot understand the tactics of the Zengakuren, nor what they are after. But they seem sincere in their convictions. The fault may lie in the present political situation. The majority party overrides the minority's wishes without adequate debate; and the minority believes its only mission is to oppose whatever the majority proposes. Frustration because of this situation may be responsible for the apparently insane acts of the students.

"But the students' true path is study, so they can build for the future. My wish is that the students will return to their studies, and have faith in their ability to make a brighter future for themselves.

"I am not trying to evade responsibility. Even now, I can see my daughter's eyes when I visited her in jail. She looked resentfully at me, as I scolded her. Her eyes seemed to say scornfully: 'Adults are cowards.'

"I must reflect on my past behavior towards my children, and study the causes that permitted the Zengakuren to capture my daughter."

But some other parents adopted a higher posture. (And the unhappy Professor Kamba was later to have his own mind changed for him, tragically and dramatically.)

In Hata-Yuguri, our Mr. Tanaka turned in fury on his son Yoshio. "Get out!" he shouted. "Communist! Bolshevik!"

Mrs. Tanaka, that patient woman, began to sob, but did not dare to intervene.

"And it's not just this Zengakuren nonsense, either," continued Mr. Tanaka, enjoying his own rage. "Running after a movie actress—I know all about it—I keep my eyes open—"

Mrs. Tanaka stopped quivering and moaning. For perhaps the first time in her life, she looked her husband straight in the eye. "I do not know which one of you is right about politics. But his way of life is more respectable than your way of life. He is young, with hot blood; and you are getting old, and your blood should have cooled. But it is your life that is unhealthy, not his; for it is you who go pleasure-seeking at night, not he."

Mrs. Katama's seed had fallen on receptive soil, after all. Sano-san, who was in the kitchen with the Tanakas's driver and overheard the whole thing, said with glee that it was the turn of the neighborhood association chairman to quiver and moan.

II

FUJI:

DEATH UNDER THE CHERRY BLOSSOM

In the cemetery, people had unrolled strips of straw matting to sit on, and families were merrily picnicking. They ate hard-boiled eggs, hot bean curd, and fried chicken, and drank bottles of rice wine. Hucksters had set up stalls, and were selling live goldfish in plastic bags, and dwarf orange trees a foot high which grew tiny oranges. Everywhere one looked there were masses of cherry and peach blossoms.

In Japan the traditional way to celebrate spring is to visit temples, shrines, and the graves of one's ancestors. Thousands of Tokyo citizens were spending the spring holiday in Aoyama cemetery. The graves on either side of the crowded narrow roadway were overhung by the pink and white blossom, and the scene was gay with the bright-purple paper parasols carried by the living.

Aoyama cemetery was filled with old people, married couples, and small children in holiday kimonos, their thick black hair cut in square bobs and the backs of their necks carefully shaved. But there were few teen-agers. The teen-agers had spent the bright spring day standing patiently in a line three blocks long, to get tickets for a rockabilly jamboree at the Theater Kyoritsu, which means "stand-togetherness."

On the stage, a young man who wore a rose-pink coat, a flame-colored shirt, and lobster-colored skin-tight trousers frantically thrummed a guitar and sang: "Rub me tender, rub me tloo." Teen-age girls threw colored paper ribbons at him, and screamed *"Maa-chan ai sh'teru wa yo,"* which means, "I love you."

65

Yumiko Showa was amused, but Yoshio Tanaka took a darker view.

The young man on the stage, busily untwining colored paper ribbons from his guitar, said he would do "anoth-ah lock-and-loll numb-ah."

"Rock-a-baka!" snarled Yoshio, which means "rocking idiot."

Later, as we sat in a coffee shop—one whose hi-fi set only played Bach, for Tokyo coffee shops cater to all tastes—Yoshio turned his lowering good looks on me. "You need no longer fear our yellow skins," he sneered. "But we fear your yellow culture!"

Yoshio was having a bad time. It was not just his father, and "lock-and-loll," that he disapproved of. He had become sufficiently proprietory to disapprove Yumiko's movies also. Like many young Japanese, he found himself living a split-level existence, and he did not know which he hated most, the old Japan or some aspects of the new. As a Communist, he was inclined to blame it all on the West.

"You are decadent!" cried Yoshio. "A citadel of evil; a festering leper!"

"You said last night that as a man of the new Japan you welcomed American influence."

"Only because it is good for destroying our old, bad values," said Yoshio. "We use you as if you were gunpowder, to blow up the thick walls of feudal customs."

What was really worrying him was Yumiko's new film. It was very sexy, and full of symbolism. In one scene she lay in bed smiling enticingly at her lover, and eating an apple. Her jealous husband meanwhile had found out about the affair, and was rushing home from the other end of Japan as fast as the railway could bring him. The bedroom scene closed with the lover standing beside the bed unbuttoning his shirt, and was followed by a close-up of a railway locomotive's pounding piston.

Yoshio loudly preached freedom verging on anarchy for

66

everyone, but I strongly suspected that if he ever got around to marrying Yumiko he would expect her to be a well-disciplined Japanese woman, pure and demure as the plum blossom.

Yumiko drank her coffee, and wisely changed the subject.

"Ryo and Sasa are to be married," she said.

Yoshio forgot his grievance, and looked amazed. "Ah *so?* I thought her father and mother were dead against it."

Ryo was a pretty, rather fragile girl of eighteen who lived in Hata-Yuguri, and Sasa was a student at Tokyo University and an intensely solemn young man. Neither of them spoke English so we had had to be content with exchanging stiff bows and grave smiles. I chiefly recalled Sasa as a round-shouldered youth, awkward and shambling, in the ugly black uniform all the students wore.

Ryo and Sasa had fallen in love. Ryo's parents immediately dismissed this as ridiculous; their daughter was much too young. In fact, they had decided to marry her off to the son of a neighbor, the managing director of a shipping company.

Sasa's father was currently having a wild affair with a geisha, and all his energy was bent on keeping his wife and grown-up son from learning about it, though the whole of Hata-Yuguri knew. Ryo and Sasa were so insistent that Ryo's mother finally hit on a plan to dissuade them without, as she hoped, driving them to any extreme step, like elopement or a double suicide. She pretended to agree to their becoming engaged but insisted that they first let her call in an astrologer. When Sasa said indignantly that this was all feudal nonsense, and Ryo gently wept, Ryo's mother said it was perfectly true, she was a silly, old-fashioned woman, but wouldn't they humor her, for if they were really well matched, what harm could it do?

Hardly any Japanese really believes in the marriage horoscope. But it is used to save "face." For the horoscope is such a complicated affair that it can be made to mean almost anything. If one side wishes to back out of a marriage, the horoscope is adduced in justification. If, however, both sides want the marriage to take place, no horoscope warnings, however dire, will have the slightest influence.

Ryo's mother of course arranged for the horoscope of her daughter and Sasa to be as black as possible, then threw hysterics at the very idea of their marrying. This was as far as the affair had gone when last I had heard about it. Now it seemed there was a further installment.

"They went to Enoshima for a week end," said Yumiko. "It's caused a terrible scandal. I don't think she's pregnant, but now of course the shipping man's son won't have any more to do with her. Ryo says she doesn't care."

I was as surprised by this story as Yoshio. I knew of course that young Japanese couples went off on week ends together, for chastity was now supposed to be very feudal. I had read a letter, printed in a newspaper, from a girl who blandly explained: "I am living with a man who wants to marry me, but unluckily he has a hooligan brother who will always keep him poor. I want to go on living with him until I find another man who will not be poor, but how can I set about finding one, without his knowing?"

But I hadn't thought Ryo and Sasa were that sort.

"They must have been made very desperate," said Yoshio, as if reading my thoughts. "I hope nothing will happen to them. The spring is a bad time."

In the spring, when the cherry trees are in blossom, about twenty-two young Japanese commit suicide *every day;* and a third of these are *shinju,* or "love suicides." The ritualistic bowel-slashing called hara-kiri is scarcely ever practiced, being despised as feudal. Young people take sleeping pills, or throw themselves under trains.

"But why suicide?" I demanded.

We had come out of the coffee shop into the gaudily neon-lit ant heap of the Ginza, which makes Broadway look like an empty and ill-lit thoroughfare.

"It is better to die for love than to have to live without it," said Yoshio promptly.

"Aren't there other things to live for in this world besides love?" I said, hoping to appeal to his politics.

But Yoshio was a Japanese first and a Communist second.

"Is life in fact so worthwhile as you Westerners seem to imagine? Doesn't it have more burdens than pleasures? The thought of death can often be very enticing!"

(2)

One spring week end, Jane and I and Mr. Shima drove west from Tokyo, towards Mount Fuji, a white cone hung in a clear blue sky.

There is never any breathing space in Tokyo. Each year the monster city swallows another 300,000 people and packs them away somehow in its convoluted streets and lanes. Subways and elevators are crammed; the traffic thunders day and night; pedestrians move in solid regiments. After a while, one feels like a brick that has been firmly mortared into a wall.

Yet on clear days it is possible to look up from a Tokyo street and see Fuji set invitingly in the pale blue sky, and quite near Tokyo are deep green ravines and sparkling bays, some of the world's most beautiful scenery.

The people of Tokyo rush to the mountains and the beaches whenever they can and especially when the cherry trees briefly blossom. But still they are living bricks in a homogeneous wall of humanity, for it is the whole wall that moves.

The 20-odd miles from Tokyo to Yokohama were one vast traffic jam. Beyond Yokohama, the young men on motor bicycles, whom the Japanese call the "thunder tribe," roared along with their helmeted heads down and their girl friends clinging on behind.

"One spring my father and mother were traveling together and were arrested by the thought-police," said Mr. Shima.

"Whatever for?"

"My father was seen kissing my mother. They had not been long married. The thought-police took a very strait-laced view. They scolded my father for being un-Japanese."

"What did your father say?"

"He explained that my mother and he were going to visit my grandfather's grave. The police decided this was sufficiently Confucian to atone for his offense."

Jane was watching the girls on the pillions of the motorcycles. "Why do Japanese girls dye their hair red?" she asked.

"Because it is boring to be just one of forty-five million brunettes," said Mr. Shima. He thought for a moment. "Did you know that in feudal times, before the war, a man sometimes chose a girl as his wife because of her big ears? She was not supposed to speak or even raise her eyes. Her ears were about all he had to go by. Big ears were supposed to be lucky."

"Now they talk more than the men do," Jane said.

"They are spritely, and blithe," Mr. Shima agreed. "Japanese men are too often cheerless and discontented. It is the contrast between a glorious sunlit morning and a drizzly afternoon."

There were six hundred traffic policemen on duty on the road to Kamakura. Traffic helicopters rasped low overhead, to help sort out the road tangles. The streets of Kamakura were louder than a fair, with people who had come to see the famous Buddha, and the Shinto shrine with its rows of god-carts and suits of black-lacquered Japanese armor. A shrine *miko*, or virgin priestess, was selling 20-yen admission tickets. She wore a scarlet skirt and a white silk blouse, and had flowers in her black hair. But part of the shrine was being repaired, and a large sign in English declared it "Off Limits." None of the Japanese visiting the shrine seemed to think the sign incongruous. It was part of their split-level world.

After lunch we drove to Enoshima, parked the car, and strolled across the long wooden bridge to the rocky pointed island. Shops lining the single steep street sold seashells, and *papier-mâché* skulls with snakes coiling out of the eye sockets. A series of escalators rode us smoothly to the summit, where the shrine stands cheek by jowl with a small zoo. There were Japanese students everywhere.

Mr. Shima planned that we should drive towards Fuji, go around the base of the sacred mountain, then turn south again and spend the night at Atami. This was an excellent scheme, except that a great many other people had had the same idea. The roads were dangerously crowded, and thick clouds of dust smothered the cherry blossom. On the twisting mountain road, buses passed us at an abandoned speed. The passengers waved to us and held up sake bottles. " 'What good is cherry blossom without wine?' " Mr. Shima quoted cheerily; at lunch, he had had a few sake cups himself.

On a good day, the pure cone of Fuji can be seen from twenty-two of Japan's forty-six prefectures, which means by about fifty million people. Most of them seemed to have chosen this particular day to try to get nearer the mountain. Fuji's five attendant lakes were crowded with boats; the woods around them swarmed with visitors.

"We had better try to reach Atami before the tourist buses do," said Mr. Shima. "Otherwise, we may lose our rooms at the inn."

"But first we will have tea," said Jane firmly.

There were teahouses all along the road, some with English signs. One exhorted: "Please visit us in your kill time." But we chose a little inn, beside a stream that was crossed by an arching bridge made of wood and painted bright scarlet.

In the inn garden, a young man and a girl sat at a table under a big sun umbrella. Yoshio Tanaka's friend Sasa. The girl was Ryo. They were eating sweet bean-paste balls out of a lunch box, and laughing as they ate. They looked very happy.

71

"No!" I said, and turned back towards the car, before they could see us.

"You do not want to have tea?" Mr. Shima asked, surprised.

"Not here," I said.

When I had seen them before, the language barrier towered high as Fuji, and a great deal had happened to them since. I felt sure the last thing they would care for would be to have their spring idyll interrupted by two *gaijins* and a possibly inquisitive court chamberlain.

Atami is a pleasure city that clings to a steep hillside overlooking the curve of a blue bay. The express trains that dash between Tokyo and Osaka stop at Atami, then vanish into a hole in the mountainside, with their loads of *zaibatsu* millionaires and Japanese politicians. Atami is full of "hotels for couples," and its narrow streets swarm with ugly, bald little men and pretty girls. The shops all sell as a souvenir a fat-bellied beaver made of wood, with enormous testicles. The beaver is the Japanese symbol of virility.

The town was packed with rollicking sightseers who had come to look at the cherry blossoms; and much sake was being drunk. But the rooms we had engaged at a hot-spring inn were still ours. Before dinner, we changed into bath kimonos, and shuffled our way in oversized slippers along a passage with a highly polished wooden floor as slippery as glass. At the end of it, Jane entered the bath chamber for ladies. Mr. Shima and I stepped the other way, into an anteroom where we took off our bath kimonos and laid them, neatly folded, in large wicker baskets. Then, naked and each carrying a cake of soap, a little wooden stool, and a small wood bucket, we stepped into a spacious, steam-filled, white-tiled grotto. In the center of the grotto, immersed in boiling water in a huge sunken marble bath, the sake drinkers were recuperating.

We filled our buckets with hot water, then sat down on the wooden stools and thoroughly soaped ourselves. After doing so, we emptied bucket after bucket of water over our heads, and sluiced ourselves down like horses. Only when we were scrubbed clean did we step into the marble tub, to soak in the boiling water along with the others. We lay languidly breathing the steamy air, until we were cooked as red as lobsters. The other occupants of the bath took not the slightest notice of us.

When we returned to the anteroom, towels were waiting for us. We dried ourselves, got into brown kimonos and our big slippers, and shuffled back to the rooms. In one of them we dined, attended by three inn maids, for Japanese inns do not have communal dining rooms. We squatted on plump cushions on the straw-mat floor, wooden chopsticks in hand, and leaned hungrily over a very low, round, black lacquer table, on which were many small bowls containining different kinds of fish, two kinds of soup, chicken, pickled vegetables, and great quantities of snowy rice.

The walls were literally paper-thin, and we could hear our late companions of the bath troop back to their rooms, and settle down to similar feasting. There was much male laughter, and a lot of feminine squealing. The three inn maids who knelt in a row on the floor beside us looked at first as solemn as judges. But, as they eyed Jane and myself, they one by one put their hands over their mouths, and giggled. They plainly were thinking that only a stupid *gaijin* would visit an Atami hot-spring inn with his wife. I hoped Mr. Shima would not lose face by being in our company.

Mr. Shima, however, was beaming at the girls. He had already helped himself liberally to more sake, which one of them poured for him into a tiny eggshell cup from a slender sake jar. The girls were worth looking at. All were in bright kimonos drawn tight at the waist by the *obi* but flared at the top to expose the nape of the neck, which the Japanese prefer to admire rather than girls' legs. They had round faces, powdered white, and pert black eyes. They wore very red lipstick, and their eyebrows were thick black arches.

None of the girls ate. It would not have been etiquette for them to do so; also, their tightly tied *obis* made eating impossible. But they smoked the cigarettes we offered them, and exchanged sake cups with each of us.

Mr. Shima became witty in Japanese, but he overreached himself. The girl kneeling beside him asked him his name, and he promptly gave her the name of a great *sumo* champion, winking at us as he did so. She pointed a finger at herself, and said: "Elizabeth Tay-rah." All three girls laughed behind their hands. Mr. Shima decided, red-faced, that it was time to go to bed.

Our beds were the straw-mat *tatami* floor, with a *futon* beneath us and another thick quilt as covering. The pillows had paper frills, and were shaped like sausages. They felt as if they were filled with stones. One is supposed to rest the back of the neck on them, not one's head. Only Japanese can do this.

Also, I was bothered by what I thought was the paper pillow slip. Only in the morning did I discover it was really a cover I was supposed to remove before using the pillow, and that it was inscribed in Japanese characters with a graceful poem, intended to lull me to sleep.

After breakfasting lightly off seaweed and bean soup, we drove back the way we had traveled the day before, passing the inn whose English sign invited us to visit it in our kill time. When we came to the inn with the scarlet bridge, a white ambulance stood before the door, and excited people were watching two stretchers being carried into it. Sasa was in one stretcher and Ryo in the other. The doors banged and the ambulance sped away.

"Not that going to hospital can do them any good," a man said, when Mr. Shima asked what had happened. "I know dead bodies when I see them."

Sasa and Ryo had left clippings from their hair and from their fingernails, wrapped carefully in white paper, as mementos for their parents. Also, Ryo had left her college notebook (containing copious comments on Japanese literature) and a suicide note. Apparently Sasa's father had disengaged himself from his entanglement with a geisha long enough to announce that he had other plans for his son than marrying Ryo. Sasa had then decided it would be best if they both died, after a brief "honeymoon."

Ryo in her suicide note mentioned timidly that she felt Sasa might be acting hastily, and that perhaps they ought to try to find some way out before they took the irrevocable step. But he was against this, so she let him overrule her. Even for a girl suicide, Japan was still a man's world.

I thought of them, eating bean-paste sweets in the garden beside the arching scarlet bridge and the little stream, and looking at Fuji for the last time; then going indoors as the sun set, to have their hot baths, put on their kimonos, and lie down to swallow their sleeping pills. The words of the little pillow-poem came back to me: "Go peacefully, and good night."

But it was the innkeeper who had the last word. He was loudly disgusted with thoughtless youth. "You never know what these young couples are up to!" he declaimed. "So gay and carefree—then they die without paying the bill!"

(3)

There are so many "love suicides" in Japan that any one case is soon forgotten. But there was something about the deaths of Ryo and Sasa that caught the public fancy. They immediately had youthful imitators. Another Tokyo student and his girl were found lying in the rain forest above the Amagi Pass, in beautiful Izu. At Nikko, five couples leaped to spectacular deaths in a single day, breaking the record set in 1875. At almost every celebrated beauty spot in Japan, young suicides mingled with the tourists, eagerly seeking death under the cherry trees.

Not always did things go according to plan. One young man lost face very badly. His girl successfully threw herself into the crater of a volcano, but he only broke his ankle and was brought out alive.

In Yokohama, a hospital nurse who had had an unhappy love affair wrote a note saying she had taken twenty sleeping pills and beside the note she left the money to pay for them. But as she sank into a coma, a burglar broke into her room. Another nurse saw him leave it, and gave the alarm. The noise woke the suicidal nurse, who discovered that the burglar had not only stolen her money but raped her before leaving.

Romantic suicides were grist to the songwriters' mill. They turned out lyrics like "O sad! two lovers gone in spring," and "They promised to be together when the camellias bloomed." It became difficult to turn on a radio without hearing a song about suicide.

Yumiko's film producer decided to make a movie about the affair, with Yumiko playing the part of Ryo. When Yoshio heard about it, and furiously objected, the producer cunningly suggested that Yoshio appear in the film also, as Sasa. "It could be your big chance!" he cried.

Mr. Shima prophesied that once the blossoms fell, signifying the end of spring, the suicide rate would drop off. "The spring is the bad time," he said.

III

ISE:

THE PRINCESS AND THE GODDESS

If you think we are worked by strings,
Like a Japanese marionette,
You don't understand those things:
It is simply Court etiquette.

THE MIKADO

O<small>N THE ROAD TO</small> I<small>SE</small>, where the most important Shinto shrine is located, a policeman stepped out in front of our car and put up his hand. When we stopped, he beckoned us peremptorily to the side. I hastily went through my pockets for my driving licence (which I was never able to read because it was all in Japanese), our alien registration cards and passports, and began framing a suitably humble apology that would show we were determined to adopt a low posture. But, as it turned out, we had done nothing wrong. The policeman just wanted us to let another automobile go by.

Its arrival was heralded by an advance party of motorcycles equipped with wailing sirens. It was a huge, square, lumbering, wine-colored Mercedes-Benz, built in 1931. It had golden chrysanthemums painted on its door panels, and it contained the Crown Prince of Japan and Princess Michiko, his wife, on their way to visit the shrines of Ise.

There was no one on the road save us and the policeman, and the royal couple appeared to be having a quiet chat. But, when they saw us, they instantly went back on duty, and bowed and waved. We bowed, too, and the policeman stood at attention, and saluted.

The occupants of thrones, and their heirs, notoriously lead

77

cribbed and confined lives. The Japanese Imperial family, which is supposed to be twenty-five hundred years old, has hitherto had a sadly circumscribed time of it, even by royal standards. The children of the Emperor and Empress have, for instance, until now been taken away from their parents at the age of three, and brought up by court chamberlains. An aunt of the present Crown Prince met her father, who was the Emperor Taisho, on her wedding day. He asked her, "Who are you?" They had not set eyes on each other since she was a little girl.

The present Crown Prince, Akihito, who was born in 1933, was similarly removed from his parents when he was three, and housed by the chamberlains in an enormous Versailles-style palace, in Tokyo but outside the Imperial moat. Akihito was eight years old when Japan attacked Pearl Harbor. His huge palace was burned down during the war, and the boy prince was moved from place to place until the war ended. When Japan surrendered, Crown Prince Akihito was living in a dilapidated wooden cottage, in a wood near Tokyo, with a sixty-seven-year-old chamberlain as his only companion. He was not even allowed the companionship of his younger brother, Yoshi.

Emperor Hirohito seized the chance provided by the American Occupation to have his sons taught by an American Quaker lady. But the chamberlains were not defeated yet. Akihito always lived apart from his family, and his home in Tokyo was overrun by chamberlains, who kept a constant watch on him. They permitted him a few tennis-playing friends of his own age, these being mainly old college chums—who naturally did not live with him, just visited. The chamberlains did live on the premises, and he had to take all his meals with the gouty old men, and was lectured long hours each day by special "tutors." One of those elderly pedagogues was once asked if the Crown Prince's unnatural seclusion, especially from girls, did not mean he was being reared in fearful ignorance of the facts of life. "Not at all," replied the tutor. "His Royal Highness is receiving his sex education through his studies of ichthyology."

The lonely prince was also reported to busy himself with observing the differences in the haemoglobin content of the blood of different sorts of eels, and with experiments in which he removed the optic nerves of fish, to discover if they could react to light without them.

Meanwhile, the court chamberlains began to look around for a suitable bride for the Crown Prince. By age-old custom, the chamberlains would choose the girl, from among only a few families of the bluest blood. The Emperor would then be asked to approve formally the chamberlains' selection. Crown Prince Akihito would be advised last who his bride was going to be. It was at about this juncture that the Japanese began to be aware that Crown Prince Akihito might after all have a will of his own.

For years, the court chamberlains planned Akihito's marriage. But each time they seemed to be closing in on him, he, as it were, won another reprieve and leaped once more to freedom. When they wanted to confine the selection of a bride to exalted court circles, he told them firmly that he would consider girls from any good *daimyo* family, "because I will not have a chrysanthemum curtain between throne and people." This gave Akihito a wide choice, for hundreds of contemporary Japanese families can plausibly claim to be descended from some past *daimyo*, or feudal lord.

It also gave the chamberlains plenty of work, for in Japan no marriage, least of all a royal one, is arranged without the minutest scrutiny of the bride's family background, physical attributes, and education. The marriage of Akihito's father and mother was deferred for years, because a courtier who had hoped that Hirohito would marry *his* daughter discovered, and gleefully let it be known, that the future Empress had a first cousin who was color-blind.

In the case of an ordinary marriage, the groom's family may employ private detectives to find out all about the bride's background. The chamberlains spent anxious months traveling about Japan, always incognito and sometimes in disguise, look-ing up family registers and interviewing startled principals of girls' finishing schools.

Meanwhile, Akihito had his own intelligence network, for his college chums loyally agreed to keep him informed about the chamberlains' research. "The Grand Chamberlain is very fa-vorably impressed by Miss So-and-so," they would report. "But don't have anything to do with her. She is good-looking, but has a terrible temper."

Akihito carried about with him a little black notebook in which he put down all this information.

The Japanese popular press joined in the hunt. Reporters fol-lowed the chamberlains about, to spy on their activities. When it seemed the chamberlains were showing special interest in one girl, the newspapermen did likewise. One of them broke into an exclusive girls' school, wearing false pigtails and carrying a camera concealed in his middy blouse. The publicity became so onerous that several fathers of eligible girls said heatedly they would rather their daughters committed suicide than marry into the Imperial family.

Finally, Akihito ended the fearful suspense, and foiled every-one, by choosing for himself a girl called Michiko Shoda. They had played summer tennis together at a mountain resort called Karuizawa. Michiko's great-grandfather was a Yokohama sauce manufacturer. Her grandfather was the founder of the Japanese flour-milling industry. Her father, in control of seventeen mills, selling annually $93,000,000 worth of flour products, was re-puted not implausibly to be a millionaire. The family had brains as well as money. One of Michiko's uncles was a professor of geology at Tokyo University. Another uncle, a mathemati-cian, was president of Osaka University. These specialties sug-gested that the Shodas and the Japanese Imperial family might well prove highly congenial to each other. Emperor Hirohito is the distinguished author of a scientific work with the resound-ing title, "*Opisthobranchia* of Sagami Bay." Crown Prince Akihito's uncle, Prince Mikasa, is a historian and archaeologist, and Akihito's sister, Princess Kazuko, is the wife of a leading Japanese ornithologist. (Their mother, Empress Nagako, breeds silkworms, and collects birds' eggs.) But only by considerable stretching can the Shoda family claim to be descended from a *daimyo*.

Nevertheless, the thwarted chamberlains boldly claimed that, no matter what Akihito himself might assert, it was they who had picked Michiko for his wife, in accordance with ancient custom. And they attempted to present the match to the public as a singular instance of their deep attachment to the new *demokurasu*. Nobody believed a word of it.

During the engagement, Akihito and Michiko did not see each other very often, but were permitted to telephone each other every day. This was progress. During *their* engagement, Akihito's father and mother, Emperor Hirohito and Empress Nagako, were permitted to meet only once a year (the engagement lasted five) and were not allowed to use the telephone at all.

Akihito and Michiko had to fight hard to gain the slightest relaxation of absurd rules of court protocol. At the same time, the new *demokurasu* expressed its opinions with brutal frankness. One Japanese daily newspaper with a 4,000,000 circulation wrote: "Akihito will be the star at the nuptials, because of his rank, but Michiko will get top billing as far as the public is concerned." Another paper declared: "Michiko may be a commoner, but it's Akihito who's getting the best of the bargain."

The marriage was a queer mingling of the old and the new in Japan. The ceremony was held in the so-called sacred enclosure, or *Kashikodokoro*, deep in the rook-filled woods of the Imperial Palace grounds enclosed by the moat. But Western morning coats and top hats were obligatory wear for male guests, and the ladies tripped over the pebbles of the Shinto courtyard in spiked heels. The wedding rites were elaborate, and lengthy. There was much coming and going, deep bowing, Druidlike incantations, waving of sacred twigs, and so forth, at three *Ka-shikodokoro* shrines.

None of this inhibited the wedding guests from whipping forbidden miniature cameras out of such places of concealment as the insides of top hats, in order to photograph the ceremony at its most hallowed moments. Both the bride and the bridegroom were coiffured, shampooed, anointed, forbidden all but special foods, and finally garbed in kimonos so numerous and enveloping that they found great difficulty in walking. But when they drove out of the palace grounds into the bustling streets of brawling modern Tokyo, they wore European court dress and were beribboned and bemedaled with European-style decorations.

As their open horse-drawn carriage drove through the streets, a fanatical antiroyalist teen-ager first threw stones at it, then tried to climb into it, explaining later that he wanted to fight a duel with the Crown Prince.

All this and more the young couple bore with patience, dignity, and good humor. But the stone-throwing was not the only aspect of the affair that looked ill. The crowds lining the route of the carriage were inquisitive, but not enthusiastic. When in due course a baby prince was born, the Tokyo streetcars flew red sun flags that made them look like trains crossing the bridge on the river Kwai, but no rejoicing crowds rushed to the palace gates. The only ones who did turn up were a handful of fanatics of the extreme right-wing Great Japan Patriotic party, and some elderly women in kimonos who lifted thin arms heavenward and feebly intoned *banzais*. The women it was later discovered were only the palace sweepers.

(2)

If the most celebrated cathedrals of Europe were situated in the Black Forest, and were all simple wooden structures resembling very large but plain log cabins, Christianity would approximate to Shinto in its aesthetic appeal. One hundred and twenty-five shrines scattered over a considerable forest area of Ise are the chief churches of Shinto. The two grand shrines are four miles apart, and most Japanese hope to visit them at least once during their lifetimes, though probably from curiosity rather than from piety.

Ten tourist buses, filled with Japanese schoolgirls in blue blouses with big sailor collars, had just drawn up at the entrance to the main shrines. Little bus conductresses waved their arms, blew shrilly on whistles, and cried "Awri', awri', awri'!" as the drivers parked. Then, holding aloft bright yellow flags with numbers on them, the conductresses led the schoolgirls along a path between red cryptomeria trees, lecturing briskly as they went. A Japanese tourist-bus conductress never stops talking, except to sing folk songs. She pours out information like a regurgitating tape recorder and, should she run short of guide book material, will recite long passages from kabuki plays.

The schoolgirls wore hideous black cotton stockings, and their bobbed black hair hung straight and lank. St. Trinian's, almond-eyed, had come to Ise. In a year or so they would be young women, but never would they acquire bosoms, unless they paid a Tokyo plastic cosmetician to pump them up with wax. Meanwhile, they tramped about the shrine grounds, peering through their square bobs at the big windowless wooden buildings whose entrances were mysteriously hung with silk curtains, presumably to protect the innermost secrets of the sun goddess.

Trooping along with the schoolgirls, who giggled at us behind their hands, we visited the stable of the sacred white horse, the hall of sacred cookery, and the hall of the sacred dances. It was nice to be out and about in such lovely woods on a spring day, but the exhibits were on the dull side. The sacred white horse was not even wearing its blue robes, and the sacred cookery consisted of ordinary rice being pounded and steamed. The shrines themselves not only were of an extreme simplicity, being made of plain cypress logs, but they were not even old. They had been built in 1953, for it is the custom at Ise to pull the shrines down and replace them with entirely new buildings every twenty years.

The sacred dances also had limitations. A shrine guide explained that they were performed "for the sun goddess, and not for human spectators." The dancing girls wore white coats with long sleeves, and billowing scarlet skirts. But, in accordance with the guide's warning, they performed with their backs to the audience. Each dance lasted about ten minutes. To the music of a bamboo flute, a Japanese harp, and wooden clappers, the girls gravely waggled green twigs with bits of colored silk tied to them, but hardly ever moved their limbs.

When it was over, the schoolgirls turned to photographing one another with the cameras they carried slung over their shoulders, and obviously got more fun out of this than anything else they had done that day.

Next morning, Crown Prince Akihito and Crown Princess Michiko attended the shrines, he in a morning coat and top hat and she in a kimono and an ermine stole. The occasion was a little awkward, for the chief priestess of Ise was the grandmother of the girl the court chamberlains had expected Akihito to marry instead of Michiko. Everyone displayed the formal correctness appropriate to a visit made in those circumstances. It was what the Japanese call a delicate situation.

But the visit was inescapable. Until fifteen years ago, all Japanese Emperors claimed to be descended from *Amaterasu-Omikami*, the Heavenly Shining Great Goddess, otherwise the sun. Part of the price Japan paid for losing the war was that Emperor Hirohito, Akihito's father, specifically disavowed the divine connection. In more practical terms, the Shinto religion was disestablished. None of this, however, has made the slightest difference. Members of the Imperial family are still compelled by custom to visit the shrines of Ise, to pay homage and

84

report all their activities to the goddess; just as every Japanese Prime Minister has to make a pilgrimage to Ise as soon as he attains the office, in order to inform the goddess who will be included in his cabinet, and what his policies will be.

The sun goddess achieved human descendants through two lesser deities called Izanagi and Izanami. They came down to earth from the Floating Bridge of Heaven. Izanagi assumed the shape of a man, and Izanami of a woman. When they arrived on the earth, they went round a pillar they found there, in opposite directions, so that they met on the other side of it.

Izanami exclaimed: "How delightful! I have met a lovely youth." But Izanagi frowned at her. "I am a man, and by right should have spoken first," he reproached her. "This was unlucky." So they went round the pillar again, and this time Izanami remained modestly silent, while Izanagi happily exclaimed: "How delightful! I have met a lovely maiden."

Every Japanese knows this charming and revealing tale. Most Japanese women, however, hope that Princess Michiko will not be an Izanami. The matter is very delicate. Michiko was educated at the College of the Sacred Heart, in Tokyo, but when she married Akihito she had to go through all the stiff Shinto ceremonies. She approached the gods on her knees, wearing an oiled wig and twelve kimonos. Custom did not permit the Emperor and Empress to attend their son's wedding. (But, along with several million ordinary Japanese who also live on two levels, they watched it on television.) And now here was the Crown Princess, and her equally Western-minded husband, making their obeisances to the sun goddess at the grand shrine of Ise.

The question a whole generation faces in Japan is whether Japanese traditions and beliefs can be successfully combined with *demokurasu*. Michiko, while she was still a schoolgirl, composed a prize-winning essay about her own generation.

"We are called the *après guerre* generation," she wrote. "We fall into two groups, those who try to escape into a world of dreams and those who reject all ideals. Juvenile criminals are examples of the second group, and people who lose all perspective and commit suicide over some trifling incident are examples of the first. Thomas Hardy's Tess said she had been born into a world that was a worm-eaten apple, and sometimes I feel just like Tess. Then I tell myself, 'It's true we live in a most difficult period; but must we be fatalistic, and handicapped all our lives by the heavy burdens resulting from a disastrous war?' We must stop envisaging a dark future just because the past was bad. We should cherish our dreams, and look to a bright future. The way we live today determines how we will live tomorrow, and the war is now a thing of the past. Through our efforts, we can free the future from the shackles of the past. The world for us is not a worm-eaten apple."

Another Japanese princess who seems to hold similar views is Akihito's spirited younger sister, Suga, who married a bank clerk, and took a job with a Tokyo television station as a commentator and disc jockey.

That day at Ise, the Crown Prince and Michiko had a religious grievance laid before them. The keepers of the Grand Shrines felt that the world had become a worm-eaten apple. The disestablishment of Shinto, they pointed out, meant that the shrines had to raise their own funds, which hitherto had been supplied by the State in recognition of the Emperor's descent from the sun goddess. But the shrines' annual income from tourists and the devout was a mere $30,000, whereas their expenses grew heavier every year. Thus, in 1953, the fifty-ninth recorded tearing down and rebuilding of the shrines had cost $2,000,000. When the next time came for rebuilding, in 1973, it was estimated that the cost would be nearly $6,000,000.

I do not know what the Crown Prince, or Michiko, replied. What they could have suggested was that the Grand Shrines of Ise only needed a baseball stadium to put everything right. The Meiji shrine in Tokyo has one, which seats 56,000 spectators and will be used for the 1964 Olympics. The Meiji shrine is able to maintain 350 priests, and to put up new buildings, because the stadium brings in a steady $280,000 a year. When the royal couple visited Ise, the Meiji shrine had just had a new sanctuary built for use by the Emperor Meiji's ghost on its occasional visits to Tokyo from Kyoto, where Meiji is buried. The new building has 45 tons of glistening red copper on its horned roof, and cost $1,500,000.

This businesslike approach may have something to do with the enterprising spirit that moved Akihito to pick the daughter of a flour-mill magnate, instead of an effete aristocrat, as his bride and that caused the delightful Princess Suga to marry her bank clerk and to take a job after marriage, just as an increasing number of emancipated young Japanese women do. For it so happens that yet another of Crown Prince Akihito's sisters is married to the eldest son of the guardian of the Meiji shrine.

IV

NARA:

GIRLS! TO THE BARRICADES!

The five diseases of the female mind are: disobedience, anger, slanderousness, jealousy, and lack of intelligence. Seven or eight out of every ten women suffer from these faults. That is why women are inferior to men.

GREATER LEARNING FOR WOMEN
(17th Century)

From the picture window of the express, we could see what looked like long white caterpillars stretched in straight rows across the fields. They were in actuality rows of vegetables, encased in white plastic to guard them against pests. On the fruit trees, every apple, plum, and peach was growing inside a paper bag, so that the trees seemed full of Christmas presents. And over each field hung crisscrossed ribbons of bright tinfoil whose dancing glitter frightened away the birds that might otherwise eat the crop. Every Japanese farmer owns his own land, and therefore hates to lose even a solitary grain of rice or a speck of fruit.

The train had reclining seats, and attached to each chair was a tiny plastic earplug at the end of a thin cord. When you put the earplug in your ear, it emitted a very thin silvery trickle of just audible music.

Almost all the passengers were men. They lay back in the comfortable seats, smoking cigarettes and twiddling their stockinged toes, for all of them had their shoes off.

Presently, a girl in white uniform, resembling a nurse, came along the car with a basket on her arm. The basket contained little white towels tightly rolled like sausages, which she handed out with an implement that looked like sugar tongs, since the towels, called *oshibori*, meaning "honorable wring," were very hot. The girl with the hot towels was followed through the car by other girls wheeling metal carts loaded with coffee, beer, sake, tangerines, and salted rice crackers. While the passengers wiped their hands and faces with the towels, the girls with the food carts offered their wares in breathlessly sexy, department-store voices.

A conductor followed the girls down the aisle. He whipped off his cap when he reached the center, revealing a completely bald yellow head. In his other hand he held a large silver watch. He bowed very low, and spoke apologetically in Japanese.

The man in the seat next to me snapped his fingers at the conductor, to bring him his shoes, and told me disgustedly: "He says we are running forty-five seconds late." The Japanese like their trains to be dead on time.

The engineer decided to make up the forty-five seconds by cutting short our stop at Tsu. This was unlucky for my companion. He was evidently an important businessman, probably visiting some of his company's plants, and a delegation awaited him on the platform. They all carried bouquets of welcome, and they all bowed very low as the train halted. But the next instant they were hurtled aside by people fearful of not getting on, who collided violently with the businessman trying to get off. The last I saw of him as the train pulled out, he was standing disheveled, shaking his fist, amid the ruined bouquets and the frantically bowing welcomers.

There did not seem to be much to Tsu but a tall chimney or so, and fields of corn ricks. But even in this country place there were little gray apartment buildings standing at the edges of the fields. They are going up all over Japan, for the new grow-ing class of "salarymen," whose wives use washing machines and electric rice cookers and prefer having abortions to rearing large families.

I got off the train at Toba, for I wanted to see how a pearl was grown, and climbed a hill of pine trees. On either hand, wet riceland fell away in steep terraces, and below, in the blue bay, floated bamboo rafts. Suspended from those rafts, inside wire cages to protect them from being eaten by starfish, some five million especially treated oysters were silently—and, one hoped, painlessly—producing pearls.

Later I saw the plant where the oysters are treated. There two hundred girls are employed. Each is paid about $50 a month, to perform very rapidly and efficiently the delicate operation of inserting a scientifically selected irritant into each oyster shell. The chosen irritant is a speck of a Mississippi "pigtoe" oyster, used because its gravity and its coefficient of expansion are the same as a pearl's. The girls, absorbed, peered through magnifiers at their patients, spread out helplessly under the glass lenses. Then, with a thin steel instrument like a short knitting needle, they deftly inserted the irritant. Some oysters, of course, did not survive the operation.

Every door of the plant had an orange tied to it, to ward off evil spirits. The Japanese believe everything has a ghost; each year they say prayers for broken sewing-machine needles. No doubt the girls feared the oysters that died might be vengeful.

For about two hundred fifty years, the population of Japan was kept stable by the destruction of female infants. Midwives kept a piece of wet paper handy and if the child proved to be an unwanted girl they smothered it. Then, in the second half of the nineteenth century, Japan decided to become an industrial country, and the population began to go up by leaps and bounds. Girls were no longer suffocated at birth, but were put to work in cotton mills, or sold to city brothels.

Today, almost half the industrial workers are women. But women now have the vote, and the right to divorce their husbands, and are busy clamoring for other privileges as well. They have not yet got around to demanding equal pay with men. But they aspire to higher jobs than formerly, as well as to higher education. Only very ill-situated young women now want to be bus conductresses. Their more fortunate sisters hope to become air hostesses at the very least. There are still women pearl divers; but the pearl factories will probably have to offer more pay in future, to induce young women to stick irritants in oysters instead of assembling transistor radios.

Most girls, of course, hope to get married. They diligently learn to sew, cook, arrange flowers, and do the tea ceremony. Most of them hope to marry "salarymen." But few of them are willing to be entirely submissive wives. And, before marriage, the girls with higher education are as often as not to be found charging police lines and crying "*Washo! Washo!*" in the name of *demokurasu*.

(2)

O-Sei had been well brought up. Her father was a wealthy Osaka cotton merchant who, however, was ashamed of being "in trade." He boasted instead of such family connections as the lieutenant general who was decorated at Port Arthur, and the deputy governor of Formosa who was killed—and apparently eaten—by the savages there at the turn of the century. "It was the Japanese who brought civilization and religious belief to that island," O-Sei's father was fond of saying. "Until Japan took them over, the Formosans knew nothing of ancestor worship."

O-Sei went to one of the best young ladies' schools in Japan, where she was taught among other things how to eat a European cream puff cake without chopsticks but without getting her fingers sticky. The school also had liberal ideas. It encouraged the girls to read Western books like *Man's Fate*, by André Malraux, and to travel to and from school in trains and trolley buses, in keeping with *demokurasu*, instead of in their papas' chauffeured limousines.

And O-Sei's family shared those progressive notions, up to a point. For instance, they did not mind her going on week-end school trips, properly chaperoned, even though they knew their daughter would spend the night in a nine-mat room with a dozen other girls. "She shares her fish and curry rice with her chums on such occasions," said O-Sei's father, laughing. "It is very good for her to 'rough it.'"

Even so, he was chary of letting O-Sei bring one of her friends home from school with her unless he personally knew all about the chum's family. One had to be careful, so as not to lose face oneself, or make a social inferior lose face. He would have been horrified to know that O-Sei quite often sneaked off with a forbidden chum to see American movies.

O-Sei's mother probably held similar views. But this it was difficult to be sure of, because O-Sei's mother was never known to express any views at all. She was a well-disciplined Japanese woman.

All this I learned from O-Sei, as we trudged through the predawn, wet darkness of Nara, from the women's university towards the teachers' college. She and the other girls in the march, some hundreds of them, wore white raincoats, and black rubber boots, and looked altogether unladylike.

"What will your father say when he hears about this?" I asked.

"Oh, I will talk him round," said O-Sei confidently. "He will be very angry at first, but I am sure he will admit the justice of our cause. He is a fair-minded father."

I had very considerable reservations about both statements, but like O-Sei's mother I preferred not to express my views. After all, I had never met O-Sei's father, though, after her lively description of him, he was very vivid in my mind.

Nara is a city of mists, of pagodas, of bow-shaped scarlet bridges arching over streams, of parks filled with tame deer that go bounding towards park-keepers who blow deerhorns. It also contains one of the two women's universities in Japan, the other being in Tokyo. A girl has to be bright rather than well-born to get into one of those colleges, for of every twenty girls who seek admission, only one passes the stiff entrance examination. I knew, therefore, that some of the girls marching through the rain were upper middle-class, like O-Sei, and some were of poor parents, but that all of them, O-Sei included, represented the intellectual cream of Japanese young womanhood. And this made what they were doing all the more significant.

The Nara mists were beginning to thin when we got to the girls' destination, which was the main entrance of the teachers' college. The girls had come to join men students of Zengakuren in a demonstration against the authorities, and to do so they had sneaked out of their virginal dormitories, some of them climbing out the windows so that they would not be stopped by their college mentors.

The police had had warning of the demonstration, and about a thousand policemen were drawn up on the road outside the gate of the teachers' college. Inside the college were some three hundred school teachers whom the Ministry of Education had brought from all over Japan, in order to explain to them why the American Occupation educational reforms that had lasted now for fifteen years were after all not necessarily to Japan's advantage, and ought to be changed.

The Zengakuren male students and the girls from the women's university regarded those schoolteachers with scorn, as Judases who were out to betray *demokurasu* and turn the hands of the clock back to feudalism.

Yoshio Tanaka had given me O-Sei's name and asked me to look her up if I passed through Nara. I liked Yoshio; but I did not much care for what I could see, in the fast brightening light, of his Zengakuren comrades who were assembled here. First, and no doubt irrationally, I didn't much care for the idea of girls being encouraged to share in a public brawl, and pos-

93

sibly be beaten over the head by policemen. Second, I thought the Zengakuren male students who were lounging around the college gate were a scruffy lot.

They wore leather jackets and dirty trousers, and probably that was all right; but they also wore self-satisfied sneers, and not only jeered at the policemen, but were loftily condescending towards the girls who had come out to join them at considerable risk to their careers and reputation. There was nothing comradely about those particular Zengakuren. They looked as if they despised everything and everybody else on earth, including *demokurasu* and the masses.

Still, I was relieved not to see any sign of the right-wing hoodlums who with their ugly clubs had smashed the student demonstration in Tokyo the dawn that Mr. Kishi, the Prime Minister, drove to the airport to fly to Washington. The youths in the leather jackets, despite their sneers, were poor physical specimens, not liable to do much serious damage. The "Pine Leaves" of the opposite political persuasion were quite another matter.

While she was telling me about herself, O-Sei had also kindly explained what the fight was all about.

"The Japanese Government is trying to restore teaching of morals in the schools," she said.

"If you mean that they are against sin, what is wrong with that?"

O-Sei giggled. Then she remembered this was a serious matter, and frowned.

"Of course we don't object to children being taught morals. But that is not really the Government's intention. By morals *they* mean obedience. Japanese youth will be brainwashed back into the feudal past. Presently, little children will again be made to bow each morning to the Emperor, as well as to their teacher. The Japanese Government means to indoctrinate the youth into accepting State decrees unquestioningly."

"You mean, like the Communist governments do?"

O-Sei frowned again.

"No, I *don't* mean like the Communist governments. The present Japanese Government is not Communist. But in it are the buds of re-emerging fascism.

"And," said O-Sei pointedly, "they grow on the branch of American imperialism."

The Zengakuren male students began to blow whistles, and to shout orders through loud-speakers. Obediently, the girls, including O-Sei, linked arms and faced up to the policemen. The Zengakuren men, I noticed, stayed in the rear. Swaying from side to side with their arms linked, the girls sang a Japanese workers' song. O-Sei gave me a translation later. "Let us take to arms!" they sang. "The clouds lift to show the green hills. The day of the workers dawns!"

The mists had indeed lifted to show the green hills, and very pretty they were, but the policemen remained unmoved by the girls, many of whom were even prettier. The policemen, as policemen will, just stood in a stolid row, a patient human barrier drawn across the gateway of the teachers' college.

The girls broke off their song after a while, and began to get up steam in a way I was becoming familiar with. They breathed down their nostrils, and they began prancing up and down, crying rhythmically: "*Washo! Washo!*" It was very interesting to watch, for most of them seemed to be inadequately supported under their white raincoats, and such bosoms as they possessed did a definite jiggle.

But still the policemen just stood there, looking stolid, though those pretty faces and jiggling bodies were mere inches from them.

The girls tried different tactics. They began to coo such provocative remarks as: "Aren't you ashamed of yourselves? Why don't you go home, and stop your brutal persecution? Do you imagine any decent girl will marry you, after this?"

Some of the policemen, especially the younger ones, began to get angry, and lose their hitherto well-maintained impassivity

95

and mutter under their breath. But still, their discipline held firm, and they made no move.

This was too much for the girls. A Japanese girl is much the same as girls elsewhere; you may strike her, but it is asking for trouble to pretend to ignore her. The girls from the women's college stepped back a pace or so, and began taking off their rubber boots and hurtling them at the policemen, and followed this up with a shower of paper parasols.

This was the male students' chance. While the policemen's attention was distracted, the male Zengakuren got round behind the police and began tearing down the main gate with ropes and also by sheer weight of numbers. But they were forestalled, for still more policemen suddenly appeared from the college buildings inside the compound, and engaged in a brisk melee with the gate-crashing students. A few students managed to get inside. But the main body were repelled, and the police then rounded up the handful who had got in.

The Zengakuren went back to their loud-speakers, and the girls walked about retrieving their rubber boots.

"It is vengeance from heaven," said one of the loud-speakers. "Comrades! We have just discovered that the Judas teachers who came here to accept the Fascist instructions *are all dying of food poisoning!*" This produced loud applause.

But another loud-speaker declared in tones of anguish: "Comrades! The student comrades who got inside but were captured by the brutal police *are now being hellishly tortured!*" This produced loud boos and groans.

I had temporarily lost track of O-Sei; so I slipped quietly away, went right around the teachers' college, and entered by a deserted back gate, to see for myself what was happening inside.

No captive students were being tortured that I could see, and the three hundred schoolteachers seemed healthy and free from food poisoning. They sat in the main hall, on benches, diligently taking notes. On the lecturer's platform, an official of the Ministry of Education addressed them in the high-pitched, artificial squeak that all public speakers in Japan employ, and that is derived from a kabuki actor's trained delivery. Even the Emperor when he opens Parliament squeaks at the low-bowing Dietmen, like a kabuki player delivering an oration.

But the teachers found it hard to concentrate, for the lecturer's high thin voice was sometimes drowned out by the shrill whistles, loud-speakers, shouts, and songs of the students who were demonstrating in front of the college gate. I examined the teachers while they industriously scribbled, and counted only three women among them. The men looked a bit bedraggled and heavy-eyed as if from lack of sleep. They were young to middle-aged.

The official of the Ministry of Education was an older man, with a short gray beard and a peppery look. When he had finished his lecture, he came over to where I was trying to be unobtrusive, at the back of the hall, and in excellent English introduced himself. His name was Ro Atsunaga.

"We're trying to undo the errors committed by the American Occupation," he explained, rather snappishly. "Those brawling young Communists out there are the consequence of those errors."

When I said I didn't think they were all Communists, he gave me a scornful look.

"How can they be anything else? For fifteen years, naked unashamed. Marxism has ruled in our schools, planted there by General Douglas MacArthur."

I said I didn't think General MacArthur was a Communist, either.

"Of course not. But he deliberately turned the Communists loose on us, because he wished to undermine and destroy the Japanese race."

I told Mr. Atsunaga that the students who were demonstrating outside claimed the Japanese Government wished to reintroduce in the schools the old prewar "morals" called *shushin*, which had successfully inculcated in a generation of Japanese unquestioning, sheeplike obedience to the Emperor and the military.

Mr. Atsunaga heard me out, then nodded understandingly. "They're quite right about what *shushin* was used for before the war. But we're just as alert to that danger as they are. More so, in fact. In the schools we keep insisting that parliamentary democracy is the only possible form of government for a civilized nation, whereas our young friends out there are great admirers of Russia and China.

"But, if you understood Japanese, you'd have heard me tell the teachers here, during my lecture," he paused for a second, then quoted himself from memory, " 'whether the new morals course becomes the old, dangerous *shushin* or not depends entirely on you teachers; and the Government is relying on you to see that it does not.' "

Mr. Atsunaga explained that the three hundred teachers had had to be smuggled into the teachers' college, since elsewhere in Japan similar seminars had been broken up by demonstrators. Now that they were in, they were virtually prisoners for the duration of the three-day course on the new morals instruction. They could not go out into the town for fear of being attacked by the Zengakuren, or by members of the Japan Teachers' Union, who were demanding that all teachers go on strike rather than hear the lectures of the Ministry of Education.

Meanwhile, the teachers were "camping" in the college, sleeping on borrowed *futons* on the floors of the classrooms, and being supplied by the Ministry with such necessities as soap, towels, cigarettes, meals, and also what seemed to me a surprisingly generous allotment of sake, beer, and even whisky.

"We feel it's our duty to make them as comfortable as we can, since they have come to these lectures quite voluntarily, at some risk to themselves," Mr. Atsunaga said. He denied that having only three women teachers and nearly three hundred men made the siege more awkward. "On the contrary, the ladies have been invaluable."

When the lectures were over, the teachers would all be smuggled out of Nara again, probably in special buses, and returned to their home districts, presumably to spread the word about what a good thing the new morals course really was. Mr. Atsunaga explained the course to me, and it seemed innocuous enough. Only an hour or so a week was to be allotted to it. The teachers would tell their pupils that it was not in keeping with the new *demokurasu* to destroy trees and flowers in the public parks, or to refuse to give up one's seat in a crowded bus or train to an older person, or to use one's elbows and knees on other people in a crowd. All the same, I found that the majority of the teachers attending the lectures were sceptical, including all three women. They had defied their own Teachers' Union to come here, "because we felt the Ministry of Education should be given a hearing," but they were anything but Government stooges.

"I can't believe that this is all the Government intends," said one of the women, who spoke English, though not as well as Mr. Atsunaga. "Why, we've *always* taught the children in school those elementary things, without needing a special course in morals to do it!" She was a middle-aged woman, who had been a schoolteacher all her working life, and looked extremely sensible.

"Well, I'm certainly not going to come out on strike against this morals course," said one of the men teachers, speaking Japanese, which the sensible woman slowly translated. "But mind you, if the Government tries any hanky-panky later on, I'll be right on the side of the union."

Mr. Atsunaga had wandered off before this, perhaps to get himself some sake, so the teachers were evidently saying just what they thought.

The students were still being noisy outside. I made my way again to the back gate—it was unguarded and unlocked, but nobody seemed to have thought of using it to get in, except me—and walked around the college wall until I was once more at the main entrance.

O-Sei spotted me and ran up, aglow with girlish fervor. She said the police had just arrested a dozen or so of the Zengakuren males and had taken them off to the Nara police station. The girls were going to follow them there, and demonstrate outside the station until the students were released. She had barely had time to tell me this when she was summoned back to the ranks, and soon was getting up steam along with the rest, crying: "*Washo! Washo!*" Presently they all marched off, but I did not follow, feeling I had had enough of "*Washo!*" for one day.

Instead, I walked over to the women's university and talked with one of the male instructors—after an existence of half a century, the university had only fifteen women on its teaching staff of ninety. What he had to say, in Japanese and speaking through an interpreter, much enhanced my respect for the university. I asked him why almost all his young ladies had climbed out their dormitory windows before dawn to take part in a rowdy demonstration, which must be a shocking thing for their parents, and he said in effect that it was all a matter of sexual drive.

"The *après guerre* Japanese girl isn't a bit like her mother. She's got a lot more spirit. But all Japanese girls want to get married, if they can. And many, if not most, marriages are still arranged by the families. A girl with real spirit hasn't much choice, I can tell you. Her family will certainly want her to marry a conformist sheep: some young man who has obeyed his parents all his life, and who has made sure of getting a nice safe job as a 'salaryman,' with a nice safe *zaibatsu* company, and who will bow respectfully to his bosses, and expect his wife and children to bow respectfully to *him*."

"What does your girl of spirit do?" I asked.

"She either stays a spinster, or else she picks a young man who also has spirit, and defies her parents. Such a young man, in today's Japan, will almost certainly be anticonformist, anti-parents, anti-*zaibatsu*. In other words, a left-winger."

I thought of Yoshio Tanaka, and Yumiko Showa.

"Will you let me introduce you to some people?" the university instructor asked. "I think they can explain it all better than I can."

So we made an appointment, and I left. On my way out, I passed a big kitchen, where girls were busy making rice balls. "These are for the girls who are demonstrating," I was told. "They are going to snake-dance outside the police station, all night." I hoped O-Sei liked cold rice balls for supper.

(3)

The lecturer's name was Hara. He and I and the interpreter, a humorless youth called Suzuki, drove to Mrs. Nakamura's house in a taxi whose meter bounded like a Nara deer.

"In the eighth century," said Hara, "we would have driven in a black-lacquered cart, drawn by a bullock."

Hara was a short, stocky, self-confident man, with a plump, swarthy face whose most arresting features were his shrewd, glittering brown eyes. He had a penetrating mind, and he was full of odd bits of information.

"The nobles of Nara," he said, "owned vast estates, and numerous slaves. They lived in elegant mansions behind bamboo fences, and they had beautifully landscaped gardens. They also had obedient, well-disciplined wives," and with a sardonic smile, he quoted an old saying: " 'The Japanese wife needs no religion, for her husband is her sole heaven.'

"The forty-fifth Emperor was named Shomu, and his reign is known as the Period of Heavenly Peace. After a visit to the Shinto shrines of Ise, he announced that he had his divine ancestress's approval to make Nara 'Buddha's Holy City of Beauty on Earth.' His single-minded pursuit of this pious aim unfortunately ruined the nation, for he had a passion for gold statues.

"When Shomu died, his widow, the Empress Komyo, gave most of his treasures to the Todaiji Temple, and a great wooden treasurehouse called the Shosoin was built to house them. It's still there. I'll show it to you, for we pass close by the Todaiji Temple on our way to Mrs. Nakamura's."

Most of the roads in Nara run through the city's immense deer park. It was easy to imagine the black-lacquered bullock carts rolling towards the vast Todaiji Temple, and the nobles wearing grotesquely carved *gagaku* masks at the temple ceremonies for the Great Buddha that the Emperor Shomu had built.

The Shosoin, which means "square-shaped treasurehouse," is a super log cabin: just like an Ise shrine, but bigger. Built of cypress wood, with no windows, it is 100 feet long, and thick, stumpy wooden pillars raise it 9 feet above the ground. The Nara builders anticipated modern man's solution of the garaging problem by twelve hundred years.

The space under the Shosoin, as we approached, was filled with busy human figures. Most of them wore the robes of Buddhist monks, but one was conspicuous in a Western morning coat and top hat. What was more, I recognized him: it was Mr. Shima's friend, the other Imperial chamberlain.

After we exchanged bows, and I introduced Hara-san and Suzuki-san, the chamberlain explained the reason for his finery.

"The Shosoin is inspected twice a year. It is my duty to see that the seals on the three doors are intact, before the inspection is permitted to begin. I myself remove the seals and when the inspection is finished I replace them with fresh seals, which I have brought especially from Tokyo for the purpose."

We had missed the inspection, which had gone on for some days, the treasures being brought out and carefully unwrapped on the ground under the Shosoin, since there were no lights inside the huge windowless storehouse. Now the treasures were all back in their wrappings and boxes and the last of the boxes had been replaced in the dusty airless interior of the Shosoin. All that remained to be done was to reseal the three big wooden doors.

Bearing his three seals, each with the Emperor's personal signature, wrapped in a bamboo leaf, the top-hatted chamberlain carefully climbed a wooden ladder onto the veranda that ran round the building, and fixed a seal to each door, while the shaven-polled monks stood around chanting. The wooden ladders would all be removed when the ceremony was completed, and the Shosoin would stand untouched for another six months.

When we drove on, Hara said: "The Shosoin is so sacred that it has never had to be guarded, in all the centuries it has existed. The Emperor's seal is sufficient to protect the treasures."

"Then it must be full of gold statues."

Hara gave me a look of glittering irony. "No. It contains screens, paintings, and musical instruments of Shomu's Period of Heavenly Peace. But no gold."

(4)

Mrs. Nakamura was a very tiny lady, two or so inches under five foot, who lived in a wooden house that was atwitter with caged birds. She was a well-preserved fifty, with jet-black hair and dimples, and she wore a beautiful opal ring and had a black coral brooch fastened to the richly brocaded *obi*, or sash, of her kimono. Her eyes were also black, as black as her hair, but harder and shinier than the coral. Despite the dimples and the twittering birds, she gave an immediate impression of formidableness. One somehow was sorry for the birds, and felt their cages really were prisons.

Mrs. Nakamura was a widow with no illusions. After nine years of marriage, her husband died, leaving her with a seven-

year-old son and a small electrical-appliance business that was
tottering on the verge of bankruptcy. Mr. Nakamura, I gathered, had had a great fondness for the most expensive geishas.
Instead of meekly handing the frail little business over to some
male relative to continue mismanaging it, Mrs. Nakamura decided to run it herself. Now, twenty-two years later, it was a
full-fledged company, and she was its iron-willed president.

"I never considered myself inferior to men," said Mrs. Nakamura, folding her small hands in her lap so that the big opal
ring made a pale fire there. "Not even when my husband was
alive."

"All our workers deeply respect Mama," said her proud son.

The boy, who had been seven when his father died, was now
a man of twenty-nine or thirty. In looks he probably resembled
his father, having a too full chin, and an air of hearty chuckling
good will that somehow seemed uneasy. His wife, a sturdy-look-
ing country girl with thick black eyebrows, served us green tea.
They had been married only a few months and lived with Mrs.
Nakamura in the little wooden house filled with caged birds.

"Men are comical creatures," said Mrs. Nakamura, contemptuously. "Gullible"—it seemed to me she shot a sharp look at
her fat-chinned son—"and unreliable. They are also vain, tight-
fisted, and small-minded. And, on top of all that, there is their
fondness for you know what."

"Women and sake," said Hara promptly. "Women and sake.
You've been reading modern novels. Ah, but how times have
changed! Women have equal rights with men now, you know.
Even marriages are no longer arranged."

There was some mockery in his tone, and his glittering
shrewd eyes went swiftly from the mother and the wife to the
son.

Mrs. Nakamura snorted. "So they say. But what earthly good
do you think that does the young girls? Let's say a working-class
girl 'falls in love' "—she made it sound derisive—"with a university graduate. She may think he'll marry her; but she'll be

ditched like a pair of old shoes when a girl of his own class comes along and gets his family's approval!"

"Ah, but read our new Constitution!" urged Hara. "Not that it's so new, by now. We've had it fifteen years already. But it says that 'marriage shall be based only on mutual consent.' And it declares that husband and wife have equal rights."

"'Mutual consent' is all right," said Mrs. Nakamura. "So long as the couple do as their parents advise them."

She turned to me, and spoke in rapid Japanese, occasionally jerking her head towards her son and daughter-in-law. Evidently this was something she especially wanted me to know. I had to try to look intelligent, and nod sympathetically, while in reality waiting for Suzuki or Hara to interpret, for she spoke too fast for me.

What she was saying was: "My son there is almost thirty and he has been abroad more than once now, on business trips to America and Manila and so on. He is like his father and goes to the geisha restaurants and worse places also, but I don't begrudge him this; only, I decided he needed a sensible girl to keep him from throwing all the money away, when I am gone.

"Now he has married his cousin, and it was I who arranged it. We got hold of a good go-between, and he produced six candidates, but I chose the cousin as being most suitable. Although they are cousins, they didn't really know each other, not to speak to, so I let them have six months in which to get acquainted—*after* the engagement."

Hara, grinning, left the interpreting to Suzuki, who looked solemn as a young owl: I don't think it ever occurred to him that she was saying anything out of the way. The son I thought looked sheepish, and grinned in a weak way, but the cousin he had married merely nodded brisk confirmation at intervals in Mrs. Nakamura's narration.

Once having begun, Mrs. Nakamura continued to erupt, her opal ring glowing in her lap and her shiny black eyes fixed on me.

"It's become fashionable lately to say the geisha is only an 'art person' who sings and dances and makes amusing conversation, but that's all nonsense, you know. If you don't believe me, ask him!" And again she jerked her head towards her son. "But anyway I know, and I ought to, considering how many times his father— Ah well, that's all done with.

"But I don't really mind geishas, I must tell you. I hope you won't be shocked: but I believe it's very good for young wives to have to hold on to their husbands in competition with an accomplished and worldly-wise geisha. I think that sexual jealousy *flavors* a marriage. I suppose, though," concluded this astonishing woman, "that that's an old-fashioned view."

We rose, made profoundly low bows, and slowly retreated, murmuring innumerable times: *"Dom' arigato gozaimashita!!"* There really was no more to be said.

(5)

"If the geisha goes," Mrs. Nakamura had said, "there will be an unimaginably different Japan." But, clearly, she did not believe there could be a Japan without geisha.

Kazuko Hashimoto thought otherwise, and her opinion was interesting, for she was a geisha.

The geisha restaurant was a simple, two-story wooden structure in a dark little narrow lane lined with almost identical boxes. Two or three boisterous parties were in progress in each geisha restaurant. Seated on the straw-mat floor, with our stockinged feet tucked awkwardly under us, we could hear laughter and high stilted voices and the harsh plucking of *samisen* strings coming from adjacent rooms.

From time to time, the wood and paper door of our own room slid open, and another geisha appeared on her knees, bowed low to the company, and glided to her place. There were nine of us, six Japanese, who were our hosts, and three *gaijins*; and the number of geisha varied between five and eight.

"Some of us have to put in an appearance at the other parties," Kazuko explained. "We stay for a bit in one room, then slip away while another course is being served. Otherwise, on busy nights there might not be enough of us to go round."

Kazuko's English was not as fluent as I have made it sound, but she spoke enough of it to get her ideas over, and when she faltered she went into Japanese and Lionel Spencer interpreted. He was an Englishman in business in the Kansai, which is the name of the Osaka-Kyoto-Nara area, and he spoke Japanese "like a native," as his partner Gardner Baldwin put it.

Lionel was one of those thin Englishmen, with limp fair hair and pale blue eyes. Even if Kazuko had spoken perfect English, she would almost certainly not have confided the secrets of her trade to me; but Lionel knew her well and had what Gardner Baldwin loudly called "a way with Japs." Baldwin was a ruddy, stocky, bluff, hardheaded, no-nonsense Englishman who dispensed explosive, damn-your-eyes opinions at the top of his voice. After insulting someone, he generally laughed like a machinegun.

The six Japanese businessmen were short, heavy men, with broad faces wrenched into perpetual smiles. Five of them slapped their big thighs and grunted with glee as the sixth lost the game of "scissors cut paper" that he was playing with his geisha.

"How do you become a geisha?" I asked Kazuko.

"It is very hard work. There is an eight-year apprenticeship."

"But what do you learn?"

"Manners," said Kazuko.

Perfect politeness behind the painted paper fan, so that one giggled only when one was meant to giggle—and not when a middle-aged fool who had drunk too much sake lost face, or when a *gaijin* persisted in asking silly questions. But I persisted.

"What else?"

"How to open a door correctly. To bow. To kneel. To sing. To dance. And," said Kazuko suavely, "to make *intelligent* conversation."

"I've heard that instead of the geisha's entertaining the guests, the guests are supposed to entertain the geisha."

Kazuko did not laugh. It might have been difficult, since she was wearing very heavy make-up, and also balancing on her head an extremely large and heavy black wig, which gleamed with fish oil. But having darted her brilliant dark eyes around the company to satisfy herself the others were not listening, she inclined her bewigged head a fraction towards the Japanese businessmen. "Do you think we find *them* entertaining?"

The man who had lost the game of "scissors cut paper" was attempting to regain face, in a peculiar way. He sidled closer to his geisha, his eyes fixed challengingly not on her but on his five friends who laughed at him. His mouth half-open in a fishlike grin, he tried to slip a hand into the fold of her kimono.

"No," I said, answering Kazuko.

"No. But we must make them think we do! They must believe it is they who are being clever and witty. And so it's become a saying that the guests entertain the geisha, not the other way round."

The girl beside the man with the fishlike mouth did not seem to move. But suddenly it was she who was pressing against him, and saying something in his ear. Something delightfully, deliciously outrageous, evidently: he fell back with a squawk of delight, and had to support himself by putting both hands on the floor. And that girl was up and gone, bowing low and smiling coyly, and another girl had slid smoothly into a kneeling position on the plump cushion, in her place, and was humbly offering him more sake.

"But why do you say that the geisha will soon be no more?"

"Foreigners," said Kazuko.

Just as American bases are blamed for clams that chop themselves in two, so foreigners, or *gaijins*, are supposed to be responsible for ruining the morals of Japan. There is something in this. Most *gaijins* visiting the country seem to have a fixed notion that Japanese girls have no morals to start with. Hence an advertisement of this sort, appearing in that most respectable of newspapers, the *Japan Times*:

> WANTED: Attractive Japanese girl, between ages 18–22, to accompany as guide American gentleman on country-wide tour of Japan. Must speak English. Address all replies with photograph to—.

It is also true that some Japanese girls are not shy. I knew a man who passed an uneasy night in a little village I shall call Somoto. In the early days of the American Occupation it was full of GIs, but they had all long since gone, leaving tender memories, and a café called Highball Center. The man I knew dropped idly into Highball Center and was instantly surrounded by eager girls who had not seen a *gaijin* for at least eight years.

When a girl with prominent gold teeth made a grab at him, all the others began to scream, and pull her hair. My friend fled into the night, where it was dismally raining. But the gold-toothed girl chased after him. When she caught up with him, she promptly bit him in the chest. Then, grabbing him by the fly, she tried to pull him back to the Highball Center. He fought her off and regained his inn, unraped, and piled his baggage against the door of his bedroom, since the door had no lock. But the door was made of paper, and all night long the girls poked holes in the paper with their fingers, then whispered seductively to him through the holes.

But I could not see what *gaijins* had to do with ruining the geisha business. I had thought they would make it boom, and said so. But Kazuko shook her bewigged head.

"Foreigners don't want real geisha who sing in high strangled voices, do slow dances, and pluck the strings of a *samisen* to make harsh oriental music. Geisha can only be witty in Japanese, which almost no foreigners understand. Also," said Kazuko frankly, "we are much too expensive; this dinner will cost your friends at least $150, though we geisha have eaten and drunk nothing.

"The *gaijins* want girls who can do the rhumba, and understand English jokes. *Gaijins* don't care if they lose face or not, so they don't need a geisha to help them recover it.

"Japanese men are the most imitative on earth, and besides all the young Japanese men have become Western in their tastes, through the movies. I don't believe you could find a single Japanese man under the age of thirty who has ever even set foot in a geisha restaurant. They go to the movies instead, or to *pachinko* parlors; or, if they are rich, to bars with 'hostesses,' and to strip joints.

"And the old men who come here nowadays," Kazuko finished with a soft viciousness that never disarranged her set smile, "all they want to do is play baseball with their behinds."

"Play—?"

"You will see."

The door slid open. The dumpling-shaped woman who had opened it bowed perfunctorily from the kneeling position, then got up and crossed the room to the six Japanese businessmen. They greeted her with glad foolish cries.

"She is our mama-san," said Kazuko. "She and her husband own four Kansai geisha restaurants, and one in Sendai. He is a Korean."

The way she said "he is a Korean" reminded me of O-Sei abusing the policemen. Her clear voice was full of loathing and contempt. Before he died in 1592, the great Japanese warrior Hideyoshi built, in the temple of Daibutsu, at Nara, a *Mimid-zuka*, or "ear collection," of 30,000 pairs of pickled Korean ears.

In almost four centuries, the Japanese attitude towards Koreans has not greatly changed.

The mama-san, who was no longer in the first flush of youth, being about seventy, nodded indulgently as the six Japanese businessmen eagerly besieged her with an earnest plea. Kneeling beside them, in a blue kimono with white dragons that I thought scarcely suited her age, she turned her head, and briskly clapped her hands.

The door slid open again, but this time to admit two very young *maiko*, apprentice geisha, with bright lips and eyes, and white flowers entwined in their coiled black hair. They knelt side by side in the open doorway, bowing low enough to reveal the napes of their necks, the part of the feminine form that never fails to excite Japanese men.

"*Yakyu!*" cried the businessmen. "*Besu-boru!*"

"Baseball," said Lionel Spencer.

Two of the other, older geisha retired, to reappear with saxophones, which they proceeded to play, vigorously if erratically. I recognized the tune. It was a Japanese ditty called "Cherry Blossom." The other geisha, including Kazuko, obediently clapped their hands to the rhythm.

The *maiko* went to one end of the room, where they were joined by two of the Japanese businessmen. In time to the music, the girls swung their arms, as if they were pitching, and then made as if to strike out with bats in their hands. The businessmen did the same.

The object of the simple game then became clear. When a *maiko* and a businessman went to bat, they did so in such a way that their behinds collided. Thus assaulted, one of the little fat men lost his balance and tumbled down on to a cushion thoughtfully provided for just such an occurrence. The *maiko* who had upset him cheerfully hauled him to his feet again. The other fat little man lasted longer, but went down in the end, amid howls of glee. Then two of the other men peeled

off their coats, and took their places on the baseball "team."
And the geisha with the saxophones went on tootling, and
the other geisha, including Kazuko, continued to clap their
hands.

"The girls almost always win," said Lionel. "If they do lose,
it's only to save a customer's 'face.' They hit remarkably hard
with their little bottoms," he added. "Much harder than they
need to. I think that's because they don't really like playing
besu-boru."

"They know they are victims of capitalist exploitation," said
Kazuko, sternly and quite unexpectedly.

"Why don't they just refuse, then?" I asked. "Isn't there a
geisha guild, or something?"

Kazuko shook her head. "There is too much competition.
Completely untrained girls can get jobs in geisha restaurants
now, provided they are pretty, and can please the customers.
Especially foreigners," she added pointedly. "But Japanese men
are no better. They, too, are bored with the *samisen,* and traditional geisha songs, and silly, quiet games like 'scissors cut
paper.' They prefer silly, loud games, like *besu-boru,* played
with *maiko.*"

"There are still geisha restaurants that employ girls who can't
rhumba and can't play 'baseball' or the saxophone," said Lionel. "But they are becoming fewer."

"I have a delicate question," I said. "Suppose that fellow
with the fish face wanted a *maiko* to sleep with him. Would she
do it? Would the mama-san order her to?"

"The mama-san wouldn't order her to," said Kazuko. "But
if the *maiko* agreed, the mama-san would expect a share of
what the man paid. The *maiko* probably would not do it, unless
the man was very attractive, or the *maiko* was putting her little
brother through college. Very few of the men who make such
requests are attractive. But," Kazuko sighed, "so many *maiko*
nowadays are in this profession because they are putting younger
brothers through college. (A *maiko* when she becomes a

geisha is able to earn much, much more than a stenographer, or a schoolteacher.)"

The "baseball" came to an end, and the mama-san sent for an apple. When it came, she lit a match, blew it out, and stuck it in the apple, glowing head up. The fruit was then passed quickly from hand to hand. The person holding the apple when the head of the match went black drank a thimbleful of sake as a forfeit.

The Japanese found this sedentary variation on "musical chairs" wildly amusing. They squealed and grunted. Their faces were heavily flushed. When they looked at us, their gaze was amiable but vacant, as if they found it increasingly difficult to recall who we were.

"Silly lot, the Japs," Gardner Baldwin suddenly bawled scornfully in my ear. "Can't hold their liquor, y'know." I thought he was looking very flushed himself.

He chuckled. "Let's down 'em proper." He shouted at the mama-san, and the thimble-sized sake cups vanished, to be replaced by big glass tumblers.

Speaking with calm malice, Kazuko murmured something to Lionel.

"What did she say?" I asked him.

"The mama-san wanted us all to go home. It's almost midnight. A geisha party isn't supposed to go on more than three hours. Now Kazuko says it will cost our friends $300, thanks to Gardner Baldwin."

But the Japanese businessmen didn't seem to mind. Hospitality was hospitality, and besides it was all on the expense account. They applauded the ingenious notion of Mr. Baldwin, who made fun of them when they were not looking, by winking broadly at Lionel and me.

The apple with the match in it continued to circulate. I lost once, Lionel once, Gardner Baldwin twice. But the Japanese lost more often, especially after Baldwin tired of the match-in-the-apple game and substituted an orange game with the same forfeit. A geisha fed you orange slices, but first you had to try to guess how many slices the orange contained. The Japanese had long since lost the power of estimating.

"Now we have had enough of the orange," said Kazuko suddenly, to Gardner Baldwin. "You and I will play *jan-ken-pon*," which is Japanese for the scissors-cut-paper game.

He looked at her, and I could see the calculation in his reddening eye. "If you lose, you will drink a tumblerful of sake? Each time?"

"If I lose," said Kazuko.

Gardner Baldwin shouted with laughter. "You're on, my girl!"

Kazuko didn't lose. When Baldwin shot out two fingers, for scissors, Kazuko had a closed fist to represent the stone that blunted them; when Baldwin had his hand in a fist, Kazuko's hand was open, so that she was the paper that overcomes stone by wrapping it. But when Baldwin's hand was open, Kazuko had two fingers extended, in scissors-cut-paper.

One by one, the Japanese men, overcome, got up and staggered softly from the room.

Baldwin had drunk four large glasses of sake in a row.

"One more try," said he. His face had become mottled.

Once again, her paper wrapped his stone.

Baldwin drank another glassful of sake, then he got to his feet and excused himself.

"Now he is being sick," said Kazuko, with satisfaction.

"We shall look after him," said the mama-san. "There is no need for you to wait."

"We can hardly leave all our friends on your hands," Lionel began.

"Ah, we are all right!" said a brisk voice from the doorway, and the six businessmen entered, led by the fish-mouthed one. Their broad faces beamed, their big spectacles gleamed. They looked sober as judges.

"Japanese cannot drink very much," they apologized. "We

are very sorry. But, you see, Japanese also recover very quickly!"

"*Gaijins* not so quickly," I murmured to Kazuko, as she bowed low to us in the outer doorway after we had said our good-bys and put on our shoes. "I suppose this is called 'the geisha's revenge.'"

But she only smiled mysteriously. It occurred to me afterwards that Gardner Baldwin was a very well-to-do *gaijin*. Perhaps Kazuko was putting a younger brother through college.

(6)

"Please lock the windows when you go out and sleep," said one of the English notices in my hotel bedroom in Nara. Evidently the hotel was accustomed to *gaijin* guests who strayed, but was resigned to their lack of morals.

This was certainly an unfair slur on the Morisons, an American tourist couple who had something vaguely missionary in their background—I never discovered precisely what. The Morisons just loved Japan, and said so all the time. "It is all so beautiful!" Mrs. Morison would exclaim, casting eyes heavenward. "So—so delicate!"

"Lovely, indeed!" Mr. Morison would agree, following with appreciative eye the progress of a slim girl in bright kimono as she walked through the hotel lobby.

Then Lionel Spencer spoilt it all by sending them on a little sightseeing expedition to a place he knew. "It's a sort of fertility temple," he explained. "But very interesting, if you don't think you'll be too shocked."

Mrs. Morison smiled. "Come, now, we're grown up!"

"And broadminded!" Mr. Morison chuckled.

Nevertheless, the expedition was not a success. The fertility temple was situated in a sort of mountain cave, and the temple guide turned out to be an ugly little girl of about fourteen, who spoke no English. She took the Morisons in tow, and led them from exhibit to exhibit, explaining each in a flat, bored voice.

Because it was all in Japanese, the Morisons did not even begin to understand, for a while. As the little girl led them round and pointed to various objects, they merely smiled tourists' fixed smiles, and gave tourists' dutiful, uncomprehending nods. Gradually, however, the meaning and purpose of certain objects became only too clear; and the Morisons' smiles got feebler and feebler. But still the child guide led them on: now producing for their inspection a *daikon*, or giant Japanese radish, freakishly shaped like a human penis; now pointing out two stones that mimicked male and female sex organs.

Finally, an incredible hag appeared and with a lecherous leer thrust under their noses a "pillow book," consisting of silk pictures bound in brocade. Exquisitely painted on each square of silk were thoroughly pornographic imaginings.

"Now they'll spend the rest of their lives telling people that the Japanese are sex maniacs," said Lionel.

"Whereas, of course, the Japanese are just matter of fact about the business, and it's people like the Morisons who have dirty minds?" asked Jane.

"Exactly."

Arthur Kawabata wanted to take us to the Ryusenji Temple on Mount Omine. Ryusenji means "dragon spring." The temple was thirteen centuries old, and the legendary founder was a very holy man, who had ascended the mountain in order to meditate undisturbed, but first had had to overcome certain demons, who became his faithful followers, and whose descendants now lived in the village of Dorogawa, where the temple was located, high on the mountain.

The interesting thing about the temple was that for thirteen hundred years no woman had as much as set foot inside its compound. The temple belonged to the Shugen-do, a Buddhist sect that took very seriously such adages as: "woman is the root of evil that even five hundred reincarnations will not absolve," and "it is better to meet a poisonous snake than encounter a woman." Now, however, women were making determined assaults on the sacred mountain, encouraged by such breaches with ancient tradition as that, on the neighboring, no less sacred peak of Odaigahara, the Buddhist monks (of a different sect) had opened a sort of mountain hostel that welcomed girl hikers as well as males. Under pressure of such unfair competition, the monks of Ryusenji, on Omine, were grudgingly preparing to allow women worshippers into their compound for the first time.

To get to Mount Omine, we drove first to Shimanouchi, where are produced most of the wooden chopsticks that 93,000,-000 Japanese eat with. The narrow streets of the little town were almost choked with bundles of cedarwood. There were also extraordinarily large numbers of very pretty girls, while gorgeous tree orchids grew on the roofs of the houses. Shimanouchi is set amid twisting green foothills ridged with cedar trees. Beyond and above towered a mountain that was the bright green color of a dragon, with silver waterfalls for scales and heavy lowering mists for dragon's breath. On top of this mountain, at the end of a looping narrow trail, was Ryusenji Temple, and Dorogawa, the village of demons' descendants.

"The monks of Ryusenji," said Arthur, "are athletic ascetics. Every monk is a qualified mountaineer, and carries a climbing rope, an alpenstock, and a conch shell in case he has to call for help. But in addition, they practice severe rites. They walk on red-hot embers, and pray naked under icy waterfalls. Each must pass through an initiation test. He is dangled over a crag at the end of a rope, and the other monks holding the rope pretend to let go."

Higher, and still higher. The mountain is over 5,500 feet, but the steep windings of the narrow road made it seem much more. When we were halfway up, it started to rain, and from then on we traveled in a heavy, steady downpour. The villagers of Dorogawa carried bamboo and paper umbrellas, and stared at us as if we were the demons, not they. They looked remarkably like ordinary human beings.

The temple was guarded by two sorts of demons: *goki*, or back devils, and *zenki*, or front devils. Leaving Jane in the car, Arthur and I passed those carved guardians—who actually resembled Disney elves—and crossed the compound to the temple's living quarters.

First we were led to a sort of waiting-room, where we sat on straw matting and were served hot tea in large cups without handles. Nobody else was in the waiting-room. Then we were taken to an anteroom, where monks knelt on the rush-mat *tatami*, immobile, bolt upright, hands folded; they were well spaced out, so that they looked rather like chessmen in black robes, with shaven heads. They paid not the slightest attention to us. They had come to Ryusenji to see the abbot. Many of them bitterly opposed the plan to admit women worshippers to the temple.

Presently we were led into the abbot's presence. But there was a hitch. The abbot, whose name was Kiagyoku Okada, looked up from where he knelt on the floor with four monks. He thundered something, and we were hastily taken back to the anteroom.

"What did he say?" I asked Arthur.

"He said: 'When I want to see the *gaijin*, I'll send for him. Right now, I'm busy, can't you see?' "

It did not sound promising.

In the anteroom, complete silence prevailed. The black-robed monks still knelt in the praying position, utterly absorbed, not moving, hardly seeming to breathe. Time dragged on. I hoped Jane, abandoned in the car outside, was not getting too wet.

Then once again we were led into the presence of the abbot. This time he was all alone, and all smiles. He was thin, wrinkled, wiry, lively, and probably about eighty years old. "There's a lady sitting in a car out on the road," he said. "Who's she?"

"My wife," I said.

"Why is she sitting out there in the rain?"

"Why," I said, "I understood—men only—some controversy over admitting women—rather delicate situation—"

"I've sent to have her brought in," said Abbot Okada, and just then Jane appeared, escorted by a tall monk carrying a dripping bamboo and paper umbrella. The abbot amiably bade her be seated.

"Thirteen hundred years ago," he explained, "the founder of the Shugen Buddhists fled from Kyoto to this mountain. He wanted to meditate on eternal things, and he found it difficult to do so in the city of Kyoto, where he was surrounded by geisha and other worldly attractions.

"Ever since then, the mountain top has been closed to women; because there we practice our rituals, and I leave it to you to imagine— Yes, yes, what is it?" he demanded irritably, as the monks who had been praying in the anteroom put their heads round the door.

One muttered something.

"When I want to see you, I'll send for you," thundered Abbot Okada. "Right now, I'm busy, can't you see?"

The monks vanished. The abbot beamed at Jane.

"Where was I? Ah, yes. I leave it to you to imagine what would happen if the monks who were dangling a novitiate over a crag at the end of a rope were to be distracted all of a sudden by the sight of a pretty woman. H'm. Yes. Well!

"But now things are changing. Japanese women claim they are the equals of men, and go about demanding what they call their 'human rights.' They say their rights are written into this Constitution that you Americans forced through the Diet." (I did not challenge this statement, which is blatantly untrue but which apparently every Japanese believes, whether he dislikes the Constitution, or is fanatically opposed to its being altered.) "We poor monks will just have to get used to seeing women on the mountain." He did not seem at all unhappy at the prospect, it seemed to me. "There will be girl hikers, probably wearing shorts." He beamed cheerfully through his spectacles at Jane. "As a first step, we propose admitting women Buddhists into the temple compound. And you, dear lady, are the first woman to set foot in those premises for thirteen centuries!"

Jane looked gratified. We all rose. Arthur, who had been interpreting all this, transmitted our humble thanks. We exchanged bows. The abbot said he would have a monk show us around. But it was perfectly plain from the expressions on the monks' faces that they did not like this at all, and presently Jane slipped tactfully back to the car.

Arthur and I were taken to look at the spring that gives the temple its name. There was a clear pool in reddish stone, and beside it the figure of a man standing on a tortoise, with a dragon crawling up his back.

"The dragon that dwelt under the spring assumed the form of a woman," our guide explained. "A mountain dweller took her to live with him, and presently she had a baby. But she warned her husband never to enter her presence without knocking. One day he forgot. Instead of his wife, a dragon was feeding milk to his child. The dragon fled back to its cavern under this spring, but first handed the husband one of its eyes, as a keepsake. The dragon's eye socket is still bleeding, and that is why the water looks red."

After this edifying tale, we went to see the shrine of the dragon, only a few yards from the red water pool. One was permitted to climb the wooden steps, and peer into the recesses of the holy of holies. But there was little to see: only a large round mirror, and a very large, black-lacquer casket. Arthur asked what was in the casket. The monk who was guiding us round said it contained a sacred image of the dragon god. But when Arthur asked what the dragon god looked like, the monk said he had no idea, for the casket had not been opened within living memory. I deduced that the dragon god was in the same category as the Emperor's Sacred Jewel.

Then we squelched through the mud to a large stone pillar just outside the main compound gate, bearing an inscription in Japanese. This was the famous, or infamous, notice forbidding women to enter.

Its doom was upon it. Up the road from Dorogawa trooped a column of women, sheltering themselves under umbrellas. They did not look at all like O-Sei and her friends of the Nara women's university, for they mostly wore peasant costume, but they had the same resolute air. There were about three hundred women, and the leaders carried a stout rope. This was tied around the stone pillar; and then all the women heaved and strained. The pillar probably weighed a ton. But it would have had to weigh more than that to withstand three hundred determined women.

When they had pulled it down, the ladies proceeded to haul it through the open gate into the compound: the scene was rather reminiscent of one of those Biblical film epics in which slaves build the pyramids.

"They are going to give thanks to the dragon god, for being allowed into his temple," smiled the monk who had come with us. He was a young monk, and evidently not one of the anti-feminists.

Jane said she was glad the women of Japan had scored another victory over male prejudice. She was also pleased with herself for being the first woman to enter the mountain dragon temple in thirteen hundred years. She thought Abbot Okada was a dear, and insisted that we send him some bottles of choice sake. Arthur thought this a very good idea indeed. On our way down the mountain, we stopped and bought some. It came in handy, we learned later. The governor of Nara called in at the temple to congratulate the monks on their broadminded, anti-feudal attitude, and he and the abbot drank the sake.

V

KYOTO:

ON BEING FULL OF ZEN

*To prefer the exotic to the home-grown is
a usual form of 'sophistication'; and when,
as in the present fad for Zen Buddhism,
the fashion enjoins contempt for intellect,
the pleasure is double.*

JACQUES BARZUN

THE EARLY JAPANESE, like the early Britons, were barbarians.
The British painted themselves blue; the Japanese, according to
amused Chinese contemporaries, painted themselves pink and
scarlet, lived on raw vegetables, and walked about barefoot.
When they went on long sea voyages to China, Japanese travelers took with them a "mourning keeper," who was heaped
with favors if the voyage went well and put to death if it
fared ill. Japanese who turned up at the Chinese Court were
accompanied by hairy Ainu, with four-foot-long beards, who
had bows and arrows and were able to shoot a gourd off a person's head at fifty paces.

But the Japanese longed to be civilized, and, when they made
Kyoto the capital of Japan, in A.D. 794, they modeled it on a
Chinese city. There were eight streets, and nine avenues. The
Purple Palace had nine encircling walls. There were nine Ministries, and eight grades of officials. On Mount Hiei, the city's
"devil door," a giant Buddhist monastery was built, to ward off
the evil that traditionally comes from the unlucky northeast.

Kyoto in the twentieth century may be the only city in the
world that has purple and gold traffic lights, instead of the usual
red, amber, and green. Kyoto also has an elegant main street

called Kawara-machi, which contains the world's best doll shops, as well as glittering, two-story *pachinko* parlors. It also has the Far East's most exclusive bean-curd shop, with certificates of merit with huge red seals on the walls, and in the window a river with tree-covered islands, all made of bean curd. The trees are thoroughly realistic, down to the last leaf on the last twig.

Crammed with temples and palaces, Kyoto can never forget its past history: in the closing years of the thirteenth century, *four* Emperors were living in Kyoto—the current ruler, and three who had abdicated. But Kyoto also likes to think of itself as the Paris of Japan, a city of the intellect, and of beautiful women. It is probably true that the loveliest women in Japan come from Kyoto, and also that Kyoto has more artists and writers than any other city except Tokyo. There used to be a "Beret Society," so called because the members sat around wearing berets and discussing French art. Though this is unhappily no longer in existence, Kyoto still has *eight hundred* cultural societies—in a city whose population is not much over a million.

But Kyoto's real importance has been and still is in religion. The rise, decline, and fall of Japanese Buddhism can be traced here. In the tenth century, a Mount Hiei monk called Kuya danced through Kyoto's streets, with a tinkling bell round his neck, singing simple hymns about Buddhism. Kuya's creed was that all you had to do to get to heaven was to pronounce the Buddha's name once.

> *He never fails to reach the Lotus Land of Bliss*
> *Who calls, if only once, the name of* Amida.
> *A far, far distant land is Paradise, I've heard them say,*
> *But those who want to go can reach there in a day.*[1]

This was jollier doctrine than Genshin's dismal warning that sinners would be "seized and placed in an iron vat, and boiled

[1] Translation by Ryusaku Tsunoda: *Sources of the Japanese Tradition* (New York: Columbia University Press), p. 193.

as one cooks beans." As for Shinran, he refused all knowledge, of good or of evil. "Of good and evil I am totally ignorant. . . . I am an ordinary mortal, full of passion and desire, living in this transient world like a dweller in a house on fire; every judgement of mine, whatever I say, is nonsense and gibberish. The Nembutsu alone is true." [2]

For centuries, the wise men of Kyoto peered darkly through the glass of theology, looking for truth. But, on and around Mount Hiei, things have come to a pretty pass today. Where monks meditated, and plovers sang among yellow primroses, there are now toll roads that roar with automobiles and the young "thunder tribe"; playgrounds and cafeterias; and at the top observation towers that go round and round.

There are over a thousand Buddhist temples in Kyoto, and all of them are bidding frantically for a share of the tourist trade. The monks sell lucky charms ("ward off evil, and drive safely"), *tempura*, bean curd, post cards. Some young monks keep pictures of pretty nudes hung up on the walls of their cells, and slip off into the city for a night of guzzling and wenching.

None of this takes away from Kyoto's sheer picturesqueness. The city's 14,000 Shinto shrines include such charming oddities as the confectioners' shrine of Tajimamori-no-mikoto, which has a 2,000-year-old legend. The Emperor Suinin sent the saint to China with instructions to bring back some *kashi*, or candy. He returned sixteen years later, by which time the Emperor was dead, so he first offered the candy at the Emperor's grave, then committed hara-kiri on the spot. His shrine is visited by confectioners from all over Japan.

There is another shrine that is dedicated to the spirits of falling cherry blossoms, and one where prayers are said for broken sewing-machine needles.

Nevertheless, the decline of both Buddhism and Shinto is evident in the fact that since Japan's defeat in the war, no fewer than a hundred and twenty-six "new" religions, with an esti-

[2] *Ibid.* p. 218.

mated ten million followers, have sprung up. As a sample, there
is the Seicho-no-Ie, which manages to combine in one "religious" emblem the Christian cross, the Jewish Star of David,
the Mohammedan crescent—and the Nazi swastika. Buddhism
itself has become, in Japan, so materialistic—or so broadminded
—that newspapers think little of carrying advertisements that
show Buddha drinking a particular brand of whisky.

Nearly all the "new" religions seem to be flourishing financially, although both Buddhists and Shintoists lament that they
cannot raise enough money to keep their temples and shrines
in proper repair. An estimated five million Japanese adhere
to a hedonist doctrine called Tenri, "the merry life." And no
"new" sect prospers more than the one called "Perfect Liberty."

(2)

Admiring the cherry-blossoms is a favorite pastime of Japanese
politicians and big businessmen. Regrettably, there is nothing
poetic about the appearance of either the business executives
or the politicians. On the contrary, like their counterparts elsewhere, they are often the most drearily undistinguished of men.

All the more striking, therefore, was the presence, at this
particular Kyoto cherry-blossom party, of an immaculate gentleman in his late fifties who wore his morning coat, white vest,
striped trousers, white spats, and white gloves as if they actually
belonged to him and had not just been hired for the occasion.

"That," I was told, when I asked, "is Tokuchika Miki, the
Master of PL *Kyodan.*"

Mr. Miki was smilingly prepared to tell me all I wanted to
know about his highly successful *Kyodan,* or religious order.

"Life is art: that in a nutshell is our creed. We instruct our
members to live radiantly, like the sun. Life's whole purpose is
happiness. To be happy—that is to live in accordance with
divine law. Perfect self-expression means perfect living. Our

slogan is, 'Do at once whatever your first inspiration dictates!' "

He must have caught the gleam in my eye as I glanced at his shiny top hat, for he added hastily: "Self-expression must not be interpreted to mean liberty to annoy or offend others—that would be bad art."

"I'm told that 'PL' stands for 'Perfect Liberty.' Why do you choose an English name for your order?"

"Because, in Japan, English has become the rage," he replied frankly.

Nevertheless, he emphasized, the order was not really a new thing.

"My father founded it, in 1920. My father was a Zen Buddhist priest. He called it, then, *Hito-no-Michi*, or 'Way of Man.' When the militarists came along, they suppressed us, for we stood for peaceful existence."

Mr. Miki and his father were both imprisoned in 1937. His father, Tokuharu Miki, died the following year (and is now worshipped by the sect, probably as a god and at least as a saint). Miki II remained jailed until 1945, when the Americans released him. Then his father's old followers begged him to form a new *Kyodan* that would, however, revive the principles and beliefs of the "Way of Man." He did so, and almost immediately it became a resounding success—if that is the proper designation for the triumphant advance of a "religion."

"Perfect Liberty" claims to have three quarters of a million followers in Japan. The headquarters are at Habikino, near Osaka, but there are over a hundred and fifty branches throughout the country. Each branch building, like the headquarters, has a huge PL over the entrance. Anyone can join PL, by paying an initiation fee of 83 cents, and then 83 cents every year thereafter, for as long as one wishes to remain a member. In return for the money, members receive a PL badge, PL literature including a hymnbook, and a paper bag, called *hosho bukuro* or "treasure-creating bag." On the twenty-first of each month ("thanksgiving day"), members are supposed to place a donation ("whatever you can afford") in the *hosho bukuro*, and send it in to their branch manager.

The PL headquarters at Habikino decided to give a big party, to which PL members from all over Japan were invited. The entertainment included dancing, music being provided by an imported thirty-piece band. Mr. Miki danced the rhumba with girls in smart Western cocktail dresses, including Sadako, his adopted daughter. PL encourages modern dancing; any member can ask for and will get free lessons in the tango, rhumba, or cha-cha. Also, children are taught those dances, in the order's equivalents of Sunday school.

"Then, there is the brides' school," said one of Mr. Miki's five young male secretaries, briskly. "Girls who graduate from our high school here at PL may attend the brides' school thereafter, for one year. We teach them to cook, sew—and dance. Also, each girl is expected to be able to compose a Japanese poem." He laughed. "They don't, of course, all become poetesses. But it's good for both their wits and their calligraphy."

The Habikino PL high school had two hundred forty students, its own baseball team, and as coach a famous Japanese baseball star from Meiji University. "He was converted to PL," the secretary explained, "and has been coaching ever since. All members of PL are encouraged to play baseball—women as well as men, old as well as young. We think it healthy. We also have a softball team, and a coach for that, too."

"Do you have to pay the coaches?"

"Oh, no; they get their food and board, but that's all. They do it for PL—because they believe in it."

Habikino is a 2,500-acre estate, and there are guards at the gates—but all the guards are women, not men. Mr. Miki was busily building modern apartment houses for all of the fifteen hundred PLers who live at Habikino. The secretary and I drove past the high school, and also past six bulldozers, each with PL painted in white on its side. "We are making a lot of new roads," the secretary explained. Our station wagon, one of the twenty-nine vehicles owned by the estate (they include four omnibuses) halted at a big gymnasium. Inside, hundreds of young people were playing basketball and ping-pong and swinging on gym bars. Beyond the gym was a large hospital.

Back at the main building, a PL service was being conducted in the auditorium. In front of a plain white altar, a priest wearing a black robe clasped his hands on his stomach, then at his breast, and finally raised them over his head and made a circle with his fingers. All the people present did the same.

Though it was explained to me, I was never quite clear what this ritual signified. "First, we think calm thoughts," said the secretary. "Then, we reflect on our past deeds. Finally, self-assured that we have nothing to be ashamed of, we make the circle with our fingers, meaning we wish to become one with God."

There were prayers, and hymns. Then, before the closing ritual, PL members stepped forward, and told how joining PL had changed their lives. One of those was a boilerman, working on the estate. He said: "My job here is to keep the temperature constant; that is, to keep everyone warm and comfortable. By doing this, by making people happy, I am doing God's work. And, by doing God's work. *I* am happier than I have ever been before in my life."

After the service, the PL members who had come to Habikino from other parts of Japan filed into a special courtyard, where each laid a stone, brought from his own town or village and inscribed with his name, at the foot of a sacred camellia tree.

Mr. Miki, who worked with his male secretaries in a large, well-appointed office kept air-conditioned, explained that PL was about to launch into golf. "We are going to have golf courses. Golf is all the rage in Japan just now. It is also a wonderful expression of our religion, which teaches, 'Do anything you like, but do it well.'

"Besides," he added, "I like golf, and what is good for me is, I feel, good for my followers also."

One reason for PL's popularity and apparent strength is its complete tolerance of other religious points of view. This is something that all of Japan's hundred and twenty-six "new" religions have in common. "You can have any religion you like, in addition to ours," the master shrugs. Most PL members do not give up their earlier Buddhist or Shinto beliefs.

Another source of strength is that all PL members are enjoined to help one another, and usually do. The order never fails to go to the rescue of a member in financial difficulties. The result, according to one Japanese businessman who belongs to PL, is that "PL members do not go bankrupt."

The hundred and twenty-six "new" religions have formed themselves into an association, the Shin Nippon Shukyo Dantai Rengo-Kai, which simply means New Japan Religious Groups Association. Mr. Miki was chosen as the association's chairman. Under the Religious Juridicial Persons Law, most of these religions, including PL, are exempt from taxation. This is the third source of strength.

(3)

Jane and I went to see Kyoto's famous Ginkakuji, or Silver Pavilion, which has no silver and looks like a modest rustic tea-house in a municipal park. The fifteenth-century garden is what one goes to look at. The creaking branches of the ancient trees are supported by heavy wooden crutches, and look like creations of Salvador Dali. There are miniature waterfalls, silver threads veining the rocks. Here clearly was the source of inspiration of the bean-curd shop in Kawara-machi—and of much else in Japan's exquisite minor arts.

The famous fifteen rugged rocks of the Zen garden of Ryoanji Temple are half-buried in white sand that is blinding in strong sunlight, and is spread evenly over the floor of a sunken pit, 80 feet long and 25 wide. The rocks, which are blackish, with a little lichen growing on them, reminded me of the black-robed, shaven-headed monks kneeling upright and immobile like cheesmen on the straw-mat floor of the abbot's anteroom in Ryusenji Temple, on Mount Omine. They are, however, supposed to represent a tiger fleeing, from one island to another with its cubs, from the attack of a leopard.

The great Zen masters preached that the Buddha was to be found within. "Great is Mind," said Eisai. "Heaven's height is immeasurable, but Mind goes beyond Heaven." Hideyoshi, a highly successful warrior much exercised by Zen, thought that "God is Mind." Nevertheless, most Zen preachers seem to have suspected that the universe would turn out in the end to be only a cosmic joke; and some feared it might prove a bad joke. They devoted almost all their energies, and their considerable ingenuity, to devising means to startle people out of the coma of human complacency.

A favorite Zen riddle runs thus. "A man is suspended over a cliff. He cannot use his hands, but is holding on to the branch of a tree by his teeth. A friend leans over and asks him, 'What is Zen?' What should he reply?" Another riddle asks: "What is the sound of one hand clapping?"

The answer to all such riddles is that there is no answer. This is the Zen mystery, and the Zen joke, which is also the mystery and the comedy of human existence, and of the universe.

The rock garden of Ryoanji is almost certainly another manifestation of Zen humor. And the joke has worked well. For five centuries, people have been going to look at it, puzzling over it, and devising ingenious theories about its real, inner meaning. And it has no meaning.

While we were standing on the edge of the pit, shielding our eyes with our hands against the glare of the white sand, and peering at the fifteen stones, an earnest young Japanese wearing the brass-buttoned black tunic of a university student sidled up to me. I could tell, by the manner of his approach, like a leopard stalking a tiger and its cubs, that he was determined to practice his English on us.

In a hushed, reverent voice, as one speaking in church, he asked haltingly: "Do you not think those stones are wonderful?" He plainly expected us to rhapsodize.

I shook my head, in the pure spirit of Zen. "No."

He looked at us as if, being still in church, I had blasphemed, and backed away a step or two. "You do not think they express the joy of living?"

"Quite the contrary," I said, and marched him round the corner, where there is a garden that nobody bothers to look at, because it consists only of simple, fresh green moss, with a single, graceful stone lantern for decoration. "Here is life," I said. "The rock garden is only a desert, which means death."

He went back and looked once more, long and earnestly, at the fifteen stones in the pit of sand; and I could see his rapt expression gradually give way to one of criticism and disapproval.

"Now you've disillusioned him," said Jane.

"That's Zen," I said.

On our way out, we were accosted by a Japanese schoolgirl, also eager to practice her English on a *gaijin*. I knew what she was going to say before she said it. "Excuse me, please," she asked. "Are you a kind gentleman?" She said she thought that American imperialism was trying to bring back feudalism to Japan and should indulge in serious self-reflection. I reflected that if she went about accosting strangers in this way she might have some interesting experiences.

There were a number of tall young Americans, with mild sheeplike faces, who were living in Kyoto and studying Zen. Some of them had even shaved their heads, and most of them were also studying poetry, Japanese architecture, Japanese calligraphy, and flower arranging. They proudly claimed to be living "absolutely Japanese" lives, and they had rented cold and draughty little wooden houses, with tiny, drizzly, over-grown gardens.

I found one of them kneeling on the straw floor of a "six-mat" room, meditating in a black kimono. The room contained a small Japanese writing desk, six inches high and eighteen inches wide; a *kakemono*, or long scroll painted with birds and flowers, hanging in a wall niche called the *tokonoma*; a small vase of flowers at the foot of the *tokonoma*, as well as an incense burner; and a tiny hanging bookcase containing a novel by Kafka, one by Thomas Mann, and a book of winnowed wisdom by Lin Yutang. He had been living in Kyoto and studying Zen for six months, and I asked him how he liked it.

He disapproved of the question. "Zen," he explained, "excludes pleasure *and* pain, happiness as well as sorrow." Then he asked me, rather hungrily, for a cigarette, and after I had lit it for him, told me: "It isn't good to *force* oneself to relinquish desires; you have to eliminate the *cause* of the desire to smoke, not just the craving, which is merely a symptom."

In California, where he came from, he had sold enough used automobiles to be able to afford a brand-new one for himself every year. But one day, strolling through the San Francisco redwoods, he read a Zen poem. The poem asked: "Before your father and mother were born, what was your original face?" This decided him to come to Kyoto, live on the $100 a month he managed to earn by teaching English, and try to reach *satori*, or enlightenment, through *zazen*, which means meditation.

"Can't Christians become enlightened?"

"Not through Christianity, which is intolerant, guilt-centered, and literally bloody-minded. The same applies to Judaism."

All the same, the Japanese had not lived up to his high hopes. He had fallen in love with a Japanese girl, and wanted to marry her. "But she wanted me to take her back to California. That's *all* she wanted. She said she hated everything that was old and

Japanese, and longed to escape from it all, and live a thoroughly modern, Western life." He laughed bitterly. "Here was I, trying to escape from the West and its sordid materialism, and find peace of mind and spirit in her world; and it turned out that the only things she really cared about were motorcars, movies, and rock-and-roll!"

He also found the strict discipline of Zen a severe trial. "I spent some weeks in a Zen temple. It was grim. We had to get up at four every morning, and meditate for a whole hour. That means kneeling bolt upright and not moving a muscle. If you do, the *roshi*—that's the Zen master—comes and beats you with a stick. We had three meals a day: unsalted rice gruel and sour pickled plums for breakfast, more rice with bean soup and pickled radish for lunch, and unsalted rice gruel for supper. When we weren't meditating, we had to chop wood and dig for vegetables. We were also sent out each week end, to go around the district with our begging bowls and ask for alms; the *roshi* explained this was to teach us humility."

"How do you meditate?" I asked.

"I've told you. One has to kneel, bolt upright and not as much as shivering even in the coldest weather, on the wooden floor of the *sodo*, the meditation hall. The *roshi* walks up and down with a stick, and if you make a single move—"

That stick had really impressed him—as it certainly would have done me.

"Yes, but what are you supposed to think *about?*"

"You concentrate on not concentrating," he said seriously. "The *roshi* told me I had to leave desire behind, and stop planning. There is no predetermined end in studying Zen: no motive. It's like breathing."

"But then how about enlightenment?"

"If you think about *satori*, you'll never find it."

"Well, how far along do you think you are, nevertheless?"

He asked for another cigarette, and puffed on it, meditatively. Then, in a sharp burst of confidence: "Sometimes I feel I'm making progress, and then I'm so happy I could burst out of my skin. But other times I feel I've aged ten years in the six months I've been here. The truth about the Japanese, I've found, is that they're selfish, self-centered, and don't like foreigners. The temple people didn't show the slightest interest when I turned up. Of course, Buddhists and especially Zen Buddhists aren't supposed to get excited about *anything*. But if I vanished tomorrow, I don't think they'd even notice.

"I wish I could go to Thailand, and be a Buddhist there," he concluded, gloomily. "I'm told the Thai are much friendlier. The only religion the Japanese really believe in is Japan."

He said he had made only one real Japanese friend in Kyoto, a young man called Kamane, who came to him for English conversation. "As a matter of fact, he's due now. You'll like him. He's awfully intelligent."

Kamane-san was a very tall, very thin young man, with a wide mouth full of tremendously oversized teeth. There being no way to conceal them, he showed them perpetually, in a beaming smile. He had spent five years in Chicago.

"Many Americans are Buddhists without realizing it," he said. "They are looking for a spiritual lead; they have found that orthodox Sunday-go-to-meeting Christianity is a dead end. But Zen will never really catch on in the West, because Westerners are much too impatient. It takes a year just to learn the fundamental Zen rules about sitting and breathing. Anyone who is serious about Zen has to devote at least four hours a day to sitting perfectly still and meditating. And this has to be kept up for at least four years."

Presently we left the Californian to his meditation, and strolled back into Kyoto together. Kamane was silent for a while. Then he looked back towards the draughty little wooden house with its damp little weedy garden. "He is a dear fellow," he said, "but, you know, he worries me dreadfully. Why does he come all the way here, to endure those discomforts, and eat that awful temple food, when he could just as well meditate in California where the weather is so much more agreeable? Sometimes I think he must be a little touched up here!" And he tapped his forehead.

(4)

"Every Lipton advertisement," said Lionel Spencer, "is in the direct line of descent from an injunction of late twelfth-century Zen. Tea and Zen are indissolubly linked."

In the year 1191, the great Zen master, Eisai, arrived home in Japan, bringing tea from China. He urged the warrior class of Japan to embrace tea and Zen together. "Whenever one is in poor spirits," Eisai preached, "one should drink tea. Why is our country full of sickly-looking, skinny people? Simply because we do not drink enough tea."

Soon the Japanese had taken to the tea ceremony with the same fervor they had shown earlier in adopting Buddhism. The tea had to be brewed in a special way, with special implements; stirred with a bamboo whisk; and savored by being sipped thrice. Ideally, the tea was drunk in a special Zen tea hut, nine foot square and full of symbolism.

"The tea hut," lectured Lionel, "emphasizes the mutability of human existence and of the cosmos itself, and consequently the need for humility. To brew the tea, one requires both fire and water, the two most powerful elements. But the little horned roof over the entrance of the hut reminds one that the elements are changeable, and the hut's simple privy is meant to remind us that the body is both mortal and unclean. The smoke of the incense rising shows that we aspire to heaven; but to get there we must be humble, like the flagstones that are willing to be stepped on, the water that allows us to use it to wash the dirt from our hands, and the little flame inside the stone lantern that permits itself to be consumed in order to provide light. Also, the doorway is built deliberately low, to make one stoop.

"However," added Lionel kindly, "don't be afraid. The *cha-no-yu* I'm taking you to won't be held in a simple Zen tea hut: far from it."

There are several masters of the *cha-no-yu*, or tea ceremony, in Japan. Each has his own "school," and each school claims hundreds of thousands of adherents. The tea ceremony, in short, is big business—not as big as steel or cotton but perhaps as large as transistor radios; every Japanese girl who hopes to have a husband has to learn the tea ceremony, and the schools charge a fee for teaching it.

This particular tea ceremony was being sponsored by one of the great masters of the art, and it was unique, because it was especially for foreigners. The master concerned had already come under strong attack from his rivals, who declared that he had vulgarized the *cha-no-yu* among the Japanese by boldly telling pupils there was no reason why they shouldn't use an ordinary metal teaspoon, instead of a bamboo whisk, and an ordinary teacup, instead of a special bowl. He had even designed a portable tea-ceremony kit for use on picnics. I gathered that this was the equivalent of modern-minded Western clergymen holding special services for Sunday golfers.

Now the master was hoping to spread the *cha-no-yu* cult abroad, by arousing the enthusiasm of *gaijins*. All his English-speaking pupils were urged to bring their foreign friends to his big tea ceremony.

They had done their work well. The narrow streets and little lanes leading to the mansion where the affair was being held were choked with automobiles. Most of the invited guests had to get out and walk the last five blocks. It had been raining, and the tiny twisting thoroughfares were pitch black and slippery with mud. Through the darkness stumbled men in evening dress, and ladies in mink as well as in kimonos, guided to their destination by policemen who held aloft white paper lanterns containing feebly flickering candles.

In the hall of the mansion there was a receiving line that included not only the master but a famous poet, an even more famous wood-block artist, and a fabulously famous Japanese movie actress. They stood bowing deeply to the guests, in an appropriately Chinese setting of priceless Tang vases and green-glaze Han dogs. The master had thin black hair, thick black eyebrows, and a great beak of yellow nose. As wave after wave of guests crashed on the doorstep and surged into the hall, they were passed efficiently along the receiving line and then funneled into a large garden, where the stormy night sky showed in strips, between hastily erected awnings.

The tea ceremony was to be performed in the garden, but to my surprise, waiters and pretty waitresses in kimonos were serving Martinis, highballs, and old-fashioneds. "It's to make the *gaijins* feel more at home," Lionel explained. "A rumor got around that they might be made to drink some of the nasty green tea. Of course it was deliberately spread by one of the master's rivals." But I noticed that the Japanese who were present were happily downing cocktails just as fast as the foreigners were.

A space had been left clear in the center of the garden, and in the middle of this circle a girl in a black kimono and a big black wig knelt on a strip of straw matting beside a charcoal brazier. Also kneeling on the *tatami* were two women in black kimonos, holding *samisens*, the string instruments that gesha play, and a third woman, also in a black kimono, with a *koto*, the Japanese harp.

After a while, when everyone had had several cocktails, the girl in the big black wig reached out for an iron kettle, and lifted it on to the charcoal brazier. The women with the *samisens* and the woman with the *koto* immediately commenced twanging and plucking. "It is in the tradition of the tea ceremony," Lionel explained, "that the sound of the water for the tea being brought to a boil recall pine leaves rustling in a breeze. However, since we aren't likely to hear the water boiling, from this distance, the women are making music that is supposed to sound the same." I did not think they were doing too well, unless one assumed that pine leaves were made of tin. But everyone seemed perfectly happy, especially those who were close enough to the bar to whisper an order for another highball.

The kneeling girl next picked up a black-lacquered box containing powdered green tea, and wiped it with a small square of silk, called a *fukusa*. Then she picked up a long spoon, and carefully wiped that. Then she washed a bamboo whisk, which looked like a shaving brush, in a bowl, and dried it, and emptied and dried the bowl. Then into the bowl she spooned some powdered tea from the black-lacquered box.

By this time—for her movements were slow and stately, and between them, she straightened her graceful back, folded her hands, and presumably practiced *zazen*, or meditation—the kettle was boiling. The girl took it off the charcoal brazier, and ladled some hot water into the bowl. Then she took up the whisk that looked like a shaving brush, and began to stir the contents of the bowl into a green froth. While she was doing this, the three women played their instruments, and also sang a sad little song in the high squeak that the Japanese consider most suited to such plaintive ditties.

"The song is called 'Yuki,' which means 'snow,' " Lionel said. "It is about a geisha who has a tragic love affair."

"In the snow?"

"Not quite. But when it's all over, she runs out into the snow and commits suicide."

"Of course. I should have known."

Finally, the women in black ceased singing, and bowed. The girl who had made the tea bowed. It was intimated that anyone who wished to taste the green froth could do so. There seemed to be remarkably few takers. But I was anxious to try it. I took

138

the bowl in both hands, in what I hoped was the approved manner, and sipped. It had the texture of thick pea soup, but tasted bitter. I was glad of the cake of sweet bean paste that was given me to nibble.

We tried to leave the garden, but this was less easy than it sounds. Waves of guests were still crashing through the front door of the mansion and then being channeled straight out to the garden, where another *cha-no-yu* performance would shortly be held. Bushes were trampled underfoot, and waiters were frozen in strange attitudes as they held trays high above their heads in the confusion. Now and then one heard the tinkle of a cocktail glass as it fell on a flagstone and broke. But we finally made it.

The master had got tired of bowing and shaking hands. He had retreated to a small arbor, where he was talking with a fellow businessman who did flower arrangements. When the master had finished teaching the tea ceremony to brides-to-be, he passed them on to his friend, who—also for a fee—taught them the art of arranging flowers.

The master was looking a little upset, and readily explained why, without having to be asked.

"We sold two hundred admission tickets, but over five hundred people turned up. It's impossible to keep track of who bought tickets and who is just gate-crashing. Besides," he added candidly, "none of them are the kind of people one can afford to throw out, even if they haven't paid. Those minks!" He shrugged. "Oh well, if it helps the cause. . . ."

He said he wanted above all to convince foreigners that the tea ceremony need not involve stiff and elaborate ceremonial. "I just want them to enjoy it," he said. "Once they have our export tea-ceremony kit, they can do *cha-no-yu* in armchairs set around their own fireplace, if they want. Just clear the mantel, and put on it one simple art object—of course it must be Japanese: with our export kit, we packet a printed list of suitable art objects, which are available at reasonable prices on application. But there is absolutely no need for physical discomfort—kneeling on the floor, and saying Zen prayers."

"But one shouldn't let it be thought that one is running down Zen," said the flower-arrangement master, alarmed. "Zen is fast becoming the rage among people abroad. It would be unwise to divorce the tea ceremony—or flower arranging—from Zen. In reality, they are both the quintessence of Zen."

"Of course," the tea-ceremony master agreed. "Of course. But one also wants to be modern in one's approach."

"Certainly," said the flower-arrangement master. "I myself take pride in being thoroughly modern. I have just commenced a new class that is particularly appealing to foreigners, I find: especially American ladies. Instead of using flowers, I make arrangements of bare branches, stones, and even bits of old machinery. It's absolutely avant-garde."

We prepared to take our leave. Guests were still arriving, and nobody but ourselves seemed at all interested in going. The master said he would let us out a back way, so we would not have to use our knees and elbows to force a passage. The back way took us through a large kitchen, where cases of bottles, all empty, had overflowed from the bar. As we exchanged farewells on the back doorstep, a three-wheeler van drove up.

"Thank God!" said the master. "Reinforcements. My wife just told me we don't have a drop of Scotch or bourbon left."

(5)

It rained very softly in Kyoto for several days. Everything smelt pleasantly of green luxuriant growth, and everywhere was the sound of chuckling water. The hills were always half-hidden in mists, and trees seemed to be coming down the slopes and marching into the town. The damp air made mirages; stone lanterns outside houses, and the houses themselves, became ghostly. Ghostliest of all were the old temples and pavilions, with their creaking floors and dark wooden interiors; the smell of incense; and the glimpse of a great, dark, Buddha face, huge and placid and high overhead, a Dreamer dreaming universes into being and then dreaming them to an end only to start dreaming them again. Vermilion-painted wooden Shinto shrines, standing at the tops of long crumbling stone staircases, loomed out of the pearl-gray mist like phantoms seen in human dreams. Even the geisha restaurants huddled on the river bank, beside the bridges over the dark-flowing water, twanged and tinkled behind bamboo shutters with a fainter and a sadder tune, as if all the geisha were about to commit suicide. If Kyoto is primarily a city of religion, it is because of this recurrent strain of melancholy in it, when Nature quietly reminds humanity that life is essentially growth followed by decay. Earthquakes may provoke defiance: damp air and growing trees induce only acquiescence and resignation.

Lionel promised to introduce me to two men who, he said, could probably tell me more about Zen than anyone else living. One was an elderly Briton who had lived most of his life in Japan, and become not only a Zen Buddhist, but an assistant bishop. Also he was passionately devoted to cats.

"In Zen," he said, "you can believe whatever you want."

"But doesn't that lead to more selfishness instead of more selflessness?"

"Not necessarily. It depends on the sort of person you are. Only, unless you practice Zen, the chances are you never will discover the sort of person you really are. A person who practices Zen opens up like a—well, like a flower. And, as each layer of petals opens, new petals are revealed."

"But suppose the person is like an onion, not a flower—suppose you can peel off skin after skin, until you're left with nothing at all?"

He smiled good-humoredly, gently stroking one of his innumerable cats. And raised snow-white eyebrows.

"Well: so what?"

"Wouldn't it be awful to find you were just nothingness?"

"Oh, no. Not if you really believed in Zen. You wouldn't care."

"It wouldn't be a tremendous letdown—to find out, I mean, that there was to be no enlightenment for you, after all?"

"No. In a way, it would be a confirmation, and a fulfillment. Because Zen enjoins on those who believe it that they must strive for freedom—including freedom from Zen's teachings!"

"Well," I said, though it was enough just to look at him to know the answer, "will you tell me what Zen has done for you?"

"Certainly—although, mind, your asking that question shows how very far off the mark you are: Zen doesn't offer to do anything for anybody. However, it has done something for me. Years and years ago, when I was a young man, I was appalled and disgusted by Christianity. The first world war had something to do with it. But it went beyond that. I really didn't care for a great deal of Christ's teaching. He seemed to me, if you'll excuse my saying this, to be harsh, fanatical, intolerant, bad-tempered, and quite often just sheerly wrongheaded. But in recent years I have conceived a great admiration for Christ. Buddhism makes you broadminded, and Zen Buddhism forces you to be more broadminded than anything else."

Lionel's second man was even more uncompromisingly tolerant—for this is probably Zen's innermost paradox. He, too, was a Britisher, a Londoner who had turned his back on the West, in the physical sense, many years before, and as far as I could tell had lived joyously and with spiritual abundance in Japan ever since. Yet his version of the creed seemed stark enough, in all conscience.

"It's quite untrue to say, as Christians and others do, that God loves us," he stated calmly. "What Zen teaches is that an unloving Universe is nevertheless to be loved.

"Without reward, of any sort: for Zen teaches us to give up

wanting consolations, explanations, even meanings, which ）
come to the same thing.

"There is no ego in Zen. No ego whatever. But there is
plenty of ego in Christianity. Christ, Himself, was an egoist.
And, indeed, most things, except Zen, are full of ego. The music
of Beethoven is all ego—except for the final quartets, which in
my opinion are all Zen. Bach is full of Zen. Mozart is full of
Zen."

"Please define Zen," I said.

He sighed, though very patiently. "Ah, please don't ask me to
do that! No one can.

"Would you understand me if I said that a hippopotamus
has more Zen than a butterfly? It has: because it has more
humor. All Buddhism has humor; but Zen has the most, because it accepts everything, yet questions everything. As a Zen
Buddhist, I believe in everything, yet I believe in nothing."

"Does that make you a humorist?"

He grinned. "In a way, I suppose. But let's take someone
rather better known. Charles Dickens is a great humorist; and
Dickens's characters are full of Zen. That's why the whole world
loves them."

I was so impressed by this conversation that I rashly mentioned it to Lionel in the hearing of his business partner,
Gardner Baldwin. I had not seen Baldwin since the geisha party,
to which he never referred. How he had fared that evening remained his secret. But he was immediately all eagerness to try
a fall with a Zen Buddhist. I never met such a glutton for
punishment.

"Zen," he said, "is utter nonsense and as such is typically
Japanese. Only a fool would believe in it. I think this man im-
pressed you because in a subtle sort of way he flattered you.
Well, he won't impress or flatter *me*."

He didn't. He repeated much of what he had said to me, and
then, addressing Lionel, he said: "Some people have Zen, too,

you know, just as some poems, animals, and characters in books do." Lionel looked expectant. "But you don't have any, I'm afraid: none at all."

Lionel, who admitted he had no idea what Zen was, looked unreasonably crestfallen; and Baldwin, who resolutely refused to believe there was such a thing as Zen, sniggered happily.

"Now, your friend here," said the British Buddhist, turning to Baldwin, "he is full of Zen."

Baldwin looked highly gratified.

"What else, in your opinion, has Zen?" I asked.

The Buddhist looked at the ceiling. "Well: quite a number of things. Trash cans. Blotting paper. Earth toilets. . . ."

Baldwin later argued passionately that he had been deliberately insulted. Reminders that he could not be insulted by being told he was full of something he didn't believe in failed to mollify him, even when Lionel pointed out that, according to Zen Buddhist teaching, "the Buddha Himself is a stick of dry dung."

VI

OSAKA:

THE STRANGE WORLD OF JAPANESE

BUSINESS

Give as little foothold as possible to for-
eigners.
HERBERT SPENCER
TO BARON KANEKO KENTARO, 1892

Japan has incomparably more to fear from
English or American capital than from
Russian battleships and bayonets.
LAFCADIO HEARN

It was still raining softly when I left Kyoto by train for
Osaka, and the roofs of the little wooden houses alongside the
railway track glistened like black seals. In the early morning,
Japan was getting up and going to work. Two women in white
smocks marched along a farm track with buckets of milk dangling from a bamboo pole carried on their shoulders. A mechanic in blue overalls, with pliers and other tools hanging from
his broad black leather belt, went whistling down a village
street. At a level crossing, a clerk with a brief case, a gray-
haired lady wearing a gray scarf and white socks and carrying an
umbrella, and a man who wore a white cotton face mask and
sat astride a motorscooter, waited for the train to pass.

Power pylons strode over the hills like purposeful steel robots,
giant advertising billboards scrawled with huge red and black
Japanese characters disfigured the fields, and from time to time
there were black smokestacks and clumps of stumpy gray apartment houses on the edges of the rice paddies. There was an

145

abundance of schools and school playing fields, with baseball diamonds and basketball nets, and the roads were alive with schoolboys in peaked caps and black tunics, and schoolgirls in middy blouses. Many houses had television aerials on their shining black roofs, and one of the village squares was dominated by a tall pink tower with four loud-speakers.

A solitary steeple with a Christian cross flashed past; a hotel's backyard contained rows of wide-sleeved *yukatas* (lounging kimonos) hanging on wooden frames after washing, resembling crucifixes. Most of the wooden houses had tall bamboo poles planted in front, and the poles gaily flew big red, green, yellow, and blue paper carp, the number of carp denoting the number of sons in a household. There were innumerable little Buddhist cemeteries, with flat-topped plinths for gravestones, and there were timber yards galore. Women in wide straw hats and padded blue cotton trousers were working in the fields and ignoring the rain, and on a station platform stood some railway waitresses wearing black dresses and frilly white aprons.

"Pretty girls," said Mr. Ota, smacking his lips. Mr. Ota was short, bald, fat, and fish-mouthed, and I had last seen him at the geisha party in Nara. He had spotted me on the train and with many low bows persuaded my seat companion, a student with a black wool tie who was reading *The Catcher in the Rye*, to change seats with him.

Mr. Ota wore a snappy blue-gray suit, and had kicked off his sharp-pointed, bright brown lacing shoes so he could wiggle his toes inside his socks, which were bright blue and patterned with red diamonds. You may think that Mr. Ota was a frivolous middle-aged man who only thought about girls, but this was not so. He also thought about business.

"You are going to Osaka to the trade fair?" was his first question to me. I said no, not the trade fair, but he brushed this aside. "You must visit the trade fair. You will see many interesting Japanese things. Cameras. Radios. Microscopes. All made in Japan."

Mr. Ota had been a businessman in Manchuria but had lost his factory when Japan lost the war. "The Russians got it; now the Chinese have it," he said, looking at me reproachfully. But Mr. Ota had made a modest comeback. He was not the power he had been, with enslaved Chinese workers and minor Japanese officials treating him as if he were a feudal lord; but he was not doing badly. He lived in Osaka and had a wife and three children. I gathered his wife did not accompany him when he visited Nara.

There were canals, red mailboxes, and many more smoke-stacks. Then we were entering Osaka. Mr. Ota pulled from his right ear the tiny plastic disc, wired to his seat, through which he had been listening to a musical program even as he talked, and bent to lace up his hideous brown shoes. "You will like Osaka," he said. "There is a night club with one thousand pretty girls. But don't forget to visit the trade fair. Here is my card."

Osaka is a city of dealers. "When you pick up the phone," Lionel Spencer explained, "you're liable to get a crossed wire, and overhear someone offering a million-yen, tax-free, under-the-table kickback on a contract." By day it is a city of broad busy thoroughfares, overmassive office buildings, and enormous banks with marble pillars and acres of marble floors, over which clank the *geta*, or wooden shoes, of messengers.

By night, however, it takes on a certain beauty: calm where the city's many lamplit bridges are reflected silverly in the dark, smooth waters of the broad canals; hectic, with scarlet, green, and blue neon bursting into artificial flowers on the tops of tall buildings and then cascading down their dark sides like brilliant waterfalls. Above this restless surge of neon rise the eerily dis-embodied television towers with their winking red stars to warn aircraft, and higher yet are the swaying calligraphic lad-ders of electric signs dangling from floating advertising bal-loons.

Opposite my tenth-floor hotel bedroom, little Japanese workmen in overalls and crash helmets walked unconcernedly in split-toed rubber boots along the bamboo poles that scaffolded a new department store. In the hotel lobby, an American businessman shrewdly beat down the already low price that a Japanese was asking for his textiles. When the American was called to the telephone by the hotel's paging loud-speaker, I recognized his name as that of the representative of a firm that lobbied intensively in Washington to have cheap Japanese goods kept off the American market.

Lionel lived roughly midway between Osaka and Kyoto, and therefore commuted. He said it was a perilous thing to do: ten times more uncomfortable than in New York, which is generally hailed as the commuters' hell, and worse even than Tokyo. Lionel showed me an editorial in the Osaka edition of the newspaper *Mainichi*. The topic was the death of a schoolgirl, who had been literally pushed under the wheels of a train in a platform crush, and the *Mainichi* said severely: "A nation is judged by the conduct of its commuters. Such incidents show how impolite we Japanese can sometimes be."

Lionel was ready to brave the perils of commuting because he was in love with his house, which he rented from a rich Japanese merchant; the merchant let him have the house cheap because, as he explained, he didn't need the money but wanted his house to be in good hands. Lionel invited me to see it and I agreed it was a jewel. It had a large garden, into which the living rooms literally opened, because of their sliding doors. The Japanese furnishings were unbelievably elegant: tall painted screens; wonderful carved or lacquered chests and tables; and a *tokonoma*, or alcove, for *kakemono*, or hanging scrolls. The *kakemono* I saw was a beautiful piece showing a pine-shaggy mountain, waterfalls, and a lake; and Lionel explained that the owner had a treasure house filled with scrolls and paintings, and each month he allowed Lionel to pick a fresh one, and hang it in the *tokonoma*.

Meanwhile, at the insistence of his family, who were disoriented from things Japanese, the owner lived, nearby, in a Western-style house uncomfortably crammed with overstuffed chairs and sofas, a plaster Venus de Milo, 21-inch television sets, and a truly horrible brass and glass chandelier.

Lionel did not like Osaka. "It has everything," he said gloomily. "Geisha restaurants, theaters, prostitutes, and male brothels. Its social life is utterly stifling. Stupefyingly large dinner parties are set for eight-thirty. Everyone drinks and talks about business for two or three hours. Then they sit down at table, too exhausted either to eat or to talk any more."

One reason for this dismal state, Lionel thought, was that Japanese businessmen almost never took their wives to parties. "You can ask them until you're blue in the face. I know, I've tried. First you send along a formal invitation addressed to 'Mr. and Mrs. Yamaguchi.' Then you phone Mr. Yamaguchi and, after chatting a bit about trade with China and the price of rice, you ask him if he's coming to your party. He says, 'Yes,' and you say quickly, 'And, of course, you will be bringing Mrs. Yamaguchi?' He hisses like a steam kettle for a moment, but you pressure him, and he finally says, 'Yes, she'll be along, too.'

"After that, right up to the night of the party, you make a point of phoning him in order to say in the course of the conversation, 'You do know, of course, that we very much want Mrs. Yamaguchi to come to the party.' And when you meet him in someone's office or at the bank, you take the opportunity to remind him, 'We're looking forward to seeing you *and* Mrs. Yamaguchi the night of the party.'

"He keeps on agreeing," said Lionel disgustedly. "Then, just an hour beforehand, he rings you up to say he is very sorry that Mrs. Yamaguchi cannot come. They all do it. They never explain."

To prove that Osaka had everything, Lionel took me to a café where one drank coffee surrounded by genuine antiques —grandfather clocks, marble statuary, old English furniture, French paintings, Greek and Roman busts, Egyptian mummy cases and Mesopotamian artifacts. On the next floor, however, teen-agers rocked and rolled to a rock-and-roll band.

Lionel refused to visit the trade fair, so I went alone. It, too, had everything. Several huge halls were crowded with people and with massive machinery, miniature cameras, transistor radios, and electronic microscopes. All were made in Japan, including the color television sets. I got the impression there was now very little, if anything, that the indefatigably industrious Japanese could not do, but that they were still uncertain what their customers—chiefly the Western countries—wanted from them.

I was reminded of Lionel's Japanese landlord and his two homes, one lovely and one awful. Side by side with the beautiful and delicate machinery were such horrors as cheap lacquerwork, cheaper mouth organs, a set of five silver cups and a silver pot with a spout, proudly marked, "Silver Whisky Set." The Japanese have an irrational passion for making things in sets of five. The only whisky likely to be spouted into the five silver cups was the legendary Japanese brand described by its maker as having been "squeezed from purest Scottish grapes."

There was some exquisite Japanese pottery. But there were also crude, colored clay figurines of *sumo* wrestlers, very badly designed paper lanterns, tortoise-shell ash trays, brass candlesticks shaped like pagodas, plywood guitars, pendulum clocks with gilt horses, plastic yo-yos, wooden goldfish, wooden owls, and waterproof beach sandals "with high-frequency welding."

I was looking at something called "essence of salamander, recommended as the only and most effective treatment for rejuvenation, 1 or 2 pills daily," when a voice hailed me. It was Mr. Ota. Beaming, he led me to his own exhibit.

"Vitreous china sanitary ware," said the man from Manchuria proudly. "Reverse trap closets of most modern design."

One of them was in complete working order. Mr. Ota pulled the chain. There was a melodious rush of flushing water.

"Quiet operation by symphonic action," said Mr. Ota.

(2)

The workers of the giant electric company stood in stiff rows, their hands at their sides and their heads bowed in typical Japanese morning greeting. Then they straightened up, and shifted their feet to stand at ease.

"Now they repeat the company's seven commandments," the assistant manager of production whispered.

"Industrious work is the key to national prosperity," the rows of overalled men and girls chanted dutifully.

"Be just, cheerful, correct, and broadminded at all times.

"Be in harmony with others.

"Improve yourself through hard work.

"Be courteous and sincere!

"Be adaptable and tolerant!

"Be grateful and repay kindness!"

"Be! Be'! With all your being, be!" murmured Lionel, who is facetious when confronted by conformity.

"Now they sing the company song," said the assistant manager.

Somewhere in the vast hall a loud-speaker crackled, then emitted a military marching tune. The workers sang:

> *For the building of the New Japan,*
> *Unite your efforts, your hearts!*
> *For ever-increasing production,*
> *Love your work, give your all!*
> *Let us send our products to the people of the world,*
> *Our products in an unending stream,*
> *Like the waters of a stream,*
> *A stream that unceasing flows.*
> *Grow, industry, grow grow grow!*

The loud-speaker clicked off. The workers bowed again, then turned smartly and marched off to their workbenches. The assistant manager glanced at his expensive Swiss wrist watch, and said: "This morning, as on every working morning, the same ceremony was repeated in the company's thirty factories, from Kyushu to Hokkaido."

We strolled thoughtfully with him to his office, a square, bright, chilly room, with a square desk, and three armchairs frugally swathed in plain white cotton wraps. Three coarse china mugs of green tea steamed on a low table.

"But don't they feel that the company is overdoing it a bit?" Lionel asked, as he sipped his hot tea. "Especially the younger ones: the ones born during or just after the war?"

"Oh no," said the assistant manager, who had taken his engineering degrees in Manchester and Massachussetts. "Even with them, the company quickly becomes a cult. A lot of the new employees are bright university graduates. They've had a liberal education. Most of them have picked up Marxism as well. So they're vigorously anticapitalist. But that doesn't last long. Within a year, they're positively rabid supporters of the company.

"We've never had a strike, you know," he added. "Not even immediately after the war, when the unions were making the most of their new freedom and there were strikes everywhere; not even now, when Sohyo (the Japanese General Council of Labor Unions) is always calling on the workers to launch new 'offensives.' " He laughed. "The president of the company says he sometimes wishes we *did* have a strike."

"Why?" I asked.

"So that both the management and the workers could learn through personal experience just how unprofitable strikes always are!"

The president, he explained, was in his sixties. He had built the giant company from nothing. The president himself had had to leave school in the fourth grade, to work in a bicycle shop. He had seen his two brothers and his sister die of undernourishment, when their father lost his job as a shoe salesman. "When the president was twenty-two, his wages were 50 cents a day. He wanted to get married and he and the girl and the girl's parents arranged to meet the *nakodo*, the go-between, outside an Osaka theater. That was the usual thing, to meet at a theater, and see the show, and so combine business with pleasure. But the president was too poor to buy tickets, so they discussed the matter standing outside the theater."

The turning point, said the assistant manager, came a couple of years later, when the president patented his first invention, an electric plug with double sockets. Other inventions followed. Before he was thirty, the young man had formed the company that today turns out a large part of all the electric equipment manufactured in Japan.

"During the war, of course, our thirty plants were to be turned over wholly to munitions work," said the assistant manager. "But it takes a remarkably long time to effect such a transformation. Our works were to turn out two thousand Navy fighter planes a month. When the surrender came, we had in fact produced only three. The war ended just when we were about ready for full-scale production."

He smiled. "Nowadays we make everything, from food mixers to all sorts of radio communications equipment. Last year our sales were over $150,000,000. Have you finished your tea? The president can see you now."

In a slightly larger but otherwise identical room, with chairs identically wrapped in white cotton, a thin, scholarly-looking man sat behind his square desk. He got up and bowed as we came in, then also shook hands. More green tea was brought.

"The Japanese save as much as they can, but unfortunately they earn very little," he said, and paused while the assistant manager interpreted his words. His gaze was abstracted, as if his mind were on a new plug with twin sockets, rather than on us. "Look at me: I'm probably the biggest single moneymaker in the nation, and my take-home pay in a year is less than the president of General Motors gets as a bonus. There's the difference between poor Japan and wealthy America."

I murmured that the president of General Motors probably didn't have much of his bonus left, after he had paid tax on it.

"Taxes are higher here than in America. In the United States, the highest rate, 90 per cent, applies only to income over one million dollars. Here, a 75 per cent rate applies to all income over $14,000, and soon goes up to 90 per cent."

He shook his head. "We are a poor country. We have in Japan about three hundred different kinds of electric light bulbs. Do you know how many kinds are in use in Western countries? Seven thousand. A country's cultural level can be measured by the number of different kinds of light bulbs it makes and uses."

I could see Lionel's mouth open to protest, and I said hastily: "How do you retain the loyalty of your workers? I'm told you've never had a strike."

"I give them a dream," he said. "I tell them what our company hopes to achieve: in one year, five years, ten years. They work along with me to make it come true, to reach the target. I'm not afraid of strikes, or of labor troubles. What I dislike is wasting time talking with Government officials. Negotiations with the Government are as bad as having a strike, or worse. A strike means lost man-hours. Government interference in business causes greater loss of profit, through wasted man-hours, than even our high taxes. And in my opinion, a lost profit is a social crime."

"Do you still invent things?" Lionel asked.

"No: no time. But I encourage our young men to invent things, and to patent them."

"What is the latest thing they've invented?"

"Electrically heated trousers, for people who get cold because their work keeps them standing in one place," he said promptly.

"Like railway-station reservation clerks. You just put the trousers on, then plug them in."

(3)

He cocked a sharp, shrewd, humorous eye at me as his son introduced me. He was a tiny man, with thin, pointed cheekbones, and he spoke no English. But the son had been to Stanford.

"Nine thousand people work for me," he said. "And they are among the best-paid workers in Japan. We provide low-cost housing, for those who want it. For instance, in recent years we've built sixty four-story apartment houses. But these are only for bachelors. When a man gets married, he may move into a company house. And we've also got company guest houses at several hot-spring resorts. Workers who are on vacation can spend their holidays there, if they like."

We were meeting at his home, not in his office, so he was relaxing in a kimono. A board for *go*, which is a kind of Japanese checkers, was set up on a side table. On an easel was a painting by him of Osaka castle, with his signature neatly calligraphed in one corner.

"Do many Japanese businessmen paint?" I asked, for I had been briefed on his hobbies by the son.

He laughed, showing little gold teeth. "Not many, and none as badly as I! But I find it soothes the nerves." He grinned. "Americans should try it, instead of taking tranquilizers."

"We made twelve of my father's paintings into a company calendar last year," said the son proudly.

"Turn everything to some advantage—that is my motto," said the little man cheerfully. "Anyway, it's better than coming home from the office and sitting up all night reading engineering reports! That's what So-and-so does." And he mentioned the name of the president of the great electric goods company.

The little man was the son of a poor fisherman who had lived by catching sea bream. But there was a driving force in the family blood: the father was the first Japanese fisherman to give his humble little scull boat an engine. The son left school when he was fourteen, and by the time he was twenty he was captain of a 20-ton trawler.

"But after a while I decided that the men who went to sea and caught fish worked hard but stayed poor, whereas those who remained ashore and bought the fish got rich." He therefore decided to become a buyer; but unlike other buyers who purchased only small cautious quantities, by the creel, he boldly offered to buy the boats' catches "by the net." Soon, all the boats were selling to him, and he was busily building canning factories.

"We became a sort of vertical trust," explained the son. "We ended up owning our own fishing fleet as well, and we had shore bases in Korea, Manchuria, China, Taiwan, and some South Pacific islands."

"Of course, when the Pacific war began, the militarists requisitioned the lot," said the little man, when his son's words had been repeated to him in Japanese. "By the end of the war, most of my ships were at the bottom of the sea and all my shore factories were gone."

He had borrowed money to start all over again with scull boats. But just as he had boldly bought fish "by the net," so he now placed orders for as many boats as the builders cared to undertake. By the time the scull boats, and a few trawlers, were delivered, the postwar inflation of the yen had wiped out the value of his money debt. And he was in possession of a brand-new fishing fleet at a time when the American Occupation was eagerly encouraging every effort that would help solve Japan's grave food shortage.

"And so now you're once again in business with a fishing fleet, shore bases, and canning factories," I said.

But that, it seemed, was only part of the story. The Napoleonic little man had branched out in several directions, some surprising. He owned a baseball team called the Lobsters, and a chain of bars (complete with bar hostesses) as well as a chain of sea-food restaurants. He was active in Japan's young automobile industry, having big stockholdings and toying with the idea of manufacturing and marketing a "people's car" to outdo the popular Toyopet. Evidently, 200,000 tons of shipping, twenty canning plants, bars, restaurants, and a baseball team were not enough. After all, he was only sixty-five.

"Of course we want every Japanese housewife to own a refrigerator," he said. "That way, we can sell more and more of our own products. Therefore, we like to see the level of Japanese wages going up. There are twenty million Japanese families, and we've barely begun to exploit that market. People talk about the need to trade with China. But the Chinese have even fewer refrigerators and washing machines than the Japanese do, and I don't see them getting them in a hurry. Japan, on the other hand, has the highest living standard in Asia. But that only means we're now about as well off as Greeks. We can push our living standard higher still. I believe in the need to trade with Japan!"

He clearly had an exciting vision of an affluent Japanese society of between ninety and a hundred million people, most of whom he envisaged living in homes with big refrigerators and deep freezes packed with his frozen foods. But they would also on occasion dine mightily in his restaurants, off tuna, trout, and crabs; cheer on his Lobsters, at the ball game; and drive home in their Lobster automobiles. And their children would get fat and stay healthy on liberal doses of his cod-liver oil.

It seemed to me a cheerful and not ignoble prospect.

After a while, we left him to his go and his painting, and the son and I went to visit one of his bars. It was a pleasant place, with subdued lighting and high stools, and when we had got ourselves installed with our elbows on the counter, and ordered drinks, a pretty girl in a kimono flicked on a lighter for our cigarettes. She did it in a way that suggested this was but one of innumerable services she was prepared to render for our comfort.

The son who had been to Stanford was inches taller than his father, and had a well-fed look. He was in his early thirties and wore bow ties and had the confident alert air of an executive.

I said that on the strength of my talks with his father and with the president of the great electric goods company, I thought that Japan's businessmen were paternalistic rather than despotic.

To my surprise, he gave me a sceptical look.

"Do you really think so? Don't forget," he went on, in his best Stanford manner, "that the big firms that provide good company housing, steady jobs, regular bonuses, and other fringe benefits account for only about two fifths of the industrial output—and employ only a quarter of the industrial workers. The other three quarters are employed by a multitude of very tiny firms which pay very low wages and may not provide any benefits at all.

"And not all the big businesses, or *zaibatsu*, are liberal-minded, by any means. If you don't believe me, ask Yasuo Takasaki."

"Who is he?"

"He is the son-in-law of Akira Takasaki."

"Who is—?"

"You have never heard of Akira Takasaki? Dear me, you barbari—you *gaijins* are awfully ignorant about modern Japan, aren't you? But I'll give you a letter of introduction to Yasuo Takasaki and he will tell you all about his father-in-law, Akira Takasaki."

(4)

Stumping out of doors with the help of a heavy cherrywood cane, the old man—he must have been close to eighty—

climbed into a black Chrysler, respectfully followed by his confidential secretary and his personal nurse. The rest of us—sundry Takasaki executives, an architect or two, and Yasuo Takasaki—entered the other cars. The cavalcade sped on its way.

My letter of introduction had produced satisfyingly swift results. I had not yet managed to get within talking distance of Akira Takasaki, but I had been taken in charge by his son-in-law, Yasuo Takasaki, with a promise that just as soon as he had a minute or two to spare, Akira Takasaki would see me.

Meanwhile, we were on our way to watch Akira Takasaki attend the ground-breaking of a new, million-dollar, nine-story apartment house. Unfortunately, I still had no clear idea who Akira Takasaki was, except that he was the very old man with the heavy cherrywood cane who was riding ahead of us in the black Chrysler.

I eyed the son-in-law, Yasuo, a man of about fifty, with thick black eyebrows and a complacent air.

"How is it you are both called Takasaki, if he is your wife's father?"

"Because I changed my name," he said mildly. "I'm a *yoshi*."

"A *yoshi*?"

"Is a husband who takes his wife's name, instead of the other way around. When a man has no son, but only a daughter," he explained, "he usually asks his daughter's husband to do this, so that the family name can be carried on. It's quite common in Japan."

"How about your family name?"

"It will be carried on by my brothers. I have three."

Yasuo looked out the car window at the traffic. We were halted by a red light, and an unseen musical box played "The Blue Danube." The music was a recent Osaka innovation, to soothe the nerves of drivers.

"I didn't mind changing my name," said Yasuo, as the light

turned green, and we drove off to the tune of "Auld Lang Syne." "But I had pangs of conscience about marrying into the family of a business cutthroat like Akira Takasaki. I knew Harold would disapprove."

"Harold?"

"Laski. I studied at the London School of Economics."

That accounted for his English.

"I wasn't a Socialist then," he confided. "But I was on the point of becoming one. So you can see what a difficult problem it was for me."

"How did you solve it?"

"I decided to try to convert my father-in-law to my way of thinking."

"And have you succeeded?"

"I think I have. Oh, there are times when his old bad habits reassert themselves. He backslides. But on the whole he is now a model employer, and much less ruthless towards business competitors."

"You say he was a 'cutthroat,' when you married his daughter. What sort of a cutthroat?"

"He went about buying up real estate, and making railway mergers," said the son-in-law, shaking his head sadly. "If other people got in his way, he just forced them out of business. Before he was my age, he controlled six Japanese railroad companies, twenty-three trucking companies, and I don't know how much real estate. He set up a holding company, and juggled with a hundred and fifty enterprises. There were about sixty million dollars involved.

"Of course, he isn't nearly as rich as he was. He lost about a hundred million dollars in the war."

The cars climbed a hill, and parked beside a large building site. Mr. Takasaki senior got out and was escorted to a large armchair upholstered in orange-colored plush. Wearing a severe dark business suit and a gray and white striped tie, he sat clutching his thick cane, and twitching his thick gray eyebrows suspiciously. It occurred to me that Yasuo's heavy eyebrows may have been his fortune; had he lacked them, or had they been thin, not even his willingness to change his name to Takasaki would have gained him the hand of the old man's daughter in marriage.

The ceremony was performed with Shinto rites. The chief Shinto priest wore a white robe; his two assistants wore sky-blue coats. On an improvised open-air altar made of pine-wood were heaped the traditional fish, vegetable, and fruit offerings: sea bream, large and pink; huge white radishes; oranges. The priest in the white robe waved a branch of the sacred *sakaki* tree; the two priests in sky-blue coats chanted a prayer and invoked the gods' blessings on the new apartment house. Mr. Takasaki tightly gripped his cherrywood stick, and uncompromisingly scowled.

When all was over, he got up from the orange-colored armchair, bowed perfunctorily to the priests and the assembled company executives—whose bowing heads practically touched the ground—and strode back to the Chrysler, at a remarkable speed for a man of his age. Soon, we were all descending the hill once again. "Mr. Takasaki does not like wasting time," said his son-in-law.

But this was only the first of two ceremonies to be performed in the old man's presence that day. Yasuo Takasaki was looking at his watch. "Now we are going to attend the opening of a new movie theater," he explained.

The ceremony this time was indoors. The new movie theater had cost $135,000. It was next door to a department store, also owned by Mr. Takasaki. The old man sat in the middle of the front row of plush tip-up seats, and the rest of us ranged ourselves several respectful rows behind him. On the otherwise bare stage, another pinewood altar had been set up, also heaped with offerings of sea bream, radishes, and oranges. This time there were two priests in white robes, moving about the stage in heavy, lacquered wooden shoes, against a backdrop curtain of midnight black trimmed with gold and silver. The priests did not just wave *sakaki* branches, and chant prayers, as in the previous ceremony. They advanced to the footlights, and cast handfuls of tiny bits of colored paper, resembling square-shaped confetti, over the audience. "That is to exorcise evil spirits," Yasuo whispered.

The subsequent proceedings were to consist of Cinema-scope's latest offering, followed by the distribution of souvenir copper ashtrays. But old Mr. Takasaki did not wait for the show, and neither did we.

"Now we will try to beard him in his office," said Yasuo, laughing nervously.

We left the movie theater, and drove to the building where Takasaki senior had his office. In addition to offices, the building contained a wedding hall, and on the roof a planetarium. The old man's private office was on the top floor.

I was ushered into a small room, with a soft gray carpet on the floor. Sliding glass doors opened on to a rooftop garden. Flowers grew at the base of the planetarium's shining aluminum dome.

On the gray carpet were a green telephone, a brass gong, several bowls of red and yellow roses, and a small electric heater. There was also a low red-lacquer table, and reposing on it a large watch. Drawn up to the table was a straight-backed chair. And in the chair was Akira Takasaki.

The old man said to his son-in-law, in Japanese: "Bring in one more chair."

Yasuo brought in one more chair.

"Now, sit down," the old man said to me, gesturing.

I sat down.

"And now, you can go," he said to Yasuo.

Yasuo bowed, and left.

We stared at each other. I revised my estimate. He must be nearly ninety.

Then the door behind my back opened again, and a very

deferential young man entered and sank down on the gray carpet. "I will interpret your questions to Mr. Takasaki," he explained, in good but harshly accented English.

I opened my mouth to put a question.

"First," said the young man, grinning apologetically, "Mr. Takasaki wants to say something."

The old man made a whirring noise like a clock about to strike, then spoke for a long time in Japanese. When he had done, the young man said: "He says, in the war he lost $111,000,000 worth of property. He borrowed $25,000,000 from the banks, and began his business again. He has now repaid all the money that he borrowed. He—"

The door behind me opened once more. A man came in, fixed his eyes on Mr. Takasaki, put his hands at his sides so that his thumbs pressed against his trouser seams, made a deep bow, and spoke in Japanese. Akira Takasaki issued a brief order. The man bowed again, and left.

Mr. Takasaki said something to the interpreter, who said to me: "He says to tell you, that man is the boss of his department store. He has just returned from Persia."

"Persia!" I exclaimed.

"Yes: Teheran, Persia. Mr. Takasaki wants to build a department store there. The Iranian Government says, 'Fine, but Moslem women will not be permitted to work in such a place.' Mr. Takasaki has just told his department-store boss to tell the Persians he will send Japanese girls to work in the store."

Mr. Takasaki looked inquiringly at me, and his habitually severe expression, like that of a very cross cigar-store Indian, relaxed into something approximating a grin. I dutifully smiled back.

The old man again spoke lengthily in Japanese. When the young man began to interpret, it became evident that the irruption of the department-store manager had caused me to miss an entire postwar installment of the Takasaki saga. He had now backtracked and was in the war years again.

"Japanese Government during the war put Mr. Takasaki in charge of shipping. Mr. Takasaki says, he found the Ministry a madhouse of red tape and bureaucracy." (Mr. Takasaki, his old eyes fixed on my face, nodded vigorously at this point.) "Mr. Takasaki restored order. He built wooden ships, to outwit the enemy's radar. He smashed all bottlenecks. He built new railroads, from the factories to the docks. People said, 'It will take six years!' Mr. Takasaki said, 'I will do it in six months.' Mr. Takasaki fulfilled his promise."

Waving the interpreter to silence, the old man resumed in headlong Japanese. After a long while, the young man cleared his throat, and said: "Mr. Takasaki was Japan's top tycoon: top railway man, top department-store man, top theater man. Mr. Takasaki was Japan's biggest businessman."

"Bigger than Mitsui?" I protested. "Bigger than Mitsubishi?" He ignored me.

"But Mr. Takasaki says, now the world is changing. It has progressed to a point where the people's interests must be observed. The theory of Socialism is good. Communist theory is not bad, but practice makes it bad, through human frailty. However, the Socialists are prodding the conservative people into acting for the benefit of the masses. This is good."

The door behind me opened once again. Yasuo Takasaki entered and apologetically laid a bundle of papers on the low table.

Akira Takasaki snatched the papers up in a thick-veined hand, but then roared like a toilet in symphonic action.

"*Hai!*" said Yasuo, which means "yes." He bowed rapidly and at the same time edged towards the door. "*Hai!* (Bow). *Hai!* (Bow). *Hai!*"

And, seizing the chance, I bowed my way out with him.

"What was that all about?" I asked.

"Those were bills presented by a cleaning firm, for cleaning his department store. He thinks their charges are excessive. I was afraid he would."

164

"What did he tell you to do about it?"

"He says to buy them out. When we've bought the firm, he wants all the top people fired. Then he is going to rename the firm the Takasaki Building Maintenance Company. He says he'll award himself a contract for the cleaning of all the buildings controlled by his holding company, and get his money back that way."

I compared this with the elder Mr. Takasaki's remarks on Socialism.

"Yes," I said. "I see what you mean about backsliding."

(5)

"We construct for endurance," wrote Lafcadio Hearn complacently; "the Japanese for impermanence." Hearn was thinking about chopsticks, straw sandals, wooden houses, paper umbrellas. But Hearn lived before the era of the wastemakers, before the heyday of Madison Avenue and automobiles with fins. It could never have occurred to him, or to any of his solid Victorian generation, that a time would come when impermanence rather than durability would be the royal road to economic fortune. He could not have foreseen a Japan that successfully flooded the markets of the West with dollar blouses, transistor radios, and miniature cameras.

The Japanese, of course, are now building durable things also. Chewing up prodigious quantities of scrap steel and other imported raw materials—for she has almost no mineral resources of her own, and her coal is poor and increasingly hard to get at—Japan is spitting out no less prodigious quantities of ships, factories, office buildings. The rate of economic growth has been close to 12 per cent in a good year. Capital investment grows by a fantastic 50 per cent every year.

But rapid growth is not simply a phenomenon of the past fifteen years or so. On the contrary, Japan's economic resurgence shortly after her defeat in the second world war is a resumption of a former trend. In the seventy-two years between 1876 and 1948—a single lifetime—Japan's national income increased ten times. This means that each year it was increasing considerably faster than the national income of the United States is now doing. Income per head doubled, even though the Japanese population increased two and a half times.

But "income per head" is only a statistical abstraction. The standard of living of the broad masses of the Japanese people did not double in the seventy-two years. The fast-growing national income before the second world war bought more babies, and more battleships. Both were needed by the militarists, who were concurrently fighting and defeating the Chinese, the Koreans, and the Russians. What Japan bought with its growing wealth was not a higher standard of living for its people, but reluctant recognition by the West that Japan was a Great Power, ranking fifth in the world after Britain, Germany, France, and the United States.

To generate rapidly increasing national incomes is the dream of all the world's so-called underdeveloped countries in the second half of the twentieth century. How did Japan contrive to do the trick in the second half of the nineteenth century?

The new Japanese ruling class that came to power in 1868 decided to industrialize the country. The decision was taken in the interests of nationalism, just as the governments of underdeveloped countries today decree that at all costs there shall be steel mills. These governments generally obtain the money for the steel mills either from the West on the ground that otherwise they will succumb to Communism, or from the Communist world by pledging to resist "imperialism." The Japanese Government borrowed from abroad to finance its wars with China (1895) and with Russia (1905). But, generally speaking, it was afraid to ask the West for money, believing this would lead to foreign control of Japanese economic life as had occurred in China; and there was then no Communist world to offer them long-term loans at 2½ per cent. The Japanese ruling class, therefore, like Stalin in the 1920's, built the new factories out of the sweat of the peasants.

Farm rents financed the railways and the industries. Japan has very little arable land, and what it has is intensely cultivated. The great upsurge in population meant that at least two out of every five farm children had to leave the farm and seek work in the towns. They did so, and the urban population of Japan trebled. Awaiting the newcomers in the towns were the textile factories.

Japanese tenant farmers were humbly accustomed to handing over much of the rice they grew to their landlords, as rents. The rents built the new factories. The surplus people squeezed off the land got jobs in factories that were owned by their familiar landlords; and feudal custom kept their wages as low as their rents had been high. Whether working in the fields or in the factories, the average Japanese remained at mere subsistence level. The factoryowners' profits were correspondingly large; but the capitalists of Japan lived frugally, and plowed most of their profits into financing the building of still more factories.

This is a simplified but generally accurate picture of how the Japanese economy grew so rapidly in the space of a single human lifetime. One refinement of the process should be mentioned. The Japanese top people early grasped a cardinal principle of banking. The State Central Bank encouraged the commercial banks to lend even more than they could afford. The consequence was a steady inflationary process, which made the real income of most Japanese workers even smaller than their very low money intake suggested, and which benefited the entrepreneurial class that was plowing both profits and borrowed money into further expansion. It all helped to speed the process of capital accumulation.

What has happened in Japan since the end of the second world war is not, economically speaking, essentially different from what went on before that colossal interruption. The tenant-farming class has largely vanished, and today most Japanese who farm own tiny plots of land. But there is not much more arable land than there was before, so that the problem of rural overpopulation has not diminished. If anything it has increased, for the small size of the plots, a couple of acres or so, means that all save one of a farmer's sons must find jobs in the towns.

This constant pressure from the rural areas keeps Japanese wages low. There is counterpressure from the labor unions; and since the Japanese are no longer spending immense sums on battleships, there is more wealth available for consumer goods. Moreover, the population, thanks to contraception and abortion, is no longer growing as fast as it had been, though it is still too large in relation to Japan's resources. Nevertheless, although the standard of living of Japanese workers has definitely risen, Japanese wages remain appallingly low in comparison with those of other "developed" countries. A Japanese white-collar worker earns only one tenth the salary of his American counterpart—and he still pays income tax on it.

But capital accumulation proceeds as briskly as before, with the result that by 1956 the productivity of industry and mining in Japan was double the prewar level—despite the enormous scale of destruction by air bombings during the war.

Japan now confronts a dilemma similar to the one facing Mr. Khrushchev. When is the fast-rising national income going to benefit the people in the form of consumer goods, instead of being continually devoted to the creation of more and more durable capital goods, in the form of new plants? Khrushchev has promised to resolve his dilemma by gradually raising living standards. Among the Japanese capitalists, there are quite a number of, as it were, old Stalinists, who fear any relaxation of the iron laws of economics and regard every wage increase as another gain by the Communists. But there are others who see the matter quite differently, and argue that what the Japanese economy now requires is a rapidly broadening mass market at home for the goods the economy is able to produce.

The latter school of Japanese businessmen is all in favor of wages going up—though they would, of course, prefer that if possible the higher wages be paid by their competitors and not by themselves.

(6)

In Osaka I met an American whose large and powerful company was building a factory for synthetic rubber for the Japanese. For its expert services his firm was getting a considerable fee, but the prospect nevertheless filled him with gloom.

The plant when it was completed and in full operation would, he said, turn out about 150,000 tons of synthetic rubber, which was five times Japan's total rubber consumption. It seemed obvious to him that Japan intended to become a rubber exporter, in competition with other rubber exporters, including the United States.

"I thought the United States was a net importer of rubber," I said hazily.

"If it were just rubber!" he said, and with an impatient wave of his hand conjured all of Malaya into limbo.

What he really feared was that, once they had sufficiently mastered the techniques of the new rubber plant, the Japanese would not stay content with selling most of its output abroad, but would proceed to construct whole new factories by themselves, and start exporting *them*.

Yet there was little he could do about it. Other American companies not a whit less powerful than his were eager, he told me, for the Japanese business and were prepared to put up the rubber factory for Japan if his firm did not. This seemed to be an illustration of what critics of the system call the contradictions of capitalism.

169

Since Japan's surrender, the Japanese have drawn extensively on the vast and growing fund of American, British, and German technological know-how: but chiefly from America. Without such lavish borrowing, Japan's astonishing economic recovery would not have been possible, for all through the war the Japanese industrial scientists were cut off from discoveries and inventions outside, and Japan's own industrial research languished under the militarists.

But though they have borrowed know-how, and been willing to pay fees and royalties for the privilege, the Japanese as always have been much less keen to put themselves in debt to foreign capitalists by importing private capital. In raising the necessary funds, they have tended to confine themselves to financial institutions like the Export-Import Bank and the World Bank. In ten years, said the representative of the concern building the synthetic-rubber factory, Japan had borrowed about $600,000,000 from those sources.

"This means that Japanese big business can use its own funds to build automobile assembly plants in Latin America and pulp mills in Alaska."

In the United States itself, he said, the rate of Japanese investment was three times that of American private investment in Japan. This seemed to him a poor return for the rescue of Japanese industry by American technological know-how after the destruction and devastation of the war years.

"And yet, Japanese businessmen are always muttering nervously about a great American take-over of Japan's industries. Japan's Foreign Investment Law specifically says its purpose is to 'create a sound basis for foreign investment, by limiting the induction of foreign capital.' "

"How do they limit it?"

"If an American invests in Japan and makes a profit from his investment, he can't take the profit out of the country without the Japanese Government's permission."

Since bureaucrats were involved, the way this worked was,

of course, more complicated than his simple sentence seemed to indicate. Say a foreigner wanted to put money into an Osaka noodle factory, but first wanted to be assured that if he made a profit he would be allowed to take the profit out of Japan. To obtain such an assurance, he had to apply to the Japanese Government for "validation" of his investment. Such applications customarily remained "under consideration" for twelve months. They were not really being considered in most cases; the bureaucrats just hoped the applicant would get tired and go away.

"I never understand those things," I said truthfully, but from then on I pestered Japanese businessmen as well as foreign businessmen in Japan with questions about such mysteries as validation, convertibility, the Foreign Investment Law, import licenses, and 51–49 stock participation allotments. I gave a lot of people headaches and got one myself, but in the end I reached some conclusions.

The Japanese *zaibatsu*, or big businesses, had with the aid of the Government bureaucrats evolved a very satisfactory system, from their point of view. They were paying out some $45,000,000 a year for imported know-how, but otherwise were holding foreign capitalists at arm's length. When they needed foreign money, they obtained it easily enough from the international bankers. This meant that the fast-growing Japanese home market, of 93,000,000 people with a rising standard of living, was virtually all theirs; for, in addition to official clamps on foreign capital, there were high duties as well as tight controls on foreign goods. At the same time, the thriving Japanese industries were turning out goods that by virtue of their sheer cheapness, combined with good quality, were invading foreign markets with sensational success.

No doubt there was a catch in it somewhere; I was brought up to believe that protection, like crime, does not pay. All the same, I thought that if I were a Japanese I should feel pleased that the motorcars, washing machines, refrigerators, television sets, radios, and cameras which more and more Japanese were acquiring were all made at home. Foreigners might grumble, and even mutter about economic reprisals; but the representative of the American synthetic-rubber plant had admitted, ruefully, that if his firm did not sell the plant to Japan, another firm would. Nor was a shut-out of Japanese goods from other countries very likely; and if such a shut-out did occur, the Communist Chinese would no doubt be ready to accommodate Japanese exporters, even at a political price. Finally, the international bankers apparently believed there was no catch at all. Japan's credit stood high with them, and they were lending the Japanese large sums of money.

The Japanese banks were also willingly lending Japanese industries large sums of money; but this was really only transferring funds from the right to the left pocket, since the top Japanese businessmen, or *zaibatsu*, who borrowed the bulk of the funds also happened to be directors of the banks that made the loans. Investment trusts were the rage in Japan—a rather startling counterpart to Zen's becoming the rage in America. The trusts had "consultation offices" in such improbable places as railway stations and department stores. The notion was that the emancipated Japanese "salaryman" had (thanks to the overthrow of feudalism) become a true partner of big business in the egalitarian democratic but intensely capitalist New Japan.

"Feel free to drop in any time," the investment trusts urged. "For the convenience of the workers, we are open all through the lunch hour." The "consultation offices" willingly provided the most innocent shopgirls with stock-market information. For workers in a hurry, there were huge, electrically controlled boards that revealed the state of the market at a glance. And this state was almost uniformly encouraging: in three years electrical goods, oil, and automobile shares all showed rises of 30 to 50 per cent. The shares were leaping and bounding like Nara deer.

Before the overthrow of feudalism, the Japanese stock market was the almost exclusive preserve of the *zaibatsu*, who used it chiefly as a battleground for fights over subsidiaries and affiliates. An ordinary Japanese would no more have thought of playing the stock market than he would have of strolling uninvited into the Imperial Palace.

The rise of investment trusts and the rapid spread of their "consultation offices," which catered to the middle, lower-middle, and even the working classes, was hailed as a striking and encouraging phenomenon. "The most wonderful thing that ever happened in Japan," said one investment-trust director. But though the Japanese stock market had come largely under the influence of the investment trusts—one trust was reported to handle over a quarter of the turnover of shares on the exchange, and to have successfully and singlehandedly beared the market by unloading ten million shares in one day —the truth was that the big industries relied on the stock market for only a fraction of the capital they required. The leading investment trusts had assets worth a billion dollars. But the *zaibatsu* issued shares to the public for only about a tenth of their new capital needs. The other nine tenths they provided themselves, out of reserves, or by borrowing from the banks they largely controlled.

"I thought the *zaibatsu* had been abolished," I said, when all this was explained to me. I was talking to a *zaibatsu*, whom I shall call Chibara Mukata, who is the chief executive of a well-mannered Japanese economic octopus that has sixteen large plants and employs 78,000 men. Mr. Mukata does not speak English, but his male secretary, trained in London and Harvard, speaks that language and four more.

The secretary shudderingly interpreted my insolent remark, but Mr. Mukata only smiled and nodded. "They were abolished," he said.

Then he explained. The octopus had had its tentacles lopped off by the Americans when Japan lost the war; and the original *zaibatsu* family that owned most of the shares had been compelled to sell them. At this point, Mr. Mukata was merely a director who had risen through the ranks because of his engineering knowledge.

But it was he who had restored the octopus's tentacles; and he had done so by borrowing money, with nothing to pledge against it—for the octopus's factories were mostly in ruins—save his rosy picture of Japan's economic revival and expansion. He raised a little money and had the fires relaid in some of the cold furnaces; and then the Korean war came, and in no time more and more plants were rebuilt, and the latest machinery was installed in them.

Now Mr. Mukata was the boss of the reborn combine; but he was careful to emphasize that he was still only a salaried employee: the owners of the revivified octopus were the bankers.

I happened to know that Mr. Mukata was almost as prominent on the board of the biggest investing bank as he was on the board of the combine itself. But it would only have embarrassed him if I had mentioned this, and the secretary had been sufficiently horrified, so I asked instead: "What happened, then, to the family that controlled the combine before—the old *zaibatsu* family?"

"Oh, we have since awarded them a pension," said Mr. Mukata.

Just so might a Shogun have referred to a pre-Meiji Emperor.

(7)

The skilled workers among Mr. Mukata's 78,000 employees received a bonus of a month's pay in June, and another in December. They also received bonuses when output was high. In addition, they got free medical care and subsidized housing and low-cost canteen meals and a travel allowance. All this added about $25 a month to their basic monthly wage of $100. Seldom if ever was anyone fired.

But $125 a month is not a high wage; it is only high for Asia, and the people of Asia are tired of being treated like Asiatics. When I was in Osaka, the Japanese General Council of Labor Unions, or Sohyo for short, launched one of its periodic offensives for more pay. All over the country, from Hokkaido in the north to Kyushu in the south, 160,000 coal miners quit work, followed by 60,000 chemical workers and over three million federal and local Government workers: railroad men, teachers, postmen, telegraphists, clerks, foresters, and tobacco workers.

Government workers in Japan are forbidden by law to go out on strike, so these three million or so streamed from locomotives, benches, desks, and forests to "attend union rallies." In a few hours, industrial activity had largely come to a standstill. Railway stations were filled with abandoned passengers, and sidings with silent freight trains. The marshaling yards meanwhile blossomed with red flags, and big crowds sang the *Internationale.* Japanese railroad workers are rather strongly under the influence of the Communists, whose party cells operate in the railways under the code name of "Cloud Number 20."

Sohyo was demanding a raise of $5.55 a month for all workers, and a national monthly minimum wage of $23.61. The coal miners got a raise of $3.61; and the railway workers, of $3.75. The coal miners' raise brought their monthly pay to over $50—suggesting that a raise was badly needed—but it also put the price of coal up 69 cents a ton. Workers in other industries had their pay increased by about eight per cent, though this only brought their average monthly pay to $70.

I went to see a Sohyo official, a podgy man who wore a splendid red sash across his chest like a foreign decoration. He told me softly in excellent English: "We are sincerely sorry if the public have been inconvenienced; but it is the fault of the Government and the capitalists for refusing to share Japan's vaunted prosperity with the workers."

Sohyo urges its 3,600,000 members to vote for Japan's Socialist party. The Socialist party is so afraid of being called Communist that it translates its name Shakaito, which means Socialist party, to mean Social-Democratic party. Sohyo also dislikes being called Communist, for the Japanese Communists are not popular.

But the Communists, as is their custom, have managed to get some of their people into important union jobs; an anti-Communist and correspondingly annoyed chemical worker rather wittily put it to me that "the Socialist party dog is wagged by its Sohyo tail, and this tail is full of Communist fleas."

Sohyo oddly enough began its existence in the summer of 1950 as a reaction *against* Communism. The general council's first leaders were moderates anxious to ensure that the entire Japanese labor-union movement was not plowed under by the Americans, who, after having released thousands of Communists from Japanese military jails, were now trying to put them back in, suspecting that the Communists if left free would do their best to help the wrong side win the Korean war. As the years slipped by, Sohyo consented to take part with the Communists in "joint struggles," and was infiltrated by them; but Sohyo's increasingly vocal leftism—culminating in the Eisenhower incident of 1960—was due as much to an inferiority complex as to anything else.

There are over forty million Japanese workers, but only seven million are members of labor unions, and only half the members of labor unions belong to Sohyo. In short, the Japanese labor movement is woefully weak. Over 40 per cent of all workers are unorganized women—who undercut the men's wages, for they are paid far less. Three quarters of the industrial workers—men, women, and children—are employed in tiny establishments and earn a mere half of what the workers employed by the big firms get. These favored workers also get most of what social security there is in Japan.

Sohyo, finally, has few real contacts with the bulk of the poorly paid workers; these belong to thousands of tiny shop unions. Sohyo makes a great fuss twice a year with its offensives for higher wages, and at these times it musters schoolteachers, miners, railroad workers, and Government clerks. But the higher wages, if obtained, seldom apply to the workers in the "matchbox" factories, who rarely dare to strike. If they do, there are always, at their local and district level, strikebreakers of the "Pine Leaves" type, ready to deal with them.

The broader-minded Japanese businessmen with whom I talked thought that Japanese industrialists had made a shortsighted choice in driving Sohyo leftward and neglecting to encourage healthy unions—for which company paternalism was scarcely an adequate substitute. But most businessmen thought quite differently. They were, I discovered, inverted Marxists, who believed more or less fervently that every rise in wages meant a fall in profits and therefore should be resisted.

In the week that the red flags were unfurled in the railway yards, I attended by invitation a meeting of a chapter of the employers' federation. The invitation came to me through the secretary, an energetic man with jet-black hair and thick spectacles. "Strikes, strikes, strikes!" he cried, wringing his hands. "Those terrible Communists. You are studying Japanese problems (I wasn't) and we want intelligent foreigners like you to understand our point of view."

Japan loses fewer man-hours through strikes than most countries, and considerably fewer than the United States, but it was not for me to contradict him.

We sat around a big gloomy room in chairs wrapped in white cotton. In almost all public and semipublic rooms in Japan, the

Western furniture is thus carefully swathed, giving one the queer feeling of being in a house whose owners are on an extended vacation. In front of each of us was carefully set a tiny handleless cup of hot water faintly tinctured and flavored by one small leaf of green tea. Then the discussion began.

"The fundament of our policy," said the first speaker, in a barely audible squeak, "is the struggle against Sohyo." The chief backers of Sohyo, he went on to explain, were the railway workers, and the schoolteachers. "The teachers and the railway workers must be forbidden to support Sohyo, which will then collapse."

While the tedious business of interpreting—done solely for my benefit—dragged on, I studied the men who sat sipping green tea around the big gloomy room. Nothing could have been less like the traditional capitalist meetings portrayed by cartoonists. I had met Japanese businessmen who were large, bull-necked, and fat. But these were little shrunken men, who resembled gray ghosts in plain dark suits—the ghosts, moreover, of confidential clerks rather than of tycoons. Here, evidently, were the representatives not of the great *zaibatsu*, like Mr. Mukata, but of Japanese middling-sized businesses.

Another speaker got up to talk about the schoolteachers. What the teachers needed, he said, was disciplining. They should be forbidden to take part in politics and in labor disputes, and should be compelled to teach the children to respect their parents, and to obey their employers when they grew up and got jobs. The Japanese Government had been forced by the Americans to hand the schools over to local authorities and parent-teacher associations, and as a result the schools were now in the hands of the Communists. The Government should put the schools back under the control of the Ministry of Education, and the Ministry should keep a careful check on teachers who expressed dangerous thoughts.

This got some applause, but the meeting was clearly more

anxious to hear what was going to be done about recalcitrant workers than what might be done with teachers who had dangerous thoughts. The next speaker obliged. The thing to do, he maintained, was to forbid the collection of union dues directly from the workers' pay envelopes, and also to prohibit workers from becoming full-time union officials. This would cripple the unions financially and at the same time deprive them of leadership; at which point, he suggested, the employers ought to put their own nominees forward as rival leaders within the unions. "What we have to do is to try to split each union in two, and also create on the national scene an entirely new labor front that will smash Sohyo."

The man who had denounced the schoolteachers got up again and commenced a long harangue, which the swarthy secretary rapidly interpreted, while the others nodded their heads like Japanese mandarins.

"It is all the fault of the Americans. The first thing they did when they landed in Japan was to open the jails and let out the Communists. They also hastened to impose labor laws and labor unions on the country, things for which Japan is not yet ripe. The unions were overrun by the Communists the Americans let out of jail. The same thing happened with education. The Americans encouraged teachers with dangerous thoughts, and the schools became filled with Marxists. This was intended, by the Americans, to destroy the fiber of the nation by undermining the ideals and patriotism of our youth. We now have frightful juvenile crime, and the laborers are completely out of control. The Americans will be sorry if Japan goes Communist. They should, therefore, help us to destroy the dragon of Sohyo. We are not opposed to labor unions that are properly led. But the leadership must be responsible. We know some excellent men. . . ."

Sohyo had critics within the Japanese labor movement. Almost a million Japanese workers, for instance, preferred a rival federation called Zenro. But Zenro, while assailing Sohyo, refused to live up to the expectations of the employers as a responsible alternative labor front. Not long after my meeting with the chapter of the employers' federation, Zenro denounced that particular band of thinkers as "egoists with reactionary tendencies."

VII

SHIKOKU:

CHAOS IN THE CLASSROOMS

In the first-class lounge of the *Kochi Maru*, a steward handed around "honorable-wring" hot towels from a bamboo basket. On the wall, two white sailing boats forever crossed a pale blue sea towards a bright green island. A large plate on the mahogany sideboard contained two rice cakes shaped like dumplings, a piece of black seaweed, and seven dried persimmons.

A pair of newlyweds, returning to Shikoku from a honeymoon in Kobe, were accompanied by the bride's sister, already busily knitting a small wool garment, and her brother, a high-school student in a peaked cap, with his nose deep in a book. The bride was a pretty, discontented girl in a green dress and a hat of white feathers. "I am going to be sick," she said. "Nonsense!" said her husband, a black-haired young man with a mole in the middle of his forehead. "We'll have a game of cards." And he produced a pack, and made the sister stop knitting and the student put down his book. It would be a good marriage.

A bald man with gold-rimmed spectacles and gold teeth began to tell me about the famous *onaga-dori* of Shikoku. The *onaga-dori* is a long-tail fowl. The tails may grow to 30 feet, and in Japan the birds are classed as national treasures. An *onaga-dori* spends most of its life perched on a bar inside a tall roosting box. The tail hangs down inside the box, looped over a wooden peg like a lariat hung on a wall. Whenever the bird is allowed out of the box for exercise, three men hold up its tail as if it were a bride's train. The birds are hand-fed with white rice and little fishes, and twice a month the tail feathers are washed with warm water and carefully dried, for the *onaga-dori* is extremely delicate.

"In Shikoku you will also find our famous *tarutos*," said the bald man. "Try them, they are delicious."

"What are *tarutos*?"

"A sort of spongecake. The name is derived from your tart. But Japanese tarts are quite different from Western tarts."

Shikoku means "Four Provinces," and is the smallest of the four main islands of Japan. It is also the most backward, for the famous land reforms could not be applied to its thick forests and steep mountains. Consequently, forest landlords still rule the roost in feudal style. No one there doubts that Japan was created by Amaterasu Omikami, the Sun Goddess and the Emperor's divine ancestress.

However, the wind of change had begun to blow gustily even in Shikoku, and this rather than an interest in *onaga-dori* or *tarutos* was the reason for my being on board the *Kochi Maru*, bound for the port and city of Kochi.

Nikkyoso, the Japan Teachers' Union, was still fighting against the re-introduction in Japanese schools of a *shushin*, or morals course, which it declared would "march the children back into the dark feudal past." In some parts of Japan, the teachers had the support of parents, but not in Shikoku. Schools in Shikoku taught children to revere the Emperor, and to sing the "Kimigayo," the Japanese national anthem, and salute the flag of the Rising Sun. All such patriotic gestures and emblems had long since been swept out of schools elsewhere in Japan, as feudal remnants; but in Shikoku schoolteachers who condemned them got tossed into the nearest pond.

Matters had now come to a head. In country districts, teachers were being expelled from the classrooms by force, and their places taken by self-appointed amateurs who admitted they had no teaching degrees but promised to save the children from dangerous thoughts.

The second-class lounge of the *Kochi Maru* was full of island teachers loudly discussing their problems. The floor was spread with blankets, seagoing substitutes for *tatami*. The teachers sat on the floor and smoked cigarettes. They were on their way back from a conference in Tokyo with the Nikkyoso executive. Jiro Yaro, a member of the Kochi chapter of Nikkyoso, was a middle-aged man with tousled hair and a high-bridged nose. He was the only one of the teachers who admitted he spoke English, though I suspected the others could but were too shy to try. After I had introduced myself and the usual bows and visiting cards had been exchanged, they made me welcome and bought me beer.

"We travel second class because a Shikoku teacher is paid only 20,000 yen a month," said Jiro Yaro. (20,000 yen is about $56.) "They want to chop 10 per cent off that, to punish us."

"They" were the prefectural authorities. They proposed to punish the teachers, he said, for rejecting the Government's new teacher-rating system. Under the rating system, teachers were to be judged according to whether they had "correct beliefs" and "a healthy attitude towards life."

There was serious trouble in Shikoku, Jiro Yaro said, because school principals refused to apply the rating system. The authorities were now threatening to suspend or fire the principals.

"What about the morals course?" I asked. "*Shushin?*"

"Of course we are fighting the morals course, also," said Mr. Yaro. "It is intended to sweep us back to the bad old days when children blindly obeyed their teachers and parents, and the teachers and parents blindly obeyed the military."

One of the other teachers spoke rapidly in Japanese. Mr. Yaro listened, nodding between sentences and remarking: "Ah, *so!*"

"What does he say?" I asked.

"He says the Government no longer wants school children to be told the truth about the war." He laughed sarcastically. "The Ministry of Education says we must not let them forget that the war also had a bright side."

But what is really wrong about a morals course?"

"Were morals so high among the prewar Japanese who were taught *shushin* in school?" he asked ironically. "Have you heard what they did to prisoners, those blind obeyers who went blindly to war?"

"It is said that teachers who belong to Nikkyoso are Communists."

"All of us here belong to Nikkyoso, the Japan Teachers' Union. None of us is a Communist."

"But it's said that you are not objective in your teaching: that you see everything from a Marxist point of view."

"That is different. One can be a Marxist without being a Communist."

"You are Socialists?"

"Yes; most Japanese schoolteachers are Socialists."

"But should you be preaching Marxist doctrine to schoolchildren?"

"*Ano-nē!*" said another teacher, meaning, "Look here!" He spoke at length.

"He is saying," Mr. Yaro explained after a while, "that teachers naturally wish to tell the children about the real forces that shape events."

"Which real forces does he mean?"

"The class struggle. The capitalist wars for markets and profits."

"Do you believe that also, Mr. Yaro?" I asked.

He shrugged. "But of course; the story of Japan proves it! Right up until she was defeated in the war, Japan's history was of oppression and exploitation at home, and aggression and conquest abroad."

"Now you are just repeating what the Communists say."

"Oh, no," said Mr. Yaro. "I am now repeating what General MacArthur told us Japanese."

(2)

The *Kochi Maru* sailed for fourteen hours through the Japanese Inland Sea. Cone-shaped islands covered with pines and firs floated gently by on either side. It was rather like sailing through a collection of Tessai scrolls. We reached Kochi in the early morning. The teachers traded bows with me, then scurried off to find out what was happening ashore. I made my way to an inn near the town's pagoda-shaped castle and requested a room.

In Japanese inns, eating is private but washing is communal. The washroom was a narrow, tiled apartment with a row of square washbasins under a long mirror. But the only occupant was an elderly man in a *yukata*, or light kimono, with a short gray beard and a peppery look—Ro Atsunaga, the Ministry of Education official I had met in Nara.

He said he had arrived in Kochi from Takamatsu the previous day, on official business (whose purpose I could guess), and invited me to have breakfast with him.

Over bowls of white rice, dried bonito, pickled plums, and the inevitable bean soup, I asked him if it were really worth antagonizing over half a million Japanese schoolteachers in order to reintroduce *shushin*, which was obviously deeply suspect.

"Before the war, children were taught to obey. Since the war, parents have lost all authority over their children, and the family system has completely broken down. Do you know that in ten years, cases of juvenile delinquency have risen from 45,-000 to almost a quarter of a million a year?"

"Juvenile delinquency has increased in other countries also."

"But in Japan the police are now compelled to arrest 14,000 primary school children every year; and 33,000 junior high school children; and 10,000 senior high school children."

"What for?"

"For theft, robbery with violence, sexual assault, and murder."

"But you won't correct the situation just by telling children to be good to their parents, and to give up bus seats to their elders."

"No. But we will correct it by replanting patriotism in our children's hearts. We must restore the best of our old way of life, before it is too late. We don't want to bring back militarism. But do you know that no Japanese history whatever is taught to any schoolchild in this country under the age of twelve?

"That," said Mr. Atsunaga, eying me fiercely, "may be quite all right for American children. America, after all, really has no history. But we are an ancient race. Our history is long, and not inglorious. We have a right to teach it. If we do not, the children lose their roots. They learn no Japanese history, but are exposed to every sort of alien influence." I could see the word Hollywood form in his mind, as if he were a cartoon character with a balloon coming out of one ear. "Our postwar educational system was deliberately devised by the American Occupation to weaken and confuse the Japanese people."

Then he finished his bean soup, and went off to see how the Kochi education authorities were faring in their struggle with the powers of Marxist darkness.

I did not care to follow him immediately; if he had wanted me to attend his confabulations, he would have invited me along. He had already asked me to breakfast, and I did not wish to seem pushing. Therefore, I took an after-breakfast stroll up the steep hill to the three-hundred-year-old castle, then toiled up its twisting wooden stairs until I stood on the topmost of its several upturned roofs, looking down on the spread-out city.

I came down in a hurry. There was a good deal of movement around the city hall, and it seemed to me I could hear faint cries of "Washo!"

Mr. Atsunaga had walked into a trap. Over four hundred Shikoku school principals, backed of course by the teachers, but also by the Kochi "Society for the Defense of Democracy" and by the local Zengakuren, had closed in on the town offices to blockade the board of education and Mr. Atsunaga.

The town offices presented an animated scene. Traffic was moving, though at a crawl, but on the stone steps of the building were squatting scores of middle-aged to elderly, bald or shock-haired, benign but resolute school principals. They also squatted in the corridors, and roosted on the staircases. I proceeded to climb the stairs, apologizing profusely as I climbed past their knees, until a hand reached out to detain me and a scholarly voice said: "We wish you to tell the American people what is happening."

I squatted down beside him so he could first tell me.

His name was Riki Higashi and he was the principal of a village school in the countryside north of Kochi. He said that what had got almost all the principals on the island steamed up was a report that Mr. Atsunaga had been authorized by Tokyo to offer the school heads some fifteen million yen, which is over $40,000, as "special allowances" if they would crack down on their teachers and point a finger at the ones they felt were dangerous thinkers.

"We do not want their special allowances," said Mr. Higashi, heatedly. "If they give us special allowances, we will hand the money over to the Japan Teachers' Union, who will use it to finance further struggles against *shushin* and the rating system. The Government is trying to destroy the Constitution and lead Japan into another beastly war!"

I said I very much wanted to see what was happening upstairs, and I excused myself and went on. The room where Mr. Atsunaga and the board had been holding their meeting was guarded by Zengakuren students, with red arm bands, and white towels tied round their heads. But they had no objection to anyone going in, provided their prisoners did not try to get out.

Mr. Atsunaga was standing at the head of a table covered with a vividly patterned cloth, appealing to everyone to be reasonable. On one side of him were the members of the local board, looking peevish, and on the other side were more Zengakuren students. Several wore white cotton face masks, which gave the scene its only satisfyingly sinister touch. But they were wearing the face masks out of politeness, because they had head colds that they did not want other people to catch. The prisoners were being served green tea. Japanese newspaper photographers stood on chairs, taking flashlight pictures.

The parley dragged on. After a while, I went out of the building to see if the Kochi authorities had any thought of trying to stage a rescue. There were many policemen about, but they were only staring, bemused, at the squatting school principals. In Japan, a *sensei*, or teacher, may not be paid much, but he is highly respected. The police evidently felt the situation was too delicate for hasty action.

I found a Zengakuren student who spoke English, and he obligingly led me to a group of his friends. They told him to tell me that they were solidly behind the teachers in their righteous struggle. "The Japan Teachers' Union is not just defending human rights and the Constitution; it is defending peace. We are against having Japanese children led into another war."

"But who is trying to lead them into another war?"

"I will tell you what we think," said the student who spoke English. "We believe the world is divided into a peace camp and an antipeace camp. The center of the peace camp is the Socialist nations. America leads the antipeace camp."

"*Ano-nē!*" called out one of the other students.

"He says," reported the English-speaking student after listening for a while, "that we and the teachers strongly support the educational system and the Constitution that the Americans introduced in Japan."

"And do you agree with that also?"

He beamed genially at me. "Of course!"

The parley in the town offices finally ended after the board

of education and Mr. Atsunaga had agreed that school principals in Shikoku would not be asked to report teachers with
"dangerous thoughts." But by then the action had moved away
from Kochi to a mountain village called Mori.

(3)

Tough elements among the people of Mori drove the teachers
out of the village primary school. "We can no longer leave our
children in the hands of Communists" became a village slogan.
Another, perhaps no less significant, was: "Let us move to restore the worship of the gods."

A few local characters who claimed that once upon a time
they had been student-teachers came forward, and were installed
as "autonomous teachers" in the primary school. The flag of the
Rising Sun was hoisted on the school flagpole, and three hundred and fifty Mori children of all ages were jammed somehow
into the primary-school classrooms. The main activity of the
new teachers seems to have been instructing the children to
bow to the northeast, in the direction of the Imperial Palace,
and to sing the national anthem "Kimigayo," which politely
hopes that the Emperor will reign a thousand glorious years.

The ousted teachers retired into the village high school, which
they made their headquarters, and they dispatched a mission to
Kochi, to appeal for help. Flushed with their victory over the
board of education, the Kochi branch of Nikkyoso, the Japan
Teachers' Union, eagerly responded. They were especially
elated because the chairman of Nikkyoso, Mr. Takeshi Kobayashi, had come to Shikoku from Tokyo to lead their
struggle in person. Mr. Koboyashi decided to visit Mori and
confer with the teachers there.

But the situation in Mori was deteriorating fast. Teachers
were set on and beaten up by villagers, who organized themselves into anti-union, antiteacher militia and went about

with the Rising Sun painted on their shirts, singing the Japanese Imperial Navy war song, "Warships, Attack!"

The news that Mr. Kobayashi was coming to Mori got blown up into a report that he was bringing with him three thousand unskilled laborers, in special buses, in order to recapture the village primary school and reinstate the teachers. The villagers placed sentinels on all the surrounding hills, with instructions to light bonfires the moment the invaders' buses were sighted. They also got hold of a wartime air-raid siren, and installed it in the village firewatchers' tower. When the siren went off, everyone was to stop whatever he was doing, and rush to the primary school.

Amid this excitement, it was particularly unfortunate that Mr. Kobayashi turned up the night the village shrine held its annual festival. All day, young Mori men zigzagged through the streets in a frenzy of religious enthusiasm, sweating under the weight of the village *omikoshi*, or portable shrine. They staggered from one side of the street to the other, grunting: "*Washo! Washo!*"

The *omikoshi* is the palanquin of the shrine god, and it is he who indicates where he wants to go and whom he wishes to punish for the misdeeds of the past year. Those who carry the heavy shrine, of wood covered with plates of brass, cannot be held in the least responsible for whatever damage is done.

With a crash of broken glass, the *omikoshi* rammed straight through a store window, knocking over mounds of fruit and barrels of fish.

"*Washo! Washo!*"

Wood splintered and paper screens tore, as the *omikoshi* smashed the side of a flimsy wooden house amid the wails of a terrified family.

"*Washo! Washo!*"

Villagers remarked, with quiet satisfaction, how frequently the victims of the disasters were Socialists, or sympathizers with

Nikkyoso and Sohyo. Truly, the shrine god knew whom to punish as well as whom to bless!

Mr. Kobayashi drove straight through the village to the high school. He was accompanied neither by buses nor by laborers. Only the chairman of the Kochi teachers' chapter, Mr. Zenjiro Togen, was with him. The two leaders were conferring with twenty Mori teachers when the villagers burst in.

"Get out of our school, Communists!" shouted the villagers, who were flushed with sake and with the satisfaction of their sublimely sanctioned orgy of destruction earlier in the day. "Go to Russia, you Red teachers!"

The chairman of the Japan Teachers' Union was hit by a fire basin, the porcelain pot filled with sand and embers that the Japanese call a *hibachi*. He fell. Someone switched the lights off. The frightened teachers cowered behind desks, but were routed out and beaten with sticks. As they writhed groaning on the floor, the villagers sprayed them from head to foot with white foam from a school fire extinguisher.

Mr. Kobayashi spent three weeks in the hospital. The teachers' union indignantly demanded action by the authorities, who eagerly complied. The police searched the union offices for Communist literature, and arrested eleven teachers.

VIII

HIROSHIMA:
A THOUSAND SUNS, A THOUSAND
CRANES

*There is in all of us an indolent capacity for
suffering evil and dangerous things, that I
contemplate each year of my life with a
deepening incredulity.*

H. G. WELLS (1917)

In NAKAJIMA PARK in Hiroshima the Japanese have built an
up-to-date Western-style hotel a step away from the horror museum that tells the story of the devastation wrought by the
world's first atomic bomb. The hotel is crowded in August,
when thousands of people visit Hiroshima to take part in the
anniversary ceremonies. After a substantial Western breakfast,
one strolls to the Peace Hall to look at the relics. The Peace
Hall is even more up to date than the hotel, being a fashionably
harsh lump of squat stone on pillars.

I visited it on the anniversary morning of August 6. Long
lines of Japanese schoolboys and schoolgirls were slowly filtering
along the corridors and past the exhibits. They walked in total
and gloomy silence—a fact that ceased to be a surprise when
one glanced at the things on show. For these Japanese children
were looking at photographs of other children just like themselves, in some instances wearing identical school uniforms,
who had been most horribly done to death.

Nowhere in the world today is there anything quite like the
Hiroshima Peace Hall, unless somewhere on permanent exhibi-
tion there are photographs and relics of the victims of the Nazi

concentration camps and gas chambers. Ghastly as the photographs are—in many cases the effect of the tremendous heat released by the explosion was literally to skin people alive—the bits of cloth and shrivelled scraps that are also on show are grislier still. Many of these relics of the Hiroshima martyrs do not belong to the holocaust of August 6, 1945, but to the period of intolerable agony that ensued for many of them, until death mercifully ended their sufferings. Those shrivelled scraps, those fingernails dropped off the victims while they lay on the floors of ruined hospitals—and were, presumably, carefully collected on the spot, to be brought here and exhibited for all the world to see.

Though the written explanations attached to each glass showcase did not contain a single word of reproach, the lesson was plain enough. White men had done this to Asians—and to Asians, moreover, the vast majority of whom were helpless civilians. Though Hiroshima was the headquarters of the Fifth Division of the Japanese Imperial Army, and a supply center for the Kure Naval base just across the bay, most of the 340,000 inhabitants of Hiroshima can have had no direct military function. They were merely sample Japanese, chosen as targets to test a new weapon. The schoolchildren politely stood aside, to let me look my fill. But they kept their eyes averted, and nobody tried to speak English to me.

The Peace Museum should, of course, be anywhere but in Japan. The Japanese appear to have taken its lesson fully to heart. Their detestation of nuclear weapons, whether these are being pointed at them or offered to them for their "defense," seems genuine and deep-rooted. It is in Moscow and Peking, in London and Washington that the photographs and the bits of blasted human beings ought to be on display. Exhibited in Hiroshima, they can only remind the Japanese of their helplessness, and fill them with deep anger against the West.

Yet a remarkable number of Japanese strive to be fair-minded. Anger, of course, is unavoidable; but thoughtful Japanese fight strenuously against falling into the trap of one-sidedness. As I walked away from the Peace Hall, a little poem was thrust in my hand:

A plane flies 10,000 miles, and kills 200,000 people.
The strong Powers of East and West are proud of
their arms.
Their hydrogen bombs are tested in distant seas,
Scattering poison over all the world.
Is such the ultimate end of human knowledge?
Where is the Hero who will go down into the darkness
of death that humanity may live?
The Savior of the World is not in existence anywhere.[1]

The huge park was rapidly filling up. Near the gaunt stone canopy where the names of known victims are inscribed, and not far from the huge grass mound where thousands of the unknown dead are buried, ten Buddhist priests in black robes settled down to a slow, grave chanting of prayers, which would continue until sundown. From other parts of the park came the sound of other voices also raised in hymn and prayer—for all religions, including the various Christian denominations, take part in the observance services. Then the voices temporarily died away as a bell tolled heavily to signal the commencement of a one-minute interval of silence. When the minute was up, hundreds of white doves were released to circle the blue sky. At just this moment of time, on August 6, 1945, a single object falling out of the same blue sky had instantly obliterated some 80,000 people, and doomed thousands more to lingering death.

People moved forward slowly, and carefully planted little sticks of incense in the soil beside the stone canopy and around the great grass mound. Soon smoke was rising from thousands of clusters of lighted incense sticks. Hundreds of Japanese

[1] Poem by Chiku Tsuchiya, translated by Kakuko Okada.

schoolgirls carried pieces of white paper, each folded into the shape of a flying crane, a traditional Japanese symbol to ward off sickness. They carried them in memory of Sadako Sasaki, the Hiroshima schoolgirl whom many Japanese regard as a sort of atomic Joan of Arc.

Sadako was only two years old in August 1945. At the instant of the explosion she was half a mile from its epicenter, and suffered no burns and apparently no other ill effects. She grew up a normal, lively girl, but a month before she was to graduate from grammar school, at the age of twelve, she fell ill. She was taken to the hospital, and there, as her body slowly wasted away, she folded bits of paper into flying cranes. The Japanese believe that a thousand folded paper cranes will ensure a sick person's complete recovery. Sadako managed to make 664 before she died. There is, of course, a monument to her, and to all the other child victims of the bomb, in the Peace Park.

(2)

The victims of the bomb include children born in Hiroshima *after* the explosion.

So frightful was the appearance of the city after the "flash of a thousand suns" that the first, appalled rescue workers to reach the devastation concluded that the entire area was doomed to remain an "atomic desert" for at least seventy-five years. In fact, rehabilitation went ahead fairly rapidly, and grass and trees, flowers and fruit soon grew again. Optimism took the place of the deep pessimism that had prevailed. Only very gradually did certain facts begin to darken people's minds again.

One is that of the children who have been born in Hiroshima since the bomb fell, a sixth have been stillborn, physically malformed, or mentally defective. Some of those children were in their mothers' wombs at the time of the blast. Others were not conceived until long afterwards.

Such statistics would in all probability not be available, were it not for the immense amount of work done by the Atomic Bomb Casualty Commission and other groups and individuals. Their research is still going on, and the experts display considerable reluctance to try to make the figures prove anything— yet. It is, for instance, contended that some factor other than the bomb may be responsible for the fact that one Hiroshima child in every six is born dead or defective. Dr. George B. Darling, the director of the ABCC, has pointed out that he and his colleagues "are trying to measure the effect of something that is new and that no one really understands." And Professor Akira Tabuchi, an obstetrician of Hiroshima University, has said: "I can point to many Hiroshima couples who have normal, healthy children, and to a few who have abnormal ones; there must be further research before we can reach definite conclusions."

Unfortunately, it is at least possible that the conclusion that is finally reached will be even more alarming than the facts now available tend to suggest. Some scientists, for instance, believe that there may be more victims of the bomb among the grandchildren of "atom-bomb couples" than among their immediate offspring.

Working in an entirely different field from the experts who have been trying to estimate the biological consequences of the bomb in Hiroshima, Dr. A. A. Imshnezkii of the U.S.S.R. Institute of Microbiology claims to have established that mutants can be induced in fungi by ultraviolet rays. At least one American biologist believes that yeast cells mutate in the presence of any one of four sugars. What worries the Japanese, and a great many others as well, is whether human beings mutate as a result of fall-out. (The majority of mutations known to occur in nature are harmful; little comfort, therefore, can be derived from imagining that human mutants of fall-out might turn out to be supermen.) One American scientist has advised, only half-facetiously: "Better start wearing lead pants, for the safety of future generations."

Meanwhile, there are the "atomic survivors." About 90,000 of them, according to the Hiroshima city authorities, are suffering in some degree from radiation sickness. At the very least, their normal resistance to illness has apparently been permanently weakened. This makes them liable to all sorts of ailments; in consequence, they have great difficulty in holding down steady jobs. But some of them also suffer from serious skin diseases, and from lung and liver disorders. The more severe cases succumb to leukemia and cancer.

In both Hiroshima and Nagasaki, a certain number of atomic survivors die each year from the effects of radiation. The number fluctuates, but seems on the whole to be slowly increasing. Five years ago the death rate from radiation in Hiroshima dropped sharply, and it was believed that after a decade the toll was at an end. But then the death rate shot up higher than before. As Dr. Darling has said, no one really understands how this fearful mechanism works. Bomb survivors are dying in Hiroshima at the rate of about one a week. Their names are then added to the long and growing list inscribed in the Peace Park cenotaph.

I met a man of twenty-three who was eight years old when the bomb fell and who has been in and out of hospitals ever since. He is almost certainly incurable, and told me that he longed for death but that the doctors were somehow managing to keep him alive. He looked as if he had shrunk, and in fact he was still shrinking, but in a loathsome and excruciatingly painful way. Stunted and wasted in appearance, he was under five foot. His bones, twisted and knotted as if with arthritis, had long ceased to grow; his flesh was still slowly but steadily shrivelling. The result was that his bones threatened soon to split his skin. His hands looked ready to burst, and the flesh was stretched on his skull like the skin of an ever-tightening drum.

But it is the frightful uncertainty that the atomic survivors fear far more than even a torturing death. The case of Sadako Sasaki is by no means unique. Parents watch over their growing children in an agony of doubt, wondering if they are going to show signs of the often fatal and always disabling radiation sickness. And they also watch themselves, for symptoms. Setsuko Torii is a woman over forty. She was in Hiroshima when the bomb fell, but had no burns or scars. One day ten years later she woke with a heavy, languid feeling. She had no appetite. After some weeks, she started coughing up blood. She has since been in and out of the hospital several times. Another survivor told me: "You get to be terrified of the slightest symptom. If your nose bleeds, you at once think: 'Maybe this is it; maybe I've got it, at last.' And then you begin to worry about your family, and what will become of them."

It is not perhaps surprising that many atomic survivors have committed suicide. Others have left Hiroshima, and are living and working in other places in Japan under assumed names. For one of the most melancholy aspects of the scourge is that the victims have so far encountered more panic than sympathy. Employers are reluctant to give jobs to bomb survivors for fear they will get sick. Hardly anyone wants to marry an atomic survivor, and share his or her darkened life.

"It isn't just the scars," another atomic survivor told me. "Most of us have no scars. We look like well people. We may be perfectly well people. But no one really knows, least of all ourselves. So, other persons are afraid of us. They think we will fall sick one day and thereafter be a constant burden on them, or that we will contaminate them. We have come to understand how lepers feel."

In a Japanese public-opinion poll, 40 per cent of the persons polled admitted they would not want to marry atomic survivors.

Of those who said they were not afraid of such a marriage, a much higher proportion—80 per cent—insisted that they would not consent to have children.

(3)

Buildings do not suffer from radiation sickness. Even if thousands of them are destroyed by an atom bomb, they can soon be replaced. The consequence is that hardly any physical traces of the devastation exist now in Hiroshima. Such traces as there are, like the much photographed ruined dome, have been deliberately preserved. It was too much to expect that Hiroshima would refuse to succumb to the temptation to cash in on its notoriety as the first place in the world to be attacked by an atom bomb. Each year, no fewer than two million tourists visit Hiroshima, and of these about seven thousand are Westerners.

The population of Hiroshima meanwhile has grown again, to over 400,000. When the rubble was being cleared away, the opportunity was seized to make broad new roads, and to put up modern buildings. The city has attracted new factories—including a munitions plant that manufactures a large proportion of the guns made in Japan. The streets have a gay, festive appearance—especially at the time of the bomb anniversary, which in Hiroshima happens to coincide with *o-bon*. Within sight of the Peace Hall, there is now a sports stadium, which can hold 35,000 spectators, where night baseball is played under huge floodlights. Hiroshima is proud of its local team, called the Carps.

I walked at dusk through the Hatchobori district, a gay area of bars, cabarets, and bright neon lights; Hatchobori is half a mile from the Atom Bomb Hospital where people like Setsuko Torii and the shrinking man become patients from time to time, and where Sadako Sasaki died. The stores were crowded and the street seemed to be full of pretty girls in smart summer dresses. Everyone was smiling, pleased that the day's work was over and that they were free to stroll about and enjoy the warm evening. There was an air of general prosperity. In the tiny stores, transistor radios chirruped cheerfully, and television screen blinked brightly above the counters in the cosy little bars.

But in one of the bars a man told me, though without heat: "They're saying now that *our* bomb was just a tiny baby, they've got enormously bigger ones nowadays, so why do we go on making a fuss about what happened all those years ago? But we can't help it. I don't care what their idea was, dropping it on a town. They say it shortened the war. But it was still a crime."

"The President of America should come to Japan, and apologize," said a very old man with no teeth.

"Apologizing won't bring back the dead, or save the dying," said my man. "But it was still a crime. We shall always feel that way, as long as there is a Japan."

I wandered on along the street, out of the bright-lit bar district, and came presently to a shrine where men and women in light summer kimonos were singing tuneful *o-bon* songs and dancing *o-bon* dances under hundreds of pink paper lanterns. It was a pretty scene, and I stayed there and watched a while.

But after I had left it behind, and the sound of the singing had dwindled to a whisper and then to nothing, I came to a bridge over the dark-flowing Ota River, and was brought to a halt by what I saw there. The dark water of the river was covered with hundreds of little paper boats, each holding a tiny lit candle. The little boats floated swiftly under the bridge, and appeared on the other side, going off and away with the tide, out to sea.

There was no sign of the people who must have lit the candles and sent the paper boats sailing on the bosom of the river. I was quite alone on the bridge with the little flickering lights passing beneath me and moving away, a broad flotilla of scattered bright pinpoints spread over the dark surface of the water.

And I knew that each of the little candles stood for a human soul. I had remembered that, although the Japanese have made it into a gay and noisy occasion, *o-bon* is really a solemn religious service; and I was witnessing the *Toro-nagashi,* the final rite of *o-bon,* which is the Feast of the Dead.

IX

KYUSHU:
HANDS ACROSS THE SEA

All the Central Land of Reed Plains is now completely pacified.
THE NIHONGI

AT SHIMONOSEKI, the gateway to the Inland Sea, bands were playing and flags and balloons were flying. A $20,000,000 tunnel, two miles long, was about to be opened, to run beneath the sea and link Honshu with Kyushu.

Before Japan lost the war, engineers had proposed building a bridge between the two islands. But the prewar Japanese Imperial Navy would have nothing to do with such a notion. The admirals pointed out that Japanese warships using the straits would have to pass under the bridge. People on the bridge would be able to look down on the Imperial warships' chrysanthemum insignia. This was like looking down on the Emperor.

So it was decided to dig a tunnel instead; and this was begun, but shelved because of the outbreak of hostilities. After the war the American Occupation decided the tunnel was too expensive. It was costing $280,000 a year just to keep the half-finished workings from flooding. However, the Japanese Prime Minister, Shigeru Yoshida, persuaded General MacArthur to let the work proceed.

Twenty-five Shinto priests wearing white silk robes and tall black hats had assembled at the entrance to the tunnel on the Honshu side, to ask the gods to bless the undertaking. Near the tunnel entrance, amid cherry trees, was a Shinto shrine with a red *torii* gate. Against this picturesque background, the priests waved their sacred twigs and intoned, watched by a large crowd among whom small boys predominated. Showers of square confetti fluttered down. A thousand colored balloons floated upward. A Shinto orchestra of flutes, drums, and fiddles played "Kimigayo," and a brass band played "Over the Waves." Seventy automobiles containing politicians and officials drove slowly into the tunnel.

Beyond the red *torii* gate was a white building which housed elevators for people who wished to descend to the level for pedestrians. The first man to walk, dry-shod, from Honshu to Kyushu was a Mr. Koya Yamamoto, of Shimonoseki city. "It's my sixty-first birthday," he explained. "That's why I wanted to be first."

On the Kyushu side, thirty motorscooters were lined up. At a signal, they roared into the tunnel, heading for Honshu. It was the start of a commemorative seven-day race to Tokyo, 750 miles away.

(2)

The commander in charge of an American air base in Kyushu was doing his best to make the Japanese forget the Girard case. But he was having incredibly bad luck. One of his transports crashed, and destroyed six Japanese homes; the commander rushed to the scene, to apologize and also to offer all possible help. This prompt action made a favorable impression. The commander followed through by attending the Buddhist funeral services for the people who had been killed. The same day, three of his airmen raped a Japanese girl, and killed an old man who tried to interfere.

It was of little consolation to the commander that the men were promptly caught, and handed over to Japanese justice. But he was determined. "I tell the men under my command," he said, "to go out and meet the people. I tell them they don't have to be able to speak Japanese in order to make friends. All that's needed is a great big grin."

He and his family were making an intensive study of Japan and the Japanese. He showed me with pride their week's time-table. It made impressive reading:

SUNDAY : *Sumi-é* (ink-painting)
MONDAY : Japanese language lesson
TUESDAY : Flower arranging
WEDNESDAY: *Bonsai* (how to dwarf trees)
THURSDAY : Kabuki and Noh plays
FRIDAY : Japanese cooking
SATURDAY : Japanese dancing

In addition, the commander was learning judo and *karate*: jujitsu, and a form of boxing in which one uses feet and elbows as well as hands, and is supposed to be able to kill an opponent with a single blow. I asked the commander if he and his family were not being negligent in not learning to play the *koto* and the *samisen*, and told him about the American Army major in Tokyo. The commander looked shamefaced, but muttered that every day seemed to be full, with one thing and another.

In addition to imbibing Japanese culture, he was doing everything he could to spread Western culture among the Japa-nese. He had a sergeant, born a Russian, who gave them free ballet lessons; and another who taught violin and piano. The base also gave free film shows, and encouraged the Japanese to use its libraries. The prefectural governor and the local mayor had gone on a three-month tour of the United States, all ex-penses paid; and the commander had organized an annual beauty-queen contest, to promote local industry. The base ran a school for "GI brides," so that when Japanese wives of American airmen reached America, they would feel completely at ease.

"Don't you have trouble with antibase picketers?" I asked, remembering Tachikawa.

"Not what you would call trouble. We have picketers, but they are quite friendly, really. And very polite. When they heard an American Senator was coming here to inspect the base, they came to me and asked me to help them frame a slogan in English that would express their sentiments, but not aggressively. I didn't see how I could refuse. They paraded before the Senator with banners that read: 'Kindly give us back our land.' At least it was better than 'Yankee Go Home.'"

The commander was not so busy with American–Japanese relations that he neglected the welfare of the Americans under his orders. Many of his officers had their wives and children living with them, and some of the American children had shown a tendency to run wild in a strange land. The base was faced with a potential juvenile-delinquent problem, as well as with the occasional grown-up rapist and killer. So the commander offered to put the children under military discipline for at least part of the year. He organized and personally supervised a boys' camp. He showed me the prospectus, part of which read: "All movement will be as a group, in military formation. Subjects will include: flags, drills, the serviceman's code of conduct, effects of propaganda, Communism, brainwashing, how to escape if made prisoner, atomic-warfare disaster control, principles of the internal-combustion engine."

"They only seem interested in the internal-combustion engine," he confessed.

I discovered through several conversations that not all the men, or their dependents, appreciated everything the commander was trying to do for them. One officer and his wife, who was pregnant, occupied a bungalow appropriate to his rank. But then one day he was promoted to full colonel. His wife returned from the PX to find all the furniture being moved out. "This stuff isn't full-colonel's furniture," she was told. "So we're taking it away. You and the colonel will get the right furniture in due course." Later, when she rang up her doctor, he interrupted her. "Sorry, but now your husband's a full colonel, I can't handle your pregnancy. Doctor So-and-so will take over the case. I only go up as far as bird colonels."

(3)

On the road into Nagasaki I was passed by a furiously driven white ambulance, and was told it contained a Japanese deep-sea diver who had got the "bends" and was being rushed on board the United States auxiliary submarine ship *Coucal*, to be put in its decompression chamber. Then I overtook a funeral. The bier was carried by mourners, who were followed by people holding white paper lanterns and green twigs. It did not seem a good augury for the unfortunate diver.

Men were laboriously mending the roads, which were in poor shape. About as much soil as a child could get into a play-bucket was spread on a straw mat. Then the straw mat was lifted on two poles, and carried on the shoulders of four men towards the hole it was intended to fill. For this work the laborers were paid 80 cents a day.

The farmhouses with their horned roofs stood out sharp and clear against a background of very green mountains, and there were ricks of rice straw in the fields. Young men in black uniforms, university students home on summer vacation, were helping with the farmwork. Three Japanese soldiers drove by in a jeep. All wore steel helmets, but the driver also wore a face mask. I drove through a village that had one very narrow street full of shops selling clocks and watches. Then I went through another village whose stores offered red paper lanterns and gold-painted trays. Between the two villages, little girls, in red trousers and with identical bobs, walked stolidly along. A conveyor belt of huge iron buckets clanked high above the roadway, and in the distance were smoking chimneys, and the slag heaps of coal mines. The trees were bright with persimmons. Then the road clambered into the green hills, beyond which lay the East China Sea, and Nagasaki.

At my Japanese inn, I was led to my room by a maid with a saucy look, and at the foot of the wardrobe I found a Gideon Bible and a paperback copy of Boswell's *London Journal*. Nagasaki has broad streets, and overlaps a series of steep ravines. The base commander had asked me to deliver a message at the American Cultural Center. The sidewalks were crowded with people clutching Rising Sun flags made of paper. A Japanese in the Cultural Center self-importantly assured everyone that the Crown Prince and Michiko were about to pass through the town. Almost immediately he lost considerable face, when muddy men in shorts came running down the street, cheered by the people with the paper flags. The runners were engaged in a Kyushu marathon race, and the crowd had been waiting for them.

I asked if anyone knew what had happened to the diver who had had the bends, and was told the following remarkable tale. Yoshio Oyama was one of the hundred or so Nagasaki divers who repair ships and sea walls and are on call to salvage companies. He had gone down into 32 fathoms of water to inspect a rusted Russian freighter that had been lying off Nagasaki since it was sunk in a typhoon in 1897. On his fifth descent, Oyama stayed below for an hour, and collapsed in agony when he was finally hauled up. Deducing that he was suffering from the bends, his companions put his helmet and his lead weights back on, and lowered him to 25 fathoms, at which depth they had him sit astride an iron bar that they sent down to him at the end of a rope.

Seated on his iron bar, Oyama was raised and lowered most of the night, but showed no improvement. When he declared that he was exhausted and chilled to the bone, they carried him ashore, still in his diving suit, and laid him in a beach trough. The trough was used for boiling seaweed. The kindly shipmates filled it with water, which they boiled by lighting a fire beneath the trough. But Oyama's inflated suit made him too buoyant, so they took him out of the trough, wrapped him in straw, and poured boiling water over him that way. After some hours of this treatment, they took him on board again, got into the lee of a small island where the sea was calm, and put him back in the water. Oyama objected, but was told this was the only cure for what ailed him.

At this point another diving boat appeared, whose crew, when the situation was explained to them, scoffed at the cure. The thing to do, they said, was to put him upside down on a steep hillside, in his diving suit. This was done, and Oyama was kept standing on his head all day. From time to time they opened his helmet, and fed him soup. All night they boiled him in the seaweed trough.

None of this seemed to work, so Oyama spent the next two days in the ocean at eight fathoms, with another diver to keep him company and to massage his legs, which seemed paralyzed. At this juncture, a doctor from Nagasaki turned up, ordered Oyama to be put ashore and kept warm, and set about trying to get hold of a decompression chamber.

The *Coucal*, on its way to Sasebo from Yokosuka, near Tokyo, got an urgent radio call to proceed at all possible speed to Nagasaki, a distance of 500 miles. The ship made the trip in four hours under the previous record time. When Oyama heard that he was going to be put on board an American ship, he smiled for the first time since his ordeal began.

Oyama was in the ship's decompression chamber for thirty-eight hours, and two Americans, a hospital corpsman and a lieutenant, never left his side. They reported that it was the worst case of the bends they ever saw. A man with the bends is like a soda-pop bottle that has been shaken very hard. He has to be gradually decompressed; else, like the soda bottle, he might explode. The actual "bends" are caused by nitrogen

bubbles in the blood, which press against the nerves in agoniz-
ing fashion and may produce total paralysis.

But Oyama was lucky. The *Coucal* finally took him to Sasebo,
and he was put in the hospital there, and subsequently resumed his work as a diver. As for the men who had dunked
him, boiled him, and stood him on his head, they were disgusted. "Never," said one of them, "has there been such a fuss
over a simple case of the bends. One more day in the seaweed
trough, and he would have been right as rain."

(4)

On Takachiho Mountain, near Kagoshima, at the southernmost
tip of Kyushu, middle-aged to elderly men, wearing floppy
white hats, open-neck shirts, and thick-soled shoes, were busily
going around in jeeps, with spades, cameras, and tape recorders.
They were Japanese professors, hoping to find on Takachiho
some clue to the origins of the Japanese race.

Takachiho is the place of Ama-no-sakahoko, the Heavenly
Downward-Pointing Spear; drops of water falling from the
heavenly spear, after it was dipped in the ocean, became the
Japanese islands. On Takachiho after this act of creation there
landed the grandson of the Sun Goddess, and other related
deities. One of them married the sea god's daughter, Luxuriant-
Jewel Princess, and their grandson was Jimmu, the first Emperor of Japan, whose coronation took place on February 11,
660 B.C.

The professors rushed about, digging up Stone Age dwellings,
cross-examining the local residents about festivals and folk
dances, and poring over ancient manuscripts that they found
in Shinto shrines. They were testing two rival theories. One
holds that Japan was originally inhabited by Ainus, who were
conquered by Koreans, who in turn were subdued by new-

comers from Malaya or Indonesia. The other holds that a mixture of neolithic races living in Japan were conquered by people from beyond the Yalu River who pushed south through Korea and crossed into Japan by the Tsushima straits. Both theories hold Kyushu to be the likeliest landing place of the invaders, whoever they are assumed to be.

In the days of Emperor-worship, eminent Japanese scholars earnestly debated the exact location of the spot where the Emperor's heavenly ancestors descended on Kyushu. The majority view held firmly to Takachiho; but another school of thought contended that the grandson of the Sun Goddess had landed with the other deities on a peak on the other side of Kyushu. The second peak was also called Takachiho, this duplication of names having caused the confusion.

"All that, of course, was false," one of the professors told me. "But in place of this false Japanese history, we now teach no Japanese history in our schools. A nation that loses its history becomes like a rudderless ship." (I thought of Ro Atsunaga and the angry teachers.) "That's why it's important to get at the true facts, so we can substitute them for the myth that has been discarded."

"But in that case," I said, "why concentrate on Takachiho?"

"Because Takachiho may have been the birthplace of the Emperor Jimmu."

"But I thought Jimmu was a myth, too."

"He is a legend, like King Arthur. But wouldn't it be wonderful if someone in England found evidence that King Arthur really did exist, and that there actually was a Camelot? That's how we Japanese feel about Jimmu."

There is considerable resistance in Japan to giving up the legend of the first Emperor Jimmu. The Japanese are fond of him; they named their great business boom of the nineteen-fifties the "Jimmu" boom. But some Japanese scholars agree that the ancient chronicles of Japan are unscientifically cocksure in their accounts of the minutest details of the career of an

Emperor who flourished as long ago as the seventh century before Christ. A number of the more progressive-minded, led by the Emperor's own brother, Prince Mikasa, have suggested that these overly-circumstantial accounts should be taken with a grain of salt.

They hold that to say Jimmu's coronation took place on February 11, 660 B.C., is carrying preciseness too far. They propose that the actual day, February 11, should henceforth be omitted from the historical record as unproven and even dubious.

(5)

At a Japanese inn in Kagoshima I was served *fugu*, or globefish, with leek sauce, and Japanese sea crab, with vinegar and soy sauce. This was followed by a soup called *dobin-mushi*. Fish and chicken are stewed together in a kettle, and the soup thus produced is poured into a cup and a lemon squeezed over it.

Feeling like a *sumo* champion who has dined well, I feebly called a taxi, and went to visit a local Communist leader, Mr. Yasutaro Nakamura. He had a round face, round spectacles, and a gold-toothed smile. He looked like a brightly amiable student. It was difficult to believe that he was almost fifty and had been a devoted party worker for over a quarter of a century. He was the son of a small farmer. "My father belonged to the upper classes in our village," said Mr. Nakamura; "he owned a half-acre of land." Educated at Waseda University in Tokyo, Nakamura joined the Japanese Communist party while a student. The Japanese militarists had him in prison for two years for speaking against Japan's aggressions in China. After Japan lost the war, the American Occupation put him in jail for another year for distributing the Communist party newspaper *Akahata*, the "Red Flag."

Mr. Nakamura did not criticize the Occupation for putting

him in jail. As a good Communist, he expected to be persecuted by the forces of reactionary imperialism. What really peeved him was General Douglas MacArthur's sweeping land reforms in Japan, which, he said, had put the Japanese revolution back goodness knew how many years. "The land reforms of the Occupation have been 95 per cent effective throughout Japan," he said. "We expected that the former tenants who became owners would soon be compelled to sell out again, and that the landlords would quickly repossess the land. But this has not happened. The number of tenants who have sold the land they acquired under the reforms has been quite negligible. Normally, the rural areas of Japan would have been very good soil for Communism. Because of the land reform, we Communists have temporarily lost out among the farmers."

How, I asked, did he explain all this in Marxist terms?

"The land reform was intended to keep Japan politically conservative, and also to save Japanese capitalism from collapse. The factories were built on cheap labor; but once they were established, the lack of buying power among the farming people who constitute a large part of our population became a brake on further industrial production and therefore on profits. Feudal farming became outmoded. We do not deny that because of the land reform the standard of living of the farmers has risen. But this provides Japanese businessmen with a new outlet for the goods they otherwise would not be able to sell. The capitalist crisis in Japan has been postponed, and the conservative-minded farmers keep the Liberal-Democratic party in power."

Land reform in Japan was not a new idea introduced by the American Occupation. A Japanese Imperial edict of the seventh century says: "Some engross to themselves tens of thousands of acres of riceland, while others own patches of ground too small to stick a needle into. . . . From this time forward, the sale of land is not allowed; let no man without due authority make himself a landlord." But this and similar well-meant attempts at land reform failed. The American bid succeeded because in the shock of total defeat the Japanese willingly did as they were told, and because the tenants found themselves in a position to take advantage of the American reform.

Displaying a revolutionary zeal that would never have been permitted them back home—no one is ever quite so bold as when disposing of someone else's property—the Occupation officials made it possible for a Japanese tenant farmer to buy the land he had immemorially tilled, but rarely owned, for a fraction of its value. A tenant could purchase a two and a half acre farm for the cost of a six months' supply of cigarettes. Moreover, he was permitted to stretch this comparatively trivial payment over a period of thirty years. The Japanese say that the tenants acquired the farms "at the price of sparrows' tears."

They did so at a time when farmers were the only really prosperous people in Japan. The industrial economy that the rural people had been sweated by their absentee landlords to create was smashed to bits. The city people found themselves at the mercy of the peasants, for they had to have food, and only the peasants had food for sale. Nor was this all. When they offered money in exchange, the peasants refused it. The money economy as well as the industrial mechanism was in ruins. Money had become virtually worthless. The city people were in most cases compelled to buy their food with jewels, furnishings, family heirlooms. It was a dramatic reversal of the age-old practice whereby Japanese peasants had paid for the necessities of life in hard times by selling off their daughters to the towns.

The result of the land reform, taking place as it did under such auspicious circumstances, has been to transform rural Japan into a countryside of six million families owning small farms, with tenant-farming playing only a negligible role. The farmers now own half a million tractors—compared with a mere eight thousand in 1947.

Mr. Nakamura was also correct in saying that the land reform

had made the Japanese rural mass a force of political con-
servatism. The former owners of large estates who were compelled to sell their land at ridiculously low prices hoped that
with the end of the Occupation the Japanese Government
would get them back their land. But the conservative Liberal-
Democrats rightly regard the small farmers as their best friends.
Mr. Hayato Ikeda, the Japanese Prime Minister, summed up
the matter: "By creating a large number of satisfied owner-
farmers, the land reform built an ideal *jiban* (political machine) for a conservative party."

But, though they are the best friends the Liberal-Democrats
have, the small farmers are perhaps less enthusiastic about the
Japanese political conservatives than Mr. Ikeda imagines. The
rural areas vote overwhelmingly Liberal-Democrat, but their
reason for doing so is negative rather than positive.

I visited a couple of small farms not far from Kagoshima
and in sight of Sakurajima volcano. In each case, the farmhouse
was a single enormous room, roofed with bamboo, and with an
earthen floor. In the middle of the floor was a square fireplace
that was covered with a board in summer. Sacks of rice lay
about, and kerosene cans, and there was a Buddhist altar as
well as a Shinto god shelf. Children were busily pickling plums,
and squeezing camellia nuts to make hair oil. Women were
working in the fields, which looked trim and kempt, against a
background of shaggy, Tessai-scroll mountains. The paddies
did not smell of human excrement, as they would have done
only a few years ago; the farmers all use chemical fertilizer
now.

A farmer in a turtle-neck blue sweater, with his trouser legs
tucked in high rubber boots, explained through an interpreter
that he had bought his land "very cheap": $120 for a *cho*,
which is 2.45 acres. "All the land around here was owned by
seven people," he said. "Seven big landlords. Now, thirty
families own the land. All thirty were formerly tenants."

But when I asked him if that was why the farmers voted for

the Liberal-Democrats, he smiled and shook his head. "We vote for the Liberal-Democrats," he said, "because we distrust the Socialists and the Communists." I did not know which would have been the more chagrined Mr. Nakamura or Mr. Ikeda.

(6)

An Englishman called Richardson was murdered in Kagoshima in 1862. The British immediately bombarded the port. The local Japanese *daimyo*, or feudal lord, at once responded by seeking British friendship, entering into trade, and establishing a college where young Japanese could be educated in English ways. These were the days of successful gunboat diplomacy.

British influence has been superseded by American. Enthusiastic base commanders and Cultural Centers have not wrought in vain. An indignant Englishman I met in Kagoshima told me that a Japanese businessman had said to him in surprise: "So you British people also speak English! And, moreover, you speak it very well."

I sailed from Kagoshima into the typhoon-tossed East China Sea, bound for Okinawa, 375 miles south. Presently, the wooden coat hanger on the wall of my cabin was moving through an arc of 170 degrees. I had been told that anything over 180 degrees meant the ship was doomed. Finding that the movements of the coat hanger were reducing me to a snake-rabbit state of hypnotism, I clawed my way up on deck, and was soon in conversation with an American of Polish descent, from Connecticut, who wore the black habit of a Franciscan conventual friar.

Another Francis, St. Xavier, whose jasper and marble tomb I visited in Goa,[1] landed at Kagoshima in 1569. Within twelve years, the Jesuits had two hundred churches in Japan. A Japa-

[1] See the author's *The Heart of India* (New York: Alfred A. Knopf; 1958), p. 205.

nese religious embassy was received in Rome. But then the poison of religious fanaticism got to work. The feudal lords who were converted to Christianity zealously burned thousands of Buddhist temples, destroyed countless works of Buddhist art, and slaughtered numbers of Buddhist priests. This uncivilized contrast with Japan's earlier manner of reconciling Shinto with Buddhism won for the persecutors the high praises of some European Jesuit writers.

Then the tide turned against the Christians. The dictator Hideyoshi in 1597 had six Franciscans and three Jesuits taken to Nagasaki and crucified. Elsewhere, Buddhists turned on Christians and slew them. Forty years later, there was a Christian peasant revolt, at Shimabara. The peasants put a cross on their banners, and marched against the coast castle at Hara. The castle was taken, and some 30,000 rallied to the rebels. The rulers of Japan feared that Spain would use the rising as a pretext for an invasion. The captured castle on the coast had to be retaken at all costs. The rebels held out for over a hundred days, but in the end were overwhelmed. All were butchered.

The Japanese then expelled all foreigners save the Protestant Dutch, who got permission to remain and to trade by agreeing to be confined to a small island. Fearing that Japanese who went overseas might return as Jesuit agents, the Government made it a capital offense for any Japanese to leave the country. The authorities also banned the building of ocean-going ships, with the result that the Japanese lost forever the chance to emulate the Elizabethans in voyages of exploration and in the opening up of new countries. When they tried their hand at empire-building, three centuries later, the game had become anachronistic and in any case the Japanese were far outmatched by the Western powers. Lafcadio Hearn commented on the influence of Christianity on Japan as follows: "This religion, for which thousands vainly died, brought to Japan nothing but disorders, persecutions, revolts, political troubles, and war." But naturally I said nothing of the kind to the good American father.

The ship would call at Amami Island, about halfway between Kyushu and Okinawa. There the Franciscans had a friary. He invited me to visit it, and I accepted with pleasure. "Provided we ever get there," I added. He looked at me benignly. "Ah, this is nothing. A mere capful of wind."

The five islands of Amami-O-shima were under American jurisdiction until Christmas, 1953. Then they were returned to Japan, but some at least of the 200,000 islanders, who grow rice and sugar cane and are bitterly poor, evidently did not appreciate this Santa Claus gesture. They gladly paid $15 a head to be smuggled in fishing boats to Okinawa, which remained under United States management.

The Amami port of Nasé has 40,000 inhabitants, most of whom live in wooden shacks on muddy lanes. Angry seas pound the bleak shore. Behind the town rise steep hills, laboriously terraced into rice paddies. Typhoons do severe damage, and every five years or so, Nasé is razed by wind-swept fires. Tuberculosis and elephantiasis are rife in the islands, and there are hundreds of lepers. Much feared is a snake called the *habu*, whose bite is generally fatal.

The friary was a plain square concrete building. Nevertheless, skilled workers had to be brought all the way from Kagoshima to build it. The islanders knew only how to make houses of wood and turf. The fathers had no domestic help. They cooked their own meals and did their own cleaning and mending. But they had a few comforts. One was a tape recorder, and some tapes of the music of Glenn Miller. Another was a lavatory with a toilet seat, instead of a Japanese *benjo*.

There were, said Father Jerome, 3,000 Catholics in Amami-O-shima. But they were widely scattered, so that the friars had a hard time reaching them. "We measure distance here not in miles but in mountains," Father Jerome said. The bulk of the islanders had no religion, save primitive animism. They apparently were neither Shintoists, nor Buddhists.

Among the Catholics, the *shimpu-san*, or priest, was highly revered. But even among the Catholics local beliefs remained powerful, if not paramount. The fathers were often asked to traverse a couple of mountains in order to exorcise a local devil. But good usually triumphed over evil. One old lady who succumbed to the temptation to burn her Catholic prayer book to drive away her rheumatism became doubly devout when her pains, instead of vanishing, instantly increased.

The most formidable foe of the Franciscans, however, was not local superstition, but Marxism: the great challenge of the times touched even Amami-O-shima. The Communists had an organization called Mamorukai, which means literally "Guardian Club." It slogan was: "Help Mamorukai, which helps you." Mamorukai distributed food, medicine, and free copies of the Japan Communist party newspaper *Akahata*. In Nasé, it had a medical clinic with two doctors from Tokyo.

The Japanese authorities since they regained jurisdiction over Amami-O-shima had done little to combat Communist influence. They had built schools; but this helped rather than hindered the pernicious doctrine to spread. The annual income per head among the islanders was only $84. It was easy to persuade them that they had little to lose but their chains.

Father Jerome had asked one of the doctors from Tokyo, who worked at the Mamorukai clinic, if he were a Communist. "No, father," he had replied. "But as a doctor I am glad to have the chance to heal the sick."

The leading local Communist, added the Franciscan, was extremely able. "If he turned Catholic, I believe he would be a good one."

X

OKINAWA:

MISSILES IN THE TEAHOUSE

*Okinawa is the keystone of the Pacific in
the free world's fight against the spread of
Communism.*

HANDBOOK OF THE
THIRD MARINE DIVISION

Approached on a sunny day, in a calm sea, the island looks
like a luscious pear laid on soft, crinkly blue paper. But once
a visitor goes ashore, it at once becomes evident that Japan's
other island is an American military base.

Colonel Everard Wildrake was there to greet me. We got into
a sedan painted the color of khaki, with a soldier in uniform at
the wheel, and were driven at a dignified speed along a magnifi-
cent, four-lane highway. Automobiles on Okinawa are not permitted to go above 25 miles an hour.

On our left was the blazing blue ocean, and bright silver
sands. Overhead, jets darted like steel gulls. On our right, the
woods were enclosed behind high wire fences, and green-
painted watchtowers peeped above the tops of the trees. Large
notices forbade entry.

I asked how the generals were—the Air Force general, the
Marines general, the general in charge of civil administration,
and the top general, who is also the High Commissioner of the
Ryukyus. Colonel Wildrake said they were fine.

We drove past Rycom, the Ryukyus' Command headquarters,
with its tall white flagpole. Parked military cars, all khaki-
colored sedans, were massed in front of the big glass and

219

concrete building. It looked rather like a large country club of the wealthier sort. Occasionally a staff officer appeared on the steps. One of the khaki sedans pulled out of its parking place, and circled smartly to come to attention, as it were, right beside him, a door already open for him to enter and the driver out and erect and saluting.

Beyond the Command headquarters was a pleasant area of bungalows, and a golf course. There were about 15,000 wives and families of military men on Okinawa, and they lived in identical bungalows and employed nearly 11,000 Okinawan maids. Round and about and between the trim bungalows there wound smoothly asphalted roads. No one was astir this brightly sunny, somnolent afternoon. The winding empty roads looked like the paths in the Los Angeles cemetery called Slumberland. They had names like China Sea Drive, Coral Road, and Bamboo Lane.

Colonel Wildrake had the soldier halt our sedan outside a big bungalow with green Venetian blinds, and said I could use it during my stay on the island. It was a four-bedroom bungalow, but there was no one else staying in it, at the moment. There were several other similar bungalows in the area, which was called VIP Billets and was patrolled by short-necked, short-legged Okinawan guards wearing bright yellow helmets and armed with rifles.

After he had assured himself I had no further immediate needs, Colonel Wildrake went off in the khaki sedan. I drank a Coke from the refrigerator, and unpacked. Then I walked over to the main highway, just a few yards off, and hailed a cruising island cab, a bright-red new Buick, driven by a short-necked toothy islander. "Naha," I said. "Uscar."

He decided to take a short cut and went off the highway, over a bumpy track and through villages. Instantly I was back in Japan, or at least on Amami-O-shima. The farmhouses had thatched roofs and the children had black hair cut in square bobs, and wore red jerseys, and wore red jerseys, and wood or straw shoes. There were red flowers in the green hedges, and pigs grunted in thatched sties.

We drove a while close to the sea, almost on the beach. A black lump of ledged stone twisted up out of the water, about a hundred yards from shore, and the driver nodded towards it. "Divorce Rock," he said.

"Why is it called Divorce Rock?"

"When an Okinawan and his wife have a quarrel and start talking about getting a divorce, the family row them out to the rock, and leave them there with one blanket between them."

I thought it over. "So that in the morning they've probably made up and don't want a divorce?"

"Yes."

We left the beach again, and went through another village of thatched houses. Through the open door of a home, I glimpsed a big Japanese calendar, with a color picture of Mount Fuji.

"How is the land question?" I asked.

"It's improved," he said. "The Americans are paying us more for the land they requisitioned. Still, we'd rather have the land."

"You've been promised you'll get it back, eventually."

He smiled sarcastically. "Yes; the Americans say: 'We will return your land once we have conquered the universe to make it safe from Communism.' "

"How about politics?"

"We want to be with Japan."

We drove past island shacks, and Okinawan women trudging along with huge bundles of firewood on their backs. Long coarse grass half-concealed the roadside Okinawan tombs, shaped like giant oyster shells. There is a legend that once every seven years, virgins go into the tombs and scrape the bones of the ancestors. I reflected that in all primitive communities, virgins always seem to have a lousy time.

We swung back onto the four-lane highway and entered the town of Naha, which is the capital of Okinawa. It looked a nice, polite place, though slummy. People drove and walked very sedately. There were lots of traffic policemen. The stores were all right and there were a couple of new buildings, one of them a bank; but the homes were mostly shacks.

Uscar, which means United States Civil Administration of the Ryukyu Islands, consisted of four narrow stories perched quaintly on concrete stilts. I paid off the taxi in dollars and cents, which are the only currency on Okinawa, and told the driver: "When the islands go back with Japan, you won't have those."

He looked hurt. "Why not? We can still lease the bases."

"But you want the land back."

"Not the land that's already under four feet of concrete. It will never grow rice again."

I went up in the elevator. The man I wanted to see sat behind a desk that had his name on it, on a polished slab of wood turned to face visitors, in letters made of mother-of-pearl. He greeted me cordially.

"How is the land question?" I asked.

"Oh, that's settled. We've made a very generous settlement and the natives are happy as clams."

"I seem to remember something like that being said a couple of years back. Then the happy clams went and elected a Communist as mayor of Naha."

He looked surprised. "But we got rid of him."

"You threw him out, so the Okinawans said if that was American democracy, they wanted the Japanese brand."

"You can take it from me the 'back to Japan' movement is dead. You never hear that cry now."

After leaving Uscar, I went to see one of the island's Communist leaders. His house was next door to his provisions store, and his wife and some of his seven children were busy behind the counter. He sat on a cushion on the floor of his living room, drinking jasmine tea and reading Winston Churchill's war memoirs. He wore a fisherman's blue jersey, and had a

shock of upstanding black hair and a pair of thin-rimmed
spectacles that made him look like Trotsky. But his thick black
mustache was wholly Stalinist.

He greeted me with a charming smile, offered me tea, but insisted on speaking through an interpreter. A Japanese flag was
prominent on one wall.

When I asked him whether on his last visit to Tokyo he had
met with the leaders of the Japan Communist party, he blinked
at me mildly behind his spectacles. "No, no, we have nothing to
do with the Communist party of Japan. I have never met
them."

He said that all the Okinawans wanted was to revert to the
rule of the motherland. "I am not anti-American. Why should
I be? They and I have the same cause at heart; the people's
welfare, *ne?*"

He was slyly laughing at me.

I was asked to cocktails and dinner at the Rycom Officers'
Club. The club stood on a high bluff overlooking the sea and
the twinkling lights of the bungalows. In the long bar there was
a regiment of one-armed bandits, all chinking busily. At the
bar it was "two for the price of one" night, meaning you got
two very good Martinis for 25 cents.

The talk at the bar seemed to be all about women. They
were expecting a girl called Hermione. She was reported to be a
knockout.

"You weren't here when Gloria came through, were you,
Colonel?" asked a major. "She was devastating."

"Nothing to what Hermione will do, from what I hear," said
someone else. He sounded unduly gloomy about the prospect,
I thought. "The reports say she is really fierce." He nervously
drank down one of his Martinis.

"Gloria blew half the roofs off, and damaged God knows
how many of our planes," said the major. They were talking
about typhoons.

We went into dinner. The large dining room was fashionably

dark, each table a little oasis of candlelight. Pretty Okinawan waitresses brought the large menus. Peering at the menu in the dim religious light produced a confused impression of a super-abundance of thick steaks, jumbo-sized shrimps and prawns, giant baked Idaho potatoes, followed by chocolate cake and extra-large portions of strawberry shortcake.

It was difficult to talk above the calypso jazz of a loud Filipino orchestra.

I asked the colonel how the Air Force's program was proceeding on the island. "Full utilization of all aircraft in the inventory has now become feasible," he said. He saw I looked blank. "Some aircraft were compulsorily deactivated for lack of runways," he explained.

I danced with the major's wife, and asked her how she liked Okinawans.

"Oh, I think the indigenous personnel are awfully stupid. Americans have been here fifteen years, yet a lot of the maids can't speak English."

After dinner, I excused myself and went to meet Mr. Mawashi, who had promised to show me the celebrated Teahouse of the August Moon. Mr. Mawashi was the president of an Okinawan company. He was a serious-looking, idealistic man who in his youth had flirted with radical notions. Middle age and material success had made a cautious liberal of him. But his best claim to fame was a unique connection with the American golf course.

"I was the only Okinawan who was permitted to join the club," he said. "It took a long time. My application was opposed because, they said, it would set a dangerous precedent. Also, they wanted to keep me out because I used to be a Socialist."

He said he thought that some Americans failed to understand the feelings of the Okinawans.

We went to the Teahouse of the August Moon. The geisha did not wear wigs, but they did not play "baseball" either. Instead, they performed simple but graceful island dances. We drank sake, and applauded. Presently, warmed by the sake, Mr. Mawashi said he remembered his sisters doing those very same dances and, in fact, he thought he could do them himself. He called for a plain white cotton towel, and wrapped it round his head. Then he put on a kimono, and danced. He did it extremely well. "You would make a fine *onnagata*," I said. Mr. Mawashi accepted the compliment gravely.

(2)

Sixteen thousand Americans lost their lives in the battle of Okinawa. The United States has since spent about half a billion dollars fortifying the island and erecting military installations of various kinds. Precisely what sort of installations, no one is prepared to say. A "very great concentration" of missiles is admitted. These no doubt range in size up to IRBMs that can travel 1,500 miles. This would bring Indochina, Burma, and important segments of both Russia and China within attacking range of Okinawa. The Chinese, on the other hand, have about a hundred and thirty airfields from which to attack Okinawa.

The battle of Okinawa was so fierce partly because the defenders were able to fight from the deep shelter of some 36 miles of caves. In this vast underground honeycomb they lived and, when all was over, many of them committed suicide, including young girls who had been taught to dread falling into the hands of the enemy. The girls who did not commit suicide found the enemy somewhat less than ferocious, and were soon dating him. But the caves are still there, and some of them are said to have massive steel doors over the entrances. Only the top brass know what is kept there. But, if someone else's nuclear missile struck and penetrated them, the consequences might be spectacular.

Between 50,000 and 60,000 Americans are on Okinawa. For

years, it was known as "The Rock," and men sent to serve there felt they were being condemned to a fate worse than Korea. But half a billion dollars spent on a small Pacific island only 67 miles long and between three and four miles wide is bound to make changes.

"Okinawa," I was told by a man who had lived on the island six years and was in no rush to leave it, "is the lushest overseas assignment any military man can have. It has the biggest fieldhouse in the Pacific, bathing and deep-sea fishing all year round, beautiful beaches, Scotch at two dollars a bottle, a hundred clubs, forty PXs, sixteen theaters and sixteen libraries, four bowling alleys, and two golf courses." The clubs, he added, included a flying club, a yacht club, and a sports-car club; and most of the attractions were within fifty or thirty minutes' drive, even with a 25 miles an hour speed limit on the four-lane highway.

On the highway, I saw a long, black, air-conditioned Lincoln cruising grandly along. In the back sat a solemn-faced young man in an airman's uniform, with his arms folded. A flag flapped on either side of the radiator, both flags bearing the mystic but potent words: MR. BIG. I trailed the car to the airmen's club, and was told that the young man had turned up a lucky number that entitled him to the use of the Lincoln, and its chauffeur, for four days and nights, in addition to $50 spending money.

This did not exhaust the delights of the airmen's club. Other attractions of membership were $1,000 Bingo prizes, free beer on Sunday mornings, and champagne and a 16-ounce steak on a member's birthday. The club also had seventy-five pretty Okinawan hostesses, who came on duty in the evenings.

The cultural side was not neglected, the manager of the club explained to me. "The average American is backward with girls. You could take five GIs and put them beside five of the world's loveliest girls, and the GIs would just sit and look at them. They wouldn't talk. They wouldn't dare. They'd be scared whatever they said the girls would think them stupid. So I have trained our hostesses. When a GI is sitting there, trying to figure what to say and unable to think of a single thing, the hostess gives him a lead. She says: 'What's with all those missiles, Mister—is Walter Lippmann right?' "

"Missiles? Lippmann?"

"Well, of course, it doesn't have to be either of those. But what I mean, I make our hostesses read magazines and stuff, so they can talk to the boys. I say, 'All right, girls, look in your magazine and pick a topic for discussion. Well, now, here's one, about missiles,' I say. "Miss Isahama, what do you think about missiles?' That way, I get the girls talking, and they get the GIs talking. The girls learn something interesting, and the GIs learn something interesting."

The Bingo prizes, the free drinks, and the hostesses—who were paid 45 cents an hour, were not allowed to drink anything stronger than water, and were taken home in buses each evening to safeguard their morals—as well as the rides in the Lincoln, were mostly financed out of the profits on the club's thirty-two slot machines, whose turnover was above $100,000 a month.

It seemed to me an ingenious and innocuous way to induce young airmen to spend their evenings in the club, and so help to keep them out of the Naha and Koza brothels, into which they might otherwise drift. But, when news of the club's activities got back to the United States, there was hell to pay. Moralists who had never in their lives foot-marched 40 yards denounced this lush, evil living. Parents of young draftees wrung their hands in public, and let it be known that they had hitherto believed that their sons overseas passed their evenings playing chess, or reading the good book. Apparently many civilians *like* to think that men in uniform far from home lead drab, hard lives, and become infuriated when they find that this is not necessarily so in all cases.

For years, the Marines on Okinawa fully satisfied such stern civilian requirements. An island story is that two Air Force officers were driving home late one moonlit night from the Teahouse of the August Moon, when they saw a number of mud-covered, unshaven men in steel helmets and full packs dragging themselves on their bellies across the road. "Who in God's name are they?" demanded one officer. "Marines," said the other, carelessly. "Only Marines. You know they spend all their time up to their asses in mud."

The Marines on Okinawa lived in tents, which typhoons constantly blew away, whereas the airmen lived in typhoon-proofed bungalows and were reported to have manicurists in their barbershops and Turkish baths on their base. Then the Marines moved to the north of the island, to a new, $20,000,000 camp called Schwab.

I flew to Camp Schwab in a helicopter. The pilot wanted to show off his machine. We swooped like a hawk on a sweet-potato field, then hovered like a dragonfly three or four feet above the heads of some startled indigenous personnel. Later, we descended into a canyon to watch soldiers wash their elephant-sized tanks. Northern Okinawa is thick scrub country, hilly and full of ravines. There were a great many high green watchtowers.

But the area around Camp Schwab was raw and red after the bulldozers. Trees seemed to have been cut down for miles around. Close to the big, brand-new camp, Okinawans were busily building no fewer than eighty bars and cabarets. Marines abroad are, of course, not allowed to have their wives with them, this being a privilege reserved for airmen, and visiting Marine generals.

The camp itself was of a spartan simplicity: straight rows of steel lockers, and steel-spring army cots with tight-folded brown Army blankets. The food was cooked in stainless steel kitchens. The job of the Marines on Okinawa was to drop everything and run, at a second's notice, to put out brushfires in places like—perhaps it is better not to say. The theory was that they would get there in ships and would be launched ashore in helicopters. However, it was admitted that an enemy sufficiently in earnest could thwart such intervention by simply blowing up Okinawa before the Marines had time to get off it. But this would probably start World War III, said the experts. Meanwhile, though out of tents or in hygienic Camp Schwab, the Marines on Okinawa continued to lead lives spartan and strenuous enough to satisfy the most carping civilian critics of the American military man overseas.

More romantic than the Marines, and, to hear them tell it, twice or three times as rugged, were the lives led by the Spooky Units on Okinawa. Since they were spooks, it was impossible to tell how many such units there were, except that there seemed to be no shortage. They were also the most unreticent spooks I ever met.

One unit occupied a drab, olive-green building that was constantly being visited by slant-eyed Asiatics in a great variety of uniforms. The boss of the show was, of course, an American; he wore an olive-green uniform and huge black boots, and smoked cigarettes with savage concentration, trying to look lean and hard-bitten. He explained that he and his men, who operated in small groups of eight or ten, were guerillas. In the event of war, they would be dropped in enemy territory, to collect information and also to blow up things and generally create hell. "Guerilla war-wise," he said, "we are targeted and trained for any area from Sakhalin to Malaya."

I said that if and when the twentieth century began pressing atomic buttons, there might not be leisure for guerillas.

"That's where you're wrong. In the past, it was difficult for guerilla forces to work close to battlefield areas because of the density of enemy forces. Depopulation of large areas will solve the problem. Guerillas will have more influence on communications than ever before. Uninhabited areas and fluid atomic battlefields will provide guerillas with more opportunities for effective action."

(3)

Ten per cent or so of the American servicemen on Okinawa were Negroes. Very occasionally they ran amok, especially in an area known as Koza Four Corners. The Four Corners consisted of some five hundred gaudy bars, with names like "Cotton Club" and "New York Jump." The bars were monopolized by the Negroes, and whites who entered the area ran the risk of being beaten up. Sometimes young Negroes marched up the hill from the Four Corners towards the business section of Koza, fighting and wrecking bars as they went.

The Negroes in turn complained that some of the NCO clubs and other places on the island were virtually off limits to them. A Negro Air Force staff sergeant said in his big deep voice: "It just about takes an Act of Congress for a Negro serviceman to get in those clubs, or some of them. If an Okinawan waitress in a club that has white southerners on its committee dates a Negro, or is even seen talking with a Negro, she gets fired."

I asked a white staff sergeant what he thought of that. "The white serviceman has just as much right to want his recreation spots for himself and his friends, without having Negroes around, as the Negroes have to want them integrated," he said judiciously. About Negroes and Okinawan girls, he said: "It's considered fashionable here for white and yellow to mix; but it's kind of taboo for white and black to mix." He concluded: "Anyway, you don't gain acceptance for yourself and your friends by mob violence. Not long ago, about a hundred of those young Negro hoodlums marched up from Four Corners, and tried to take the town."

A Negro from Texas, a Marine sergeant, said gloomily that the Four Corners was "just like being across the tracks in any Mississippi town." He added: "You know, it was set up to be like that; about six years back, or more, they just kind of *gave* the Four Corners to the Negroes, to keep us quiet and to try to cut down white-black fights."

On his first pass, being unaware of all this, he strolled into the "white" area of Koza. "A white MP walked up to me and tapped me on the shoulder. 'Keep moving, boy,' he said. 'I beg your pardon?' I said. 'Don't get wise with me, Nigger,' he said. 'You heard me, tar baby.'" The sergeant's jaw muscles tightened at the memory.

" 'Now, look here!' I said to him," he continued. " 'I'm a sergeant in the Marines: here's my pass.' 'Damn your pass,' he said; 'up here, you're nothin' but another loud-mouthed nigger.'

"The thing is," said the sergeant earnestly, "that the Peking radio *reports* all this, you know. Some Americans think we ought to keep quiet about it, and never tell anyone, like you, comin' in from outside. But the Peking radio talks about it. The Okinawans know all about it. Just our own folk back home in the States, *they* don' know about it."

The Okinawans to whom I talked seemed surprisingly placid about any white-black tension in their midst. Even when a Negro ran amok and threw a hand grenade that injured Okinawans, they tended to shrug it off. "Before the war, the Japanese soldiers on Okinawa also committed criminal acts," a policeman said. He agreed the Negroes were probably reacting against the race prejudice of the whites. But when it was suggested that indigenous law enforcers should carry firearms, for the protection of themselves and other Okinawans—only Okinawans guarding American bungalows and American military installations had guns—he smiled and shook his head. "That might only provoke the foreigners against *us*. Now they fight each other," he said. But this was an official view. Another Okinawan said, more bitingly: "White Americans who treat black Americans as inferiors are hardly like to think of Asians as equals."

As far as I could tell, whatever happened in Koza, which was close to the air base, the night clubs of Naha were uninterested in the color of their customers' skins. I did not see many Negroes there, but I saw some, and they seemed on cordial terms with both the Okinawans and their fellow Americans (white).

Off Peace Street, in Naha, there were plenty of bars and little clubs, mostly with gay paper lanterns hung over the entrance and steep steps going down into a basement. Some of the girls wore their straight black hair almost waist-long, and nearly all of them had skin-tight bespangled dresses. In one basement club, the dancers shuffled around a fountain in the center of the stone floor; in the middle of the fountain stood a drenched plaster nude whose head almost touched the cellar's glass chandelier. The band played in an alcove beside the bar, which was hung with mauve paper lanterns. Military policemen in white helmets came in from time to time to look around, and tiny Okinawan children sold sticks of chewing gum from trays.

The largest night club offered a stage show consisting of girl strippers who wore *Noh* masks. A noisy party at one of the tables included one of Okinawa's numerous talkative spooks. He loudly chased the Communists out of North Korea, helped the Chinese throw off their chains and topple the Peking regime, and saved the Indonesians from themselves. Then he went on to save the United States from itself.

"America has gone soft," he said, ignoring the girl strippers, who had just taken off everything except their *Noh* masks. "This is a life-and-death struggle between us and the Communists, and America has to be run as a tight ship. First thing we have to do is get rid of the States, and in their place have military districts. . . ."

(4)

Gillespie waded ashore with the other Marines but stayed on. He had lived on Okinawa ever since. He had long arms and a short body, looked like a prize fighter, and had a heart of gold. But he hated "brass" from his Marine days, and hated official-dom since exchanging his gun for a trading license. He knew everything that had happened on the island since the day the Marines landed, and was willing to talk about it, with unprint-able expletives for his two pet hates. I was ready to be a good listener.

Gillespie said Okinawa was the biggest and most densely populated of a scattering of islands called the Ryukyus. "There are about 700,000 natives—what Rycom and Uscar call 'indige-nous personnel.' That's a hell of a lot of people on a small island."

The Okinawans, he said, were under American administra-tion, but the United States publicly conceded that Japan had "residual sovereignty." "That's the red-tape way of saying Ja-pan will get the Ryukyus back one day, but they can't say when," he added.

He explained that Okinawa for about four hundred years, un-til the seventeenth century, had been under Chinese influence. Then a war lord from Kyushu moved in, and for a century or so the islanders had to pay tribute both to China and to Ja-pan. The Japanese finally took the Ryukyus under their "pro-tection" in 1872.

"They think of themselves as *min-ken*, people of Japan. All the island politicians, conservatives, Socialists, Communists—they all talk about Japan as their motherland, and they want the islands to go back to Japan as soon as possible. Most of the schoolteachers are Japanese, not Okinawans, and they fly the Japanese flag. The island didn't have a university under the Japanese, but we Americans built one. Now the students some-times yell: 'Yankee, go home.' "

Gillespie liked the Okinawans. "They're a cheerful bunch," he said, using another word. "They've got a sense of humor. You ought to hear them laugh at some of the things the poop heads do. Keerist, I've seen village elders practically bustin' their

233

sides, but of course with their hands over their mouths, so as not to be seen even smilin'."

Poop heads, in Gillespie's language, were "brass," or officials.

"What kind of things?"

"Like tryin' to teach them to knit . . . kee-rist, I'm not kiddin'. Ask Uscar."

But the thing the Okinawans found no humor in was American land policy. "Land is real serious business here. Okinawa has an awful land problem. We introduced new health services that made the population increase even faster than it was doin', but at the same time we rented thousands of their arable acres. An' when I say 'rented,' I mean we pay for what we take but the Okinawans can't refuse.

"Most of them understand military necessity," said Gillespie. "The Japanese taught them *that*. But two things shocked them. One was requisitionin' land not just for military purposes but for a golf course, for the 'brass.' The other was when some of those poop-head bureaucrats said the families that had their land taken for the golf course were far, far better off than they ever had been growin' rice, for now they could make more dough doin' an easy job like caddyin'. . . ."

And, he said, other bloopers had been made. "About 50,000 Okinawans are workin' for our Armed Forces, an' that's a lot of families. But what do you know? Damned if some poop head in the Pentagon or some place didn't lay down a law that said Okinawans should get 10 cents an hour, Filipinos 52 cents, Japanese 83 cents, and an American civilian workin' for the Armed Forces here should get a minimum $1.20. It took a visitin' Congressman or somebody, an' a rovin' delegation from the ICFTU, the international labor-union boys, to straighten things out.

"But you can imagine how the Communists played that one up. 'Okinawa, keystone of freedom,' ha ha! An' the poop heads didn't like labor unions among the indigenous personnel. There were so many laws an' so much red tape, an *American* union would've needed a smart lawyer and a good auditor to get goin', far less simple Okinawans."

"Do they really talk about the islanders as 'indigenous personnel'?"

"Yeah, a lot do. You'll find it in Rycom and Uscar reports. Used to be a lot worse, though. One Christmas, they had a big sign up in the PX: 'Gift packages for indigenous *female* personnel.' Poop-head talk for local girl friends. The items in the packages were listed, too: 'kit, sewing, one; soap, cakes of, two; comb, one; powder, face, box, one—' "

"You're kidding *now*," I said.

" 'Value of contents, $1.95,' he finished. "No, I'm not kiddin'. You should have heard some of our kids."

"Did they buy gift packages for their girls?"

"Like hell. Bought 'em Chanel, and silk stockings."

Gillespie got riotously sarcastic about what he called the poop heads' handling of the political situation on the island.

"A couple of island politicians who spoke up for Okinawa goin' back to Japan, and criticized the land payments, got fired out of posts they'd been elected to, an' then the poop heads appointed their own men. The islanders said they had *always* elected mayors an' governors an' such, under the Japanese, an' what the hell was all this talk about American democracy?

" 'Subversives!' cried the poop heads; 'that's what you all are, just subversives.'

"Of course, what happened was, all the moderates were shoved aside by the extremists. Before anyone knew what was happening, Naha, the capital city of Okinawa, had a Communist mayor.

"Well, the poop heads got rid of him, after an awful lot of trouble. But the islanders were so mad, in the end the 'brass' had to send an Okinawan *Socialist* to Washington. A Socialist! A guy they'd tossed out of office years back as a real Red. Now he was the most *moderate* man they could find on the island." And Gillespie laughed scornfully.

"What did he go to Washington for?"

"To help settle the land problem. Things had got to the point where if they didn't settle it somehow, about 50,000 Okinawans workin' for the Armed Forces here were goin' to throw down their tools and try to close the bases."

"Did the land question get itself settled?"

"Well, temporarily. The Socialist said: 'Jack up the rents you were paying, by about ten times, and furthermore, we want a right of review every five years. Land values just keep going up all the time on Okinawa'—which is true. So they agreed to everything he said, and gave him a present of a gavel, because he'd got himself appointed Speaker of the Okinawa Legislature. The American High Commissioner was supposed to tell them what to do, but lately the legislators, all Okinawans of course, have been tellin' *him*."

(5)

I went to the Uscar building, to talk about Okinawan problems with the men behind the desks with the mother-of-pearl name placards.

American bureaucrats on Okinawa have an interesting history. At first, the military would have nothing to do with civilians. When it was suggested from Washington that a civilian official or so might be a good thing, the military sat back on their haunches and howled. The first to arrive was so cold-shouldered that he went a little crazy from loneliness, and was to be seen wandering about the lovely beaches, collecting shells. Later, in his office, he fixed them up with pipe cleaners to look like little urinating men, and kept them in rows on his mantel.

But presently he applied for and was granted an assistant, and Parkinson's Law began to operate. The bureaucrats are now almost a match for the military in numbers, but there is still no love lost between them. Uscar is in Naha, and Rycom is ten miles away. They keep their distance, and communicate by memo.

Both, however, use much the same jargon. When I visited Rycom, I found in the toilets large notices reading: "Please Practice Supply Economy." This meant, save toilet paper, of which there was a shortage.

At Uscar, everyone was complaining bitterly about project 436, which had been forced on them by Rycom. I asked what the project was.

"It's predicated on the assumption that in future Uscar will supply its own logistical support, instead of relying on Rycom, as heretofore," a bureaucrat explained. "In a nutshell, Uscar has had to buy two buses."

One official had formerly been a schoolteacher, but now the mother-of-pearl sign on his desk called him "Educational Reorientator." He told me about Okinawan education. Most of the teachers were Japanese, he said, but they were too ambitious. They did not realize that Okinawan schoolchildren were in a cultural phase that lagged behind the main Japanese islands. Consequently, they tended to confuse the children by using terminology that was too advanced. "That's why we've introduced rule 19 in all Okinawan schools," he finished.

"What is rule 19?"

"It says: 'In the event of lack of correspondence between comprehension and vocabulary, it is preferred that preference be given the former.'"

"And you manage to translate that into Japanese so the teachers understand it?"

"Why not?" he asked. "It's quite clear. It simply means the teachers mustn't use big words."

"What else are you doing for the Okinawans?"

"Many things. Especially for the youth. Currently, we are launching an investigation into attitudes held by Okinawan adolescents. There may be only a few subversives, but it was decided to have the matter probed by a special research team.

"Then, our two radio stations on the island are constantly telling the Okinawans how the United States is fighting Communism. We have such programs as 'I Was a Communist for the F.B.I.,' which is paid for by the Veterans of Foreign Wars; and 'Freedom, USA!,' which is paid for by the American Legion.

"Our information dissemination is quite extensive. We supply pictures and stories to one hundred Okinawan indigenous-language newspapers. Our cameramen expose an average of fivty-five negatives weekly, in order to record pictorially the achievements of Uscar.

"We are teaching Okinawans to manufacture such articles as fiber doormats, shell figurines, table mats, bamboo and reed baskets, aprons, and knitted goods.

"We endeavor to contrast such useful activities with the havoc created by the Communists in nearby Asian lands."

Colonel Wildrake rode with me to the airport in one of Rycom's big khaki-colored sedans. On the way, he explained that Rycom received advance notice from all incoming planes of any important passengers. This made it impossible for Rycom to be taken by surprise. No matter how short the notice, an escort and an honor guard could be provided. Rycom sometimes even managed to have briefing folders ready, with the names of the VIPs inscribed on the covers.

"That's a lot of protocol," I remarked.

"Protocol is the grease the big wheels need for their smooth operation," he replied.

I looked at him sharply, but he returned my look with a bland and steady gaze. I never knew when that man was pulling my leg.

XI

HOKKAIDO:
THE NEW FRONTIER

Boys, be ambitious!
WILLIAM SMITH CLARK

WE FLEW BY STAGES up the whole length of Japan. Fukuoka by night was a neon tracery of bright electric flowers on darkness, which blossomed and died, and blossomed again. Oranges grew in Kyushu, but in Honshu snow whitened the Japanese Alps. We passed over stretches of marvelously blue water, and rice paddies that were all silver and jade. There were rice paddies everywhere, hand-carved out of steep hillsides, and out of black lava. Once we flew low over a live volcano that poured out sullen gray smoke.

In Hokkaido, 1,500 miles northeast of Okinawa, Japan is opening up a new industrial frontier close to Russia. Only 5,000,000 people live in Hokkaido (compared with over 67,000,-000 in Honshu), but Hokkaido already produces one third of Japan's coal, one third of Japan's pulp and timber, and one third of the fish catch (Japan is the world's major fish producer). The development of Hokkaido owes much to an American, William Smith Clark, from Massachusetts.

The Governor of Hokkaido in 1870 was a young Japanese named Kiyotaka Kuroda. At the age of thirty-one, he visited the United States and paid his respects to President Grant. He asked for advisers, and the President offered to lend him the services of General Horace Capron, the Commissioner of Agriculture, and forty-five other Americans who were willing to go and live in Hokkaido, a far-off island with icy winters, inhabited by black bears and hairy Ainu. General Capron, who was sixty-seven when he arrived in Hokkaido, remained there four years, and he and the other American experts introduced wheat, corn, oats, potatoes, and beans, as well as cattle, sheep, pigs, and horses.

After Capron there arrived Dr. William Smith Clark, the president of Massachusetts Agricultural College, to open a new school and to teach. Clark seems to have accepted the task chiefly in order to be able to convert the Japanese students to Christianity, though he had been warned that Christianity remained a forbidden creed in Japan, punishable by death. Undeterred, he smuggled fifty Bibles through the Japanese customs at Yokohama, in his luggage. The new school was established at Sapporo, the capital of Hokkaido. Clark was shocked to find that some of his students drank. He ordered a public smashing of liquor bottles. Each morning, the bearded American giant conducted prayers. He also introduced a biology course, principally so that he could intone at the end of each lecture: "And thus, gentlemen, we have conclusive proof that life is not the product of mere chance, but that there is a Great Author of our being."

Clark was in Hokkaido only eight months. He converted twenty-four students, who became known as the Sapporo Band of Christians. Hokkaido University, which he founded, has today over 6,000 students, of whom only about a hundred are Christians. But Clark was anything but a failure. At least 5,000,-000 Japanese think he was the greatest American. Small busts of him are on sale in every store throughout Hokkaido, and most of the 300,000 tourists who visit the island each summer take one with them as a souvenir of their stay. Clark's statue dominates the university campus. His parting message to the students has become Hokkaido's motto. He said, "Boys, be ambitious!" and the people of Hokkaido have taken this message very much to heart.

When Jane and I went to call on the president of Hokkaido

University, Dr. Harusada Suginome, we found him busy with plans for an impressive new William Smith Clark Memorial Center. Dr. Suginome is a well-known Japanese chemist, with American, German, and Swiss degrees; and the university has ten faculties. But the buildings still have a rustic air, very proper to a new frontier. We were conducted to Dr. Suginome's office along corridors adorned with fine stags' heads. The university has an institute at Muroran for the study of seaweed, and owns a research ship that cruises six weeks every summer, from the Bering Sea to Singapore, with forty students on board. And around the Sapporo campus are several hundred acres of experimental farmland, the property of the university's faculty of agriculture, which also operates a sardine-canning factory.

In the university's big gymnasium, students wearing black masks, black gloves, and black cloaks banged away with bamboo poles, in the risky fencing called *kendo*. Others practiced judo, another name for jujitsu. A *Karate* expert showed how to break a piece of wood two inches thick with a single blow of the edge of the open hand, wielded like the edge of an axe. The same blow, struck on the back of the human neck, will kill. Hokkaido students are a tough lot, accustomed to grappling with bears. Freshmen used to be made to run around the campus naked a hundred times in the winter snow. Now they practice *karate*, *judo*, and *kendo* instead, and also play baseball and rugby football; the university has twenty-six athletic clubs. But it also has forty literary, dramatic, and art societies. The biggest is the painters' club, called the Kuroyuri-kai, or Black Lily. The day we visited Dr. Suginome, the university's drama club was busily rehearsing a play by Jean-Paul Sartre, in Japanese.

The Hokkaido students were not being pampered. Some fifteen hundred of them had scholarships—but these amounted only to six or nine dollars a month. Another three hundred were each receiving a grant of up to $30 a month; but they were expected to repay the money after they got jobs. Four out of five students earned their tuition by doing odd jobs around the campus, as clerks or janitors; in the long hard Hokkaido winter, they spent half of each day shoveling snow for a dollar, and the other half munching hot corn on the cob and studying their books. When they graduated, they hoped to get into local government, banking, journalism, or into business with Snowbrand dairy products, Sapporo beer, and Fuji steel.

(2)

Like all frontiersmen, the people of Hokkaido tended to look down on others as effete, while secretly resenting what they imagined to be the others' superior airs. They derided the mad way Tokyo did things, as a Texan might scoff at "those Easterners." It is a fact that Hokkaido has very few shrines or temples, and does not practice the tea ceremony. "In Tokyo," said the deputy governor scornfully, "they think there is nothing up here but bears, codfish, and snow." The people of Hokkaido even tried to prove scientifically that the future belonged to them, not to Honshu or Kyushu. "Overcrowding sets up a stress syndrome," a biologist said. "It creates acute psychological tension, by overstimulating and then exhausting the pituitary gland, which produces adrenalin in the human body." Hokkaido has fifty people to the square mile compared with Honshu's two hundred and fifty.

In Sapporo, an extremely pleasant city of half a million people, with big straight boulevards and large public gardens ablaze with flowers in summer, workmen were busy tearing down the city's oldest building to make way for modern offices. The structure that was coming down was only sixty years old. The shop windows were full of baseball mitts, tennis rackets, ice picks, and gas stoves, and the department stores sold men's shoes decorated with gold medallions, and dresses labeled *"Mode de l'Automne."* The center of Sapporo was commanded by a 440-

foot television tower, and nearby was a gay establishment calling itself the Rumba Garden.

The countryside around the capital was startlingly un-Japanese. The village halls had gilt clock towers, and the farmhouses, of brick, not wood, had solid-looking barns, silos, fat
dairy cows, satiny horses, and sheep. People ate corn on the cob
instead of noodles, and they preferred mutton to seaweed or
bean curd. At a place near Sapporo called Shinotsu, which was
formerly a peat bog, there were giant sunflowers and corn grew
to the height of a man. It was planned to spend $30,000,000
on land reclamation in this area; to plant rice as well as corn;
and to build several dams.

We visited the Planning Bureau in Sapporo at lunch hour
in order to take the director to lunch. We found groups of
young men practicing choral singing in the corridors. The director explained that they were going to be on a television
show. He said that 50 per cent of Hokkaido's exports were manufactured goods, as compared with only 15 per cent before the
Korean war. The island sold $15,000,000 worth of plywood and
other products to the United States each year, and the figure
was rapidly rising. Income per head in Hokkaido was higher
than anywhere else in Japan, and wages, real wages, not just
money wages, had risen by 52 per cent in ten years. Hokkaido
hoped to increase its industrial output 10 per cent every year,
and to treble the number of dairy cows.

Then we went to see Mr. Toru Shimamoto, the president of
the Hokkaido Bank. He told us gleefully about his campaign
for better island roads. He got together a team of motorscooter
riders, and sent them all around Hokkaido with instructions to
note every pothole. Then he sat down and wrote a blistering
report. He was interested in improved roads, because forty-three
of the Bank's sixty-seven branches were out in the country. Better roads would also help the farmers to get their products to
market. "Because of our poor roads," he said sternly, "our dairy

farmers get only 30 cents of the milk consumer's dollar, compared with well over 50 cents in the United States." He was about to set off to Washington, to coax American bankers to make loans for further Hokkaido development.

Hokkaido had at least one very good road: the 100-mile highway between Sapporo and Asahigawa, to the north. The reason was that one-fourth of Japan's 170,000-man army (or "ground self-defense force") was kept permanently stationed at Asahigawa. Beyond Asahigawa lies Wakkanai, and from Wakkanai, on a clear day, one can see Russian Sakhalin, 26 miles across the Soya Strait. The Russians also hold the southern Kurils, off Hokkaido, islands which were once Japanese.

On August 16, 1945, Stalin asked Truman to let the Russian Army occupy the whole of Hokkaido east of a line running from Kushiro in the south to Rumoi in the northwest. This would have given the Russians most of Hokkaido's rich timber and its potential pastureland, as well as an estimated two billion tons of coal deposits. After this request was refused, Japanese Communists on Hokkaido, of whom there are still about 40,000, tried to transform Hokkaido into an independent Soviet republic—or one at any rate independent from the rest of Japan. The Communists had no hope of succeeding, partly because of the presence of American forces in Hokkaido, and also because many people in Hokkaido were refugees from the Kurils and south Sakhalin, having been driven out of those places by the Russians. But the Communists are still around, and the Russians are too close for comfort.

(3)

My friend Frank Iwama said one of the most embarrassing moments in his life occurred when an Ainu woman on Hokkaido went up to him and asked him indignantly: "What is it that is peculiar about us? Why do Japanese people look at us as if we were freaks?" She had tattooed round her lips and chin an enormous blue mustache, and a blue beard. Though the custom is now supposed to have ended, there are still many Ainu women with blue mustaches and beards. Ash bark boiled in water was used to produce the blue effect; the tattooing was done with a knife; and the operation, or rather the series of operations, commenced when a girl was eight years old and continued until she was sixteen, which was the marriageable age. Hair has a mystic significance for the Ainu. The men, as everyone knows, are luxuriantly hairy; and elaborately carved mustache lifters are an important part of Ainu art. The world's best collection of Ainu mustache lifters is to be found in the Ainu museum of Hokkaido University, which is presided over by Dr. Kodama. He has been studying the Ainu and collecting Ainu skulls and other relics for over thirty years.

No one knows where the Ainu came from originally; they are evidently Caucasian rather than Mongolian, since they lack the Mongolian spot as infants and the Mongolian folded eyelid as adults. With customary vagueness, anthropologists profess to find links between the Ainu and bearded Australoids, people from Western Oceania, and certain South Indian tribes. Since there are now almost no pure-blooded Ainu left, nearly all of them having intermarried with Japanese, probably no one will ever know.

The Japanese "discovered" the Ainu when they began seriously to colonize Hokkaido, at the end of the sixteenth century. But Chinese chronicles of a much earlier period mention Japanese travelers to China who were accompanied by long-bearded bowmen, who sound like Ainu. In Hokkaido, the Japanese fought and traded with the Ainu, much as Americans fought and traded with the Indians. The Japanese swapped sake for bearskins and eagles' feathers. But they held the Ainu at arm's length, as savages, until the nineteenth century, when they feared the Russians might invade Hokkaido and subvert the Ainu. To secure the loyalty of the Ainu, the Shogunate decreed in 1802 that the Ainu be taught Japanese language and customs, "to cultivate patriotism among them, so that they may not rebel in case of invasion by foreign powers." As a result of this very plain statement of expediency, the Ainu became Japanese citizens, and a process of assimilation began forthwith.

There are only about 15,000 Ainu, and their chiefs are very old. We visited one of them, a broad-shouldered patriarch with huge eyebrows, enormous mustaches, and a tremendous beard, wearing a crown of straw and a white shirt with loose sleeves. His daughter spoke some English in addition to Japanese.

She told us that in an Ainu home, everyone must sleep facing the east, and that all food must be brought into the house through a window, also facing east, called the god-window: never through the door. The Ainu have spears, and bows and arrows, the arrows being poisoned; but these weapons are used only for hunting animals, not against other human beings. She said that when two villages quarreled, each village picked a champion, and then the two champions talked at each other until one fell silent through sheer exhaustion.

The Ainu have a sun god (*chup-kamui*), a fire god (*abe-kamui*), a forest god, a sea god, and a bear god. The greatest of these is the bear god (*kimun-kamui*). The bear is, in fact, the special cult of the Ainu.

The Ainu go looking in caves for bears. When they find one, they plant three poles in front of the cave, and wait. When the bear sees the three poles, he cannot resist the temptation to dig them out of the ground. While he is thus laboriously employed, the Ainu shoot him full of poisoned arrows. They sell his skin, and also sell his gallbladder to drug manufacturers.

But bear cubs are kept alive for *iyomande*, the bear festival. The captured cub is tenderly and lovingly reared. He is petted by all the children, given special food, and may even be fed human milk. But, come *iyomande*, the bear is ceremoniously shot to death with arrows. This is followed by a three-day feast.

Foreigners who condemn this practice as cruel are told that

the bear is actually a holy spirit which has been trapped in a bear's skin, and that all bears long to be released and returned to heaven and therefore are extremely grateful to the Ainu who do them this good service.

When the chief's daughter had finished telling us these and other particulars of Ainu life and customs, her father, despite his great age—he claimed to be ninety—vigorously performed a grasshopper dance for us. Later, when Jane and I were returning that way, we decided to call in at the Ainu village, and see some more of the venerable-looking chief. But a disappointment awaited us. His daughter was in, but the chief was away.

"I'm sorry you missed him," she said. "But he went up to Sapporo. He's got a television show."

(4)

The smokestacks of brand-new factories rose straight out of flat fields of corn, beans, and radishes around Tomakomai, south of Sapporo on the coast, and there were thickets of television aerials on the roofs of cottages and of the new apartment houses for the workers. But Tomakomai was in the midst of a strike of paper workers, and all normal life had come to a halt.

Tomakomai was a "company town"; the Oji paper plant was said to own or control everything, including the stores. But the paper workers had a strong union, and the strike started when the management tried to get rid of the closed shop and set up a company union. About a third of the paper workers joined the "number two" union, but the members of the "number one" union picketed the plant so that "number two" union men could not enter and the management could not get out. "They can have food sent in from neighborhood restaurants," a striker said, with relish, "but if they try to leave the plant, we take their trousers off and then chase them back inside." It was evidently hoped that if the management were kept locked up long enough, and occasionally deprived of their trousers, they would relent.

Meanwhile, the strikers had seized command of the town. At the intersections they had put up wooden sentry boxes with red flags on top, and the sentries stopped people to ask them their business. The strikers' committee were prepared to give passes only to persons who were not connected with the management of the Oji paper mills. Seventeen hundred policemen had been sent to Tomakomai, but seemed to have made up their minds to stay as far as possible from the scene of the trouble. In spite of the appeals of the town council—said by the strikers to be a puppet of the company—the police remained on the outskirts.

Around the mills, in the grounds of a school, and in sunny lanes where giant sunflowers grew luxuriantly, the older men among the paper workers roosted in patient rows. The active pickets were all young men, very tough-looking, who wore white head bands, and sun glasses, and rode importantly up and down the town on noisy motorcycles. By night, the motorcycles were used to drag trains of ten or fifteen oilcans tied together up and down the streets where "number two" union men lived, to make sure they and their families got no sleep. Stones and garbage were also hurtled through their windows.

The striking paper workers had the sympathy and also the active support of other unions. The Hokkaido coal miners raised enough money to pay each striker two dollars a day for the support of his family. Local schoolteachers were running their classes in shifts, in order to be able to join the pickets round the paper mills. Post and telegraph workers tapped the paper plant's lines and listened in to its phone calls; they also intercepted all its mail, in order to keep the strikers informed of the company's plans. Railroad workers made sure that no supplies reached the besieged mills.

In the ranks of the paper workers themselves, however, the strike had split families and broken friendships. There were two thousand workers on strike, and one thousand who wanted to work. Fathers and sons, brothers, even husbands and wives, were sometimes in different camps. When the "number two" union men launched sorties to try to get past the pickets into the plant, they and the strikers fought each other with pick handles and baseball bats.

The women who supported the strike seemed especially ferocious. They had invented a terrible technique, which was called the "wringer." When the picketers went into action, the women among them threw themselves on strikebreakers who had not already been felled by baseball bats and pick handles, and twisted their testicles. One woman wept loudly when she discovered that her victim was her own husband.

None of this ugly turmoil was reflected in Noboribetsu, only a few miles farther round the bay from Tomakomai. Ainu men sat outside the little town's souvenir stores, busily carving wooden bears, and street vendors offered passers-by delicious Hokkaido crabmeat right off the charcoal brazier. Noboribetsu is surrounded by gray volcanic hills, and consists almost entirely of hot-spring hotels. The boiling volcanic water that fills the hotels' baths goes bubbling across the town, through a narrow rocky canyon. The spindly wooden hotels perched many-storied on both sides of the canyon look as though they were about to fall in.

Jane and I took a walk to see the actual hot springs, where the very earth is hot to the touch and queasy to the foot, and where steam rises from wide, sinister pools. The stores selling wooden bears seemed more fun, and a lot safer. Off the main street we found a very decent little bar called Lila. The joint was jumping, but not with customers, for there were none. The bartender fed Louis Armstrong and Dave Brubeck jazz records to a player under the counter, then beat time with his fingers. His girl friend, clearly a square, just went on laying out hand after hand of patience on the bar counter, never saying a word. The Scotch cost a dollar a nip.

The twisting road from Noboribetsu to Muroran was under

repair. Traffic was directed by women wearing white cowls, and waggling red and green flags. The houses along the route had roofs like the starched caps old ladies used to wear.

The volcanoes around Muroran regularly jetted puffs of white steam, like the chimneys of locomotives. In the bright blue sky, the white steam of the volcanoes mingled with smoke the color of oxblood, from the Fuji steelworks. As far as its setting is concerned, Muroran must be the world's most scenic steel town. In July 1945, the American Navy bombarded the steel plant and in addition to doing a great deal of damage, killed fifty workers. The plant, when we visited it, had been thoroughly modernized and was turning out over a million tons of steel a year.

The managing director, Mr. Hirase, occupied a large, pleasant office that he shared with a number of wooden bears. Punctually each day at four o'clock, he shut up shop and drove to the golf course five minutes away. He took us on a tour of his sizzling, snorting, thundering plant, shouting explanations into our ears amid showers of sparks and bursts of flame. The older men, at his approach, whipped off their caps, put their thumbs along the seams of their trousers, and stiffly bowed from the waist. But the young workers just went on practicing baseball catches, this being their lunch hour. The workers, said Mr. Hirase, earned on the average $100 a month, and also received fringe benefits amounting approximately to another $20. They had a very strong, close-knit union.

"Do you have many strikes?" I asked, thinking of Tomakomai.

"Every year," said Mr. Hirase, but added cheerfully: "The union is considerate enough to call strikes only during winter, when we can't do much work anyway, because of the snow." Less cheerfully, he went on to say that he did not know how long this reasonably happy state of affairs might last. "There are a lot of Communists in Hokkaido."

After seeing the steelworks, we climbed to the top of Muroran's highest hill, where there is a tall television tower. A number of burly men, wearing black coats and looking like bears, were grouped around the tower, taking photographs. They were Russians. The Bolshoi Circus was in town.

We spent the night in an inn on Lake Toya. Early in the morning, Jane called me to the window to admire the view. The surface of the lake was calm and smooth as a polished steel mirror. The softly rounded hills surrounding it wore gently billowing white draperies. Then suddenly out of the white morning mists there burst a big bustling ferryboat, playing loud music. It rapidly approached the shore, the canned music getting steadily more overpowering as it came. Lining the rails were pretty girls in neat blue uniforms, with shining brass buttons, wearing saucy hats. They waved and smiled hopefully towards the windows and gardens of the numerous lake hotels. They were ferryboat hostesses. The ferryboat was called the *Venus*.

In the main street of Abuta, baby bears chained to logs at the entrances to souvenir shops were being fed by Japanese tourists wearing light summer kimonos. I wondered rather uneasily what would happen to these bears at *iyomande*, the bear festival. Bearded Ainu men, evidently the owners of the bears, sat around busily carving wooden ones to sell to the tourists. The shops also had numerous one-dollar busts of William Smith Clark of Massachusetts. The other attractions of Abuta's main street were *pachinko* parlors, archery, a shooting range, and, last but not least, strolling girls in tight black pants.

The town's hot-spring hotels all had improbable murals of beckoning Venuses in the lobbies, which also disclosed neat rows of guests' shoes, patiently waiting. Before you enter a Japanese inn or hotel, you remove your shoes, and they are kept waiting for you at the entrance. Each time you go out, even if only for a moment's breath of air, you have to sit down and put your shoes on, then sit down and take them off again when you return. In the hotel lobbies, beyond the rows of shoes, there were television screens, racks of colored picture post cards of volcanoes and bears, and blasts of jukebox jazz. In the hotel gardens, fat carp plopped in ornamental lotus ponds.

We took the train from Abuta to Hakodate. Pink clouds floated over the sharp peaks of volcanic mountains, and all around the smooth vast curve of Volcano Bay, square-sterned fishing boats were drawn up on black sands. Rows of cuttlefish hung on fences, like washing put out to dry.

In the train, a skinny old man was traveling with a plump young woman, evidently not his daughter. At intervals, he drank pink tonic from a medicine bottle that he kept under the seat. Then he had the giggling young woman clean his ears, with an earpick. While she did this, he kissed her hand, then the whole of her arm. Finally, he thrust his bald head forward, and kissed her in the armpit.

A mother and daughter were traveling together. The mother wore no jewelry or make-up. Her hair was pulled back tight, and she wore a brown kimono with a dark-brown *obi*, and white split-toe socks with wooden sandals. The daughter, inches taller than her mother, wore pearl earrings and her lips and nails were bright red. Her hair was curled, and she wore a silk blouse, silk stockings, and high-heeled white shoes.

At Hakodate, we transferred to the ferry for the five-hour ride across the Tsugaru Strait, from Hokkaido to Honshu. After much bonging of gongs, the ship's gramophone played "Auld Lang Syne," and we were off. The funnels belched black smoke, which thickened steadily on the blue sea like a leaden pall. Behind us lay the sharp-pointed, grayish-pink volcanoes of Hokkaido. Ahead of us there lay the white-plumed volcanoes of northern Honshu.

It seemed strange to think that we were not returning to Japan, for we had never been out of it. Everywhere we went in Hokkaido, the flavor had somehow been un-Japanese. But there was no mistaking the flavor now. The ferryboat, as usual, was crowded. There were people everywhere—on the decks, in the lounges, cramming every nook and cranny. In September 1954, twelve hundred people drowned when one of the Tsugaru ferries sank in a squall. We were in Japan, all right, with our pituitary glands being overstimulated and then exhausted, in a stress syndrome.

XII

SENDAI:

THE DEFENDERS OF FREEDOM

The function of the press in Japan is to fight feudalism.
TAKESHI SUZUKI

THE COUNTRYSIDE around Sendai in northern Honshu is full of swift trout streams, and farmhouses with black-tile roofs and television antennas. The television mast begins to displace the firewatcher's tower as the symbol of rural Japan.

My hotel bedroom in Sendai overlooked a garden that had a tiny brook running through it, with orange-colored pebbles at the bottom. The room's *tokonoma*, or alcove, contained a long, white scroll with a single graceful red flower, and the walls were decorated with bamboo paintings. But the room smelled overpoweringly of new *tatami*, or rush mats. When I mentioned this to the hotel manager, who kept a four-foot demon made of red *papier-mâché* beside his desk, he said reprovingly: "You should be pleased; there is nothing like a new wife, or new *tatami*."

Sendai, which was bombed to bits in the war because it was the headquarters of the Northern Command, has fine, broad new streets and a twelve-story department store with a children's playground on the roof. I wandered through an enormously long, roofed-over shopping center, hung with gay paper lanterns. The stores were crammed: tasty trout and large red lobsters; luscious apples and smokily purple grapes; lots of clothing and jewelry; and caverns of books. A gaudy bar, showing through its curtained door a glimpse of red plush, girls, and rows of whisky bottles, was called The New Tiger. Other bars had six-foot sake bottles standing outside their doors, to attract the thirsty.

At least two of the movie theaters in Sendai seemed to specialize in films of social realism. One featured a movie about Japanese liberals being persecuted by militarists before the war. The other had a movie on the life and death of Sadako Sasaki, the Hiroshima schoolgirl whose symbol is a flying crane made of folded paper. I was told that movies like these were much liked by the students of Sendai University.

The university must be one of the hardest institutions of learning in the world to get into. Only one in six passes its stiff entrance examination—one in eight in the medical faculty—and, of those who manage to pass, ten per cent are failed later. But the later failures are nearly all due to malnutrition and tuberculosis, not to any slackening of effort.

I visited the university, and was courteously shown over its vast collection of half a million books, which include a very fine European collection of seventeenth-century German black-letter books, as well as Buddhist sutras, and manuscripts from Tibet. I inquired if I might ask the students a few questions, and immediately a room was placed at my disposal, and I found myself facing a dozen or so serious-faced young men and one girl. All of them could speak some English.

Sendai is a "conservative" university, and the Zengakuren, the leftist students' federation, was banned from it. Nevertheless, most of the students were Socialists, though they were very vague about the brand of Socialism they professed. They all said they wanted "a new, Socialist order of society," but admitted they did not know how to get it, or even what it would be like.

They thought the Japanese Constitution, inspired if not created by the American Occupation, was "the best in the world," but did not see why Japan needed the Emperor, "since sovereignty resides in the people." They claimed they did not fear either China or Russia, and declared that Japan should have no defense forces.

When I asked if they expected Socialism to come to Japan through the Japan Socialist party, they smiled knowingly and said they had no faith in the Socialist Dietmen, or in any Dietmen. I asked why. After much hesitating and exchanging of glances with one another, a student got up and said: "We learn from the newspapers that the conservative government we have now is no good, and that all the members of the Diet are rogues. The conservatives are reactionaries, and the Socialists are weak and useless. Perhaps the Communists are really the only people who have something."

I looked at them in astonishment. "What newspapers? The *Akahata*, the Communists' Red Flag paper?"

They chorused back: "No, not the *Akahata*; and not the Socialist newspapers. The ones that everyone reads."

There is no illiteracy in Japan, and the Japanese consume 36,-000,000 newspapers every day, as well as 360,000,000 magazines and 130,000,000 books a year. A national newspaper convention was being held in Sendai, and I had been kindly invited to attend. I mentioned my talk with the students to one of the newspapermen.

"The students are, of course, perfectly correct. The conservatives are feudal and reactionary, and the Socialists are weak and foolish."

"That leaves the Communists."

"I cannot help that. It is the duty of the press to tell the truth."

"But the press isn't pro-Communist, is it?"

"Not at all. On the contrary. But the press is anti-government."

"You mean it's against the present government, or that it's against any government, on principle?"

"The latter. If the Socialists came to power, we would attack them."

256

"If the Communists came to power, you wouldn't be able to attack *them*, because they wouldn't let you."

"But the danger at present comes not from the Communists, but from the conservatives, who are in power and who are feudal and reactionary. It is against them that we must never relax."

(2)

The Japanese journalists took a tour in a sightseeing bus, and I went along at their invitation. Away from the wide flat landscape around Sendai, the countryside was mainly thick forest, bumpy roads, mist-wreathed hills, and lead-colored lakes under a dun sky. The farmhouses were so poor they had paper doors.

The bus hostess was a little, bright-eyed creature, not five foot, with a shiny black belt tight around her tiny waist, and wearing a peaked cap at a jaunty angle. She began to talk into a microphone the minute we all got on, and she never stopped until the bus did, and sometimes not even then. She told us the local history, and the legends, and sang us folk songs. She also sang the favorite Sendai song, "Moonlight on the Ruined Castle," which was composed by a Sendai man, Bansui Doi. We were by this time a trifle tired of it, for Sendai is so proud of the tune that seven times every day it bursts forth from giant loud-speakers all over the city. But nothing could prevent the bus hostess from singing it once more.

When the bus drew up outside a temple we were to visit, she had been talking and singing for seven hours, not counting a half-hour halt at a small village for tea. We were all anxious to get out and stretch our legs, but the hostess had not finished. She had launched on a local legend about the eleventh-century Fujiwara warriors who dominated those parts, and she was determined to conclude it. She stood blocking the aisle, microphone in hand, lips rapidly moving. Finally, the man nearest the door put his hands under her elbows, and placed her to one side. We all got off, and as we climbed the steep stone steps to the temple, we could hear her still talking.

In the temple, we sat with our shoes off on a ragged *tatami* floor, and were handed wooden bowls filled with cold rice and seaweed. The Japanese journalist next me held his bowl close to his mouth and ate with flying chopsticks. "Ah!" he cried enthusiastically. "Good food, at last!"

Then we got back in the bus, and visited some seaweed farms.

Everywhere the Japanese journalists went, they were given gifts, according to the pleasant custom of the country. As one of the party, I received gifts also, despite the fact that I was a *gaijin*. The gifts were in neat wooden boxes, prettily wrapped in gay gift paper and tied with colored ribbons done up in complicated bows. After unwrapping my gifts and opening all the boxes, I found I had acquired fourteen *kokeshi* dolls made of wood ranging in height from a centimeter to a foot, a Japanese medieval castle made of china, several boxes of sweet bean-paste balls, and a black plastic brief case.

Much sake was consumed at a *sayonara* dinner, and white-faced geishas in black wigs and orange and black kimonos mingled with the guests. The dinner began with salmon eggs, pickled sea urchins, and salted entrails of cuttlefish as appetizers. There followed *sashimi*, or sliced raw fish; clear soup; baked sea bream with mushrooms, potatoes, and fern; and *tempura*, or deep-fried fish and shrimp. We concluded with pickles and rice.

A geisha got up and sang "Moonlight on the Ruined Castle."

"When a geisha decides to surrender her virginity to some favored suitor," the man on the next cushion confided, "she goes through a ceremony called 'opening the cherry.' "

But I was momentarily weary of geishas, and had certainly had my fill of Bansui Doi's masterpiece.

"Why, *specifically*, does the press think that the Government is feudal and reactionary?" I asked.

258

He considered. "The Government wants to give more power to the police, to maintain law and order. Frankly, we cannot see the necessity."

"But isn't it true that as the law stands now, the police may not even arrest persons who are carrying dangerous weapons —they can only question them about their intentions?"

"The Government wants to turn Japan into a police state."

"*Specifically*, what evidence have you for saying that?"

But the sake had induced too warm a feeling of well-being and no one wanted to bother about tiresome and especially specific questions.

"The greatest happiness for a man is to improve his own life in the world," he said. "If we all do this, mankind will be happy. So why does the Government wish to have more police, and more soldiers? This is reactionary feudalism. Have some more sake."

(3)

Nikko means sunshine. "Don't say *kekko*, or marvelous, until you've seen Nikko" is a Japanese proverb.

Feudalism was still in fashion at Nikko, not a hundred miles from Tokyo. A guardian of the gorgeous Toshogu shrine was at once overruled when he tried to tell Jane and me that Japan's feudal dictators, the Shoguns, had done much for popular culture in the spirit of *demokurasu*. "The Shoguns had nothing whatever in common with democracy," another guardian interposed firmly. "The first of the Shoguns, Ieyasu, was a despot. But he laid the foundations for two hundred and fifty years of peaceful feudalism."

Ieyasu died in 1616, and was enshrined at Nikko as *Tosho-dai-gongen*, the Great Incarnation Illuminating the East. He was a great man. "If you only know what it is to conquer, and not what it is to be defeated," he said, "it will fare ill with thee."

A later generation of Japanese militarists might have done well to heed his warning.

Ieyasu is commemorated at Nikko by a complex of shrines in the *gongen-zukuri* or rococo style. The wooden panels of peacocks and phoenixes are intricately carved and richly colored, and all the gateways have roofs resembling enormous hats. There is an abundance of grinning dogs that look as if they were made of soapsuds, and there are carved stone lanterns, Chinese sages, nude Buddhist kings, a crying dragon, a sleeping cat, and three lifelike monkeys that hear, speak, and see no evil. The Shinto priests, whose English name cards describe them as "Reverends," possessed the urbanity of Papal nuncios. One of them, the Reverend Seiji Takahashi, readily agreed that the descent on Japan of the heavenly grandson of the Sun Goddess was only a myth. But, he exclaimed, such a pretty myth!

"In Takama-ga-hara, the Plain of High Heaven, our ancestors lived in peace and happiness, loving one another. That azure sky so pure and bright is still the Japanese people's heaven. Our ancestors who lived there were all *kami*, or divine beings, and we believe we are their children. They were beautiful in heart, and we should strive to be like them." Nor was Shintoism an exclusive, standoffish sort of religion. "On the contrary, we recognize the same divine spark in all other people; and not only in every person, but in every tree and every stream." The tolerant Ieyasu, he said, was anointed a Shintoist, buried according to Buddhist rites, and had believed during his lifetime that there was a great deal of truth in Confucianism.

Jane and I drove past the scarlet bridge that was reserved for Imperial messengers, and took the steep road from Nikko to Chuzenji. There were thirty hairpin curves, and signs in English that read: "Up Priority." A score of empty buses slowly descending looked, because of the steep slope and the sharp bends, like airplanes stacked up over an airport. Great wreaths of white mist rolled in the valleys below us, and unfurled from the mountain peaks above.

At the top of this terrifying ascent, Lake Chuzenji lay placid under the green cone of Mount Nantai, surrounded by spruce, silver birch, and chestnut trees. Small pleasure boats cruised up and down the lake, and even from afar we could hear the ferry hostesses talking to the passengers through microphones.

The road that ran alongside the lake was lined with flimsy wooden hotels, which twittered like nests of young birds. Chattering Japanese schoolchildren peered from every window. The buses had deposited them. From personal observation, I would imagine that about one third of all Japanese school-children are constantly going around Japan on sightseeing bus tours, either to ease congestion in the classrooms, or because of teachers' strikes. Presently, wearing rubber boots and carrying umbrellas, for it was raining, the children descended into the town's single street, and crowded the souvenir stores, where they began to spend their pocket money on pink celluloid dolls, stuffed birds, plastic cases to hold captured butterflies, gaily painted hand towels, colored picture post cards, and soft ice cream.

We boarded a bus that was going to Yumoto. It was a small bus, badly put together, with treadless patched tires; and we quickly repented our rashness. The road was narrow and full of potholes and jagged-edged boulders. It was also very steep. Time and again, we teetered on the edge of precipices over whose rocky lips waterfalls plunged on the way to the plain below. Finally, we reached Yumoto, a hot-spring spa that stank of sulphur and boiling mud.

On the way back, the bus was filled with young hikers, boys and girls with big packs on their backs. They got off after a few stops, and strode off through a field of purple flowers, into the deepening twilight of the hills. The bus driver, a man with a deplorable mind, winked and said something about young couples.

Chuzenji's single street was now a promenade. The school-children had had their evening meal and their hot bath, and had come out again, in pink and white pajamas, to buy more souvenirs. Young men in kimonos and wooden shoes, also fresh from the bath, were playing *pachinko* machines, watched by girls wearing tight blouses and very tight plaid trousers. From behind the *shoji* screen of a well-lighted house came a pounding of drums and a plucking of lute strings. Presently, however, the lights of the town began to go out one by one, and soon the street was dark and deserted. Each silent inn displayed neatly arranged rows of shoes at the entrance.

Our hotel was Western style. One dining-room wall was occupied by a huge, carved, bright-hued, imitation *gongen-zukuri* wood panel depicting a panlike creature who played a flute while lounging on what looked like balls of wool, no doubt meant for clouds. Beneath this stood an old-fashioned phonograph that played Bach organ music. A Japanese waiter wearing a black tie and a boiled shirt front asked us if we cared to eat trout. When we said we would, he went to a glass tank in which swam what we had thought were tropical fish, grabbed out four tiny trout, and removed them to the kitchen. He reappeared with them on two plates, grilled and sprinkled with lemon juice.

The hotel lounge was hung with photographs of celebrities. The Emperor of Abyssinia. Pibul Songgram of Siam. The Shah of Persia. King Faisal of Iraq, with a big bow of black crepe attached to the frame to mourn his assassination.

A Buddhist temple stood at the edge of the lake: a cluster of red and green lacquer roofs, bronze bells, and golden Buddhas. It was protected by two deities, the god of wind and the god of thunder. They sat on either side of the entrance, each inside a wooden cage. Tied to their huge red fingers were strips of white paper representing the prayers of worshippers.

In the courtyard, an elderly priest came up and thanked us, in English, for visiting the temple. He wore a black robe and was smoking a cigarette. Thick melancholy mists had rolled down from the mountains, blotting out Mount Nantai and lying heavily on the surface of the lake. The world seemed to end a few yards beyond the weathered stone balustrade where the lake water lapped.

" 'There prevailed in Milton's time,' " said the priest unexpectedly, " 'an opinion that the world was in its decay, and that we have had the misfortune to be produced in the decrepitude of nature. It was suspected that the whole creation languished, that neither trees nor animals had the height or bulk of their predecessors, and that everything was daily sinking by gradual diminution.' "

"But Johnson could as well have cited Raleigh as Milton," Jane said after a moment's pause. "Wasn't it Sir Walter who said that 'the long day of mankind draweth fast towards an evening, and the world's tragedy and time are near at an end'?"

The priest urbanely agreed, then broke down and confessed that he, too, had been at Edinburgh University. But it had been a near thing. We never came so close to losing face.

We drove away from Chuzenji and Nikko, towards Tokyo, along a great avenue of tall straight cryptomeria trees, traversed for two hundred and fifty years by Imperial messengers, Shoguns, and *daimyos*. Going through Utsonomiya, our morale was restored by seeing a god-shop that sold ladies' underwear as a sideline.

XIII

TOKYO:

THE TYPHOON

Those who make half-revolutions dig their own graves.
GEORGE BERNARD SHAW

I PICKED UP the ringing telephone. "*Moshi mosh'!*" said a man's voice, meaning "Hello!"

"*Moshi mosh'*," said I. "Hello, who is it?"

"*Moshi mosh'!*" the voice repeated, sounding a little irritated. "*Moshi mosh'!*"

"Fellow must be deaf," I said to Jane, as she took the phone from me. She always handles those problems better than I.

"*Moshi mosh'*," Jane cooed. "*Ano-ne.*"

"*Ano-ne!*" said Yoshio Tanaka, and broke into English. "I thought nobody was going to answer. . . . *Ano-ne.* May I drop in if I pass by your house today?"

No Japanese telephone conversation can proceed unless both parties keep repeating *Ano-ne*, meaning roughly "Look here." If one neglects to say *Ano-ne*, as I had done, the other simply will not hear.

Yoshio and Yumiko Showa were now engaged to be married. Yoshio had finally succumbed to the blandishments of Yumiko's film producer and lent his dark, proud profile to a screen test. The result excited the producer, who begged Yumiko to lure her young man into a movie career. "Seduce him," he said. "Marry him, even. But talk him into it somehow." Yumiko said her forte was suicide, not seduction, as the producer well knew, but that she would marry Yoshio, who would then lose face unless he was able to support her. "How much will you pay him?" she asked practically.

264

But an engagement period is always a strain, in Japan the same as anywhere else, and Yoshio compensated for certain inner anxieties by adopting a high posture towards the complexities of a perplexing world. He was not the only one. The giant city of Tokyo is a huge organism able to absorb any number of upheavals. Scattered parades and demonstrations are simply swallowed up and lost in its vastness, while life goes on, unnoticing. But increasingly there were files and columns of people, mostly young people, marching and demonstrating with tall red banners in the main arteries. They swarmed in the area around the Imperial moat, shuffling past the Tokyo police headquarters with menacing shouts, and they thrust up thickets of placards outside the Diet and before the gates of the American Embassy. "Go home, U-2!" said the placards; and "Down with Kishi!"

"Let the Americans beware they don't take a toss, as well as Kishi," said Yoshio when he called on us later that day. "The people aren't anti-American—yet. But why does American policy in this part of the world have to be so—so two-faced?"

"Good God! Two-faced?"

"You don't see that?" He seemed genuinely astonished. "But look; *ano-ne!* How *contradictory* American policy is—if you like that better than two-faced!" He ticked off on his fingers. "This Constitution of ours; it's the best thing we ever had from the West, the best thing the United States ever did. It's been enormously, fantastically acceptable. No one in this country wants to change an iota of it, except a few diehards: known or deeply suspect old Fascists. An entire Constitution, virtually written by conquering foreigners; and, over fifteen years after the great defeat and more than a decade after the end of the American Occupation, the people still love it, cherish it, are filled with nothing but gratitude for it. Was there ever such an epilogue to a terrible war between two nations, in the whole of history? But what do the Americans now want us to do? They want us to tear the human rights and the safeguards of peace out of this same Constitution. They say that unless we do so, the United States will deem Japan to be a weak and feckless nation, not responsible enough to be left unprotected; so until we amend our Constitution, they will keep their bases here."

The reason for this outburst, it seemed, was that Mr. Walter Robertson had declared, some time before, that the Americans would stay in Japan until Japan had developed substantial military forces, but that such a build-up was unlikely under the existing Constitution. "We won't change our Constitution," said Yoshio. "And, anyhow, it's an *American* Constitution; can't they understand that?"

"But the Americans have taken all their troops out of Japan. There are no soldiers left."

"Only air bases," said Yoshio sarcastically. "Only airmen, and air bases. Places for U-2s. Just a few months ago, they swore that the U-2 was only a weather plane. They denied it was spying. And now, this Powers business! How can we believe a word they say, after that?"

Then he remembered he was supposed to be so terrible a Communist that he and his friends despised Khrushchev for "bourgeois tendencies."

"Of course, we of the Zengakuren never did believe a word they said. But this—this ruthless cynicism staggers even us." He made an elaborate gesture of helplessness. "The Americans put through a tremendous all-land-to-the-peasants reform in Japan—merely in order to keep conservative Japanese governments in power by means of the peasants' votes. But on Okinawa they do not hesitate to take land *away* from the people— by decree, by compulsion; at gun-point—so they can build nuclear bases."

Now he had touched on the exposed Japanese nerve: the fear of nuclear weapons. His lean face grew hard with contained emotion.

"Nuclear bases—on Japanese soil! Weren't Hiroshima and Nagasaki enough?"

No use to try to argue with him that American policy might conceivably be wrong, or muddled, but that at any rate it aimed hopefully to ward off another world conflagration, not begin one. Yoshio believed he was in possession of the real facts, and the only true, the only possible, interpretation of them. And this brought him to another facet of the great Japanese uneasiness over American policy.

"In the past five years or so," he said, "the United States has spent billions of dollars on military forces and installations in Asia. The amount spent on economic aid to Asia has been only a fraction of this military build-up. The whole of the Pacific is in the hands of the nuclear Seventh Fleet. And the intention is quite plain. It's to 'contain,' as they say, the new China; 'contain' her, if they can't smash her entirely. That, of course, is what they'd like to do. Smash China.

"The trouble is, the new China just refuses to be smashed. The Chinese have had the chance to learn from the Russians; they have the advantage of coming thirty years after the Russians. The revolutionary dynamism of Communism has passed or is passing from Russia to China. Even the Russians themselves admit it. Khrushchev is afraid of it.

"But just look where American policy and persistent American hostility to China puts Japan. The Americans can't hope to smash, or even stop the Chinese. But they can provoke them, perhaps intolerably. And China is growing at the rate of 15,000,-000 people every year, and must soon devise nuclear weapons, if she doesn't already have them. She very probably does have them. What has Japan got to set against that? Nuclear weapons we don't and won't have. But neither do we want to be pushed into a fight with the new China—which would be absurdity, since Japan inevitably follows along the same path of Socialist development, sooner or later. We don't wish to be pushed into a fight with China and have only transistor radios and dollar blouses to defend ourselves with!

"But that's just where American policy is pushing us. Even Kishi can't really stomach America's China policy. No Japanese can. In the first place, no Japanese seriously thinks that Formosa has a political future. . . . But put that aside. On the Formosa issue and on other grounds as well, Japan's present, American-guided policy gives deep offense to the Chinese. The Americans say: 'Japan must be maintained as the only possible counterweight to China in the Far East; Japan is now our only hope.' We are thrust out, I tell you, like a stick to trip China with. And the consequence is that China and Russia are in a military alliance that specifically mentions Japan as a threat to them. Not a threat because of what Japan is or would do by herself, or because of Japan's past behavior to China, which God knows was bad; but because Japan is for all practical purposes one big American base within nuclear striking distance of both China and Russia."

Useless, I knew, to say it was not America's fault that Japan happened to be the only highly organized and well-equipped industrial country lying athwart the path of a China that often spoke as if it were conscious of a military destiny it must fulfill; that the new, militant Chinese might, like the Japanese only a few short years before, harbor ambitions involving an arc of countries from Burma to the Philippines. What Yoshio was saying was believed to a greater or less extent by many Japanese, from the extreme left through the extreme right. Even the ultra-nationalists, who noisily denounced Russia, were remarkably soft-tongued about China; while the Japanese businessmen who voted conservative were eager for China trade. I also knew that this almost general Japanese attitude to China seemed to constitute a high blank wall of noncomprehension for many Americans; I had heard an American who carried much weight in his Government's Far East councils dismiss out of hand two Japanese conservative politicians who returned from Peking with a low posture and in a mood of considerable appeasement. "They have become a little bit strange," he had shrugged.

So I said to Yoshio: "All that is very well. Now that you've got freedom of speech in Japan, thanks to the Americans, anti-Americanism is the rage. But what is it you want? You talk about armaments being forbidden by the Japanese Constitution, and you say you want Japan to have no armed forces whatever. But you say that only because the present Japanese Government is with the West and not with the Communist world. And don't forget that it is a freely elected Government. If a Japanese Government turned right around, towards the Communist world, the Communists in Japan would be all in favor of Japan's becoming armed to the teeth."

"But the people who are demonstrating against the American U-2s, and against Kishi, are not Communists," Yoshio said. "Nor are they 'anti-American'—that cheapest of all jibes against people who won't be bullied or coaxed into agreeing with you! Even the Zengakuren aren't anti-American. But they are deeply distressed about American policies, and they do not trust Kishi. If the Americans allow themselves to be identified with Kishi, they may go down with him."

(2)

Yoshio was right about one thing. In the political typhoon that was blowing up in Japan, of which we were so far seeing only the first, wayward gusts, dislike, or lack of understanding, of American policy was constantly getting itself entangled with purely domestic Japanese issues. The chief domestic issue was the political future of the Japanese Prime Minister, Mr. Nobusuke Kishi.

Mr. Kishi was a little over sixty, which is quite young for a Japanese politician, and he had become Prime Minister with a

considerable handicap, for he had been a member of the Tojo
War Cabinet and after Japan's surrender he spent over three
years in the same jail where Tojo and other members of the
Cabinet and the armed forces were hanged. Mr. Kishi not only
escaped this fate, but was ultimately set free without even
standing trial, or being charged with anything whatsoever.
Nevertheless, in the eyes of a large minority of his own country-
men, which the turn of events or his own errors could easily
transform into a majority, he was a "war criminal" and a
"fascist."

Well aware of his handicap and ambitious to overcome it,
Mr. Kishi determined to make his political fortune by attacking
Japanese politicians who seemed overly subservient to the
United States. On those grounds, he helped drive his predecessor as Prime Minister from office. It was a well-worn tactic,
for his predecessor, Mr. Ichiro Hatoyama, had succeeded in
driving out *his* predecessor, Mr. Shigeru Yoshida, in exactly the
same way. Once he was installed as Prime Minister, Mr. Kishi
persuaded President Eisenhower to withdraw all American
soldiers from Japan. He also publicly opposed nuclear weapons
either for Japan or in American hands in Japan; suggested "a
collective security setup embracing both East and West" as a
long-range ideal; and proposed meanwhile to the United States
to amend its security treaty with Japan, to give Japan a right of
consultation on any move in the Pacific that America might
make, and a right of veto over the use of the American air
bases in Japan. He also suggested that the United States return Okinawa to Japanese jurisdiction.

The Americans agreed to rewrite the security treaty in Japan's
favor, because they were well aware of the existing danger that
Japan might drift into neutralism. They believed that Japan's
becoming neutral would be a terrible blow for the West. Some
Americans thought that Japan was going neutral anyway, and
that the best thing would be to get the American bases out of
there, but even they wanted to hang on to Okinawa. The other

school of though prevailed, and it was decided that revising the treaty to make important concessions to Japan would be better than trying to stick with the old treaty, which was being criticized by both the Government and the Opposition.

In the context of domestic Japanese politics, this was a gain for Mr. Kishi over the "anti-main stream" faction in Mr. Kishi's Liberal-Democratic party. To offset it, the anti-main-stream faction instantly began denigrating Mr. Kishi and criticizing the proposed revisions of the treaty as not going far enough. Mr. Ichiro Kono, a former supporter of the Prime Minister who had turned against him, said ten years was far too long for a security treaty, that it should run for only three years. Other Liberal-Democrats who assailed the treaty, but who were anxious lest Washington misconstrue their attacks on it, kept sending secret messages to the American side, saying that they were making a show of attacking the treaty only in order to bring Mr. Kishi down. Once he was forced to resign as Prime Minister, they said, they would faithfully carry out their obligations to the United States under the treaty, which as a matter of fact they much admired.

About this time, I had an interesting lunch with one of Kishi's critics from the anti-main-stream faction. He was a fattish, grayish man who looked not unlike a British Tory or an American Republican, but a Tory or a Republican as portrayed in *Pravda*. He dripped cynicism.

He began by remarking that the Japanese suicide-rate was now "back to normal," and explained that during the war suicides had fallen dramatically, to only around a thousand a year. The rate had now climbed to 25,000 or so, or to about a norm of one in every 4,000. "When not busily killing other people, we Japanese fall back on killing ourselves," he laughed.

When he began to speak about Kishi, however, he forgot to be cynical and flashed into anger. Kishi, he said, was a *ryuto-dabi*, a dragon with a snake's tail, meaning, "he started off all right, but he will end miserably." He complained bitterly of the

Prime Minister's ingratitude to persons like himself who had given Kishi the best years of their lives, as it were, and grumbled: "It is like having one's hand bitten by one's dog." Finally, he regained his manner of bright malice, and cheered himself up by prophesying that *"saru mo ki kara ochiru"*—"even a monkey sometimes falls out of a tree."

When Mr. Kishi did fall, a short time later, he received the further execrations of those within his own faction of the party who claimed he had promised each of them that he would succeed him as Prime Minister. One of the many dubious demimonde characters closely associated with the fringes of the Liberal-Democratic party, who also felt he had some sort of grievance against the fallen Prime Minister, stabbed Kishi in the buttocks at Kishi's own sayonara party. Another right-wing hoodlum had earlier stabbed an elderly Socialist in the courtyard of the Diet. These were the first political stabbings in Japan since the war, but they were not to be the last.

(3)

Dr. Adenauer visited Japan and drank seaweed soup with Mr. Kishi at an inn called the Palace of the Dragon King, overlooking pretty Lake Ashinoko. Dr. Adenauer addressed both Houses of the Diet. "We have both suffered heavy blows from fate, but we both begin to recover through our industriousness," said the German Chancellor, and asked for "a common effort to defend the values that give meaning to our existence." The Japanese, including the Liberal-Democrats, listened glumly to what many of them interpreted as an appeal to revive the old anti-Bolshevik pact with Germany, a pact that did Japan little good.

Nevertheless, Mr. Kishi boldly decided to link the revised security pact with the United States, which had become for him an almost fanatically cherished project, with the forth-coming visit to Japan by President Eisenhower.

The treaty was now under attack from without as well as from within. Khrushchev was keeping up an incessant barrage of notes and *démarches* against it, and coupling his criticisms with dire warnings about Japan's extreme vulnerability to nuclear attack in the missile age. Khrushchev's shrewd verbal punches did nothing to raise the morale of Mr. Kishi's dispirited Liberal-Democrats, already half-unnerved by the continual, growing parades outside the Diet.

Mr. Kishi decided on a tough answer to Mr. Khrushchev's scarcely veiled threats. Unfortunately, he did not take all of his own party into his confidence. The debate in the Diet on the revised security treaty had stretched out over a hundred days. Other parliamentary business had accumulated, and the Socialists hoped to end the Diet session without having the treaty passed, which would be a major setback for Mr. Kishi. This, however, was just what the Prime Minister was determined to avoid.

He proposed an extension of the Diet session, to allow further discussion on the merits and demerits of the treaty. Two hundred Socialist Dietmen squatted in the corridor outside the private office of the Speaker, to prevent his reaching the Chamber and putting Kishi's proposal to a vote. The Prime Minister sent for the police, and five hundred policemen entered the Diet and carried out the Socialists one by one. Some Socialists kicked and tried to bite the policemen. But a passage was cleared for Mr. Ichiro Kiyose, the seventy-six-year-old Speaker. However, when he entered the Chamber, one or two Socialists grabbed him from behind and attempted to prevent his occupying the Chair. They were hauled off by Diet guards, and the Speaker sank into his seat and in a half-fainting condition declared Diet business open.

The only business was supposed to be the Government mo-tion for extending the session. But, having got that safely passed, Mr. Kishi startled most of the Dietmen by proposing that the revised security treaty with the United States be forthwith passed, without further discussion. By a technicality of Diet procedure, the treaty would then become law on the very day President Eisenhower set foot in Tokyo. Yoshio Tanaka had told me: "Let the Americans beware of becoming identified with Kishi."

All the Socialists who were present in the Chamber, and more significantly for the Prime Minister's political future, twenty-seven members of his own party as well, walked out. The 259 Liberal-Democrats who remained passed the treaty by a standing vote a few minutes after midnight. It was not the most auspicious way to open what Mr. Kishi had called "a new era" between Japan and the United States.

A new slogan now appeared on the placards and was shouted by the thousands of demonstrators who regularly turned up around the Diet and outside the gates of the American Embassy. "Ike, don't come!"

"You said your demonstrators were not anti-American," I reminded Yoshio.

"I warned against risking identification between Kishi and Eisenhower. But they are not anti-American. Mingle with them and talk to them. You'll find them thoroughly friendly."

The Socialists had deserted the Diet, declaring the session extension illegal. The Socialist party leader, Mr. Inejiro Asanuma, led a huge crowd to the American Embassy. Mr. Asanuma was admitted, but his followers had the gates shut in their faces. They beat their fists against the bars. Then a member of the Embassy staff who had been out to lunch walked through their ranks. The crowd fell silent and patiently waited until a Marine guard had opened the gate to let him in and then closed and locked it again. When it was securely fastened, the demonstrators resumed dutifully beating the bars and chanting: "Ike, don't come!"

Mr. Asanuma asked that President Eisenhower's visit to Japan be postponed, because "it will only provoke the Japanese people, already infuriated by the passing of the security pact." But the Americans preferred to leave any change of plan to the Japanese Government, who had issued the invitation. And Mr. Kishi declared that "the greater part of the Japanese people will welcome Eisenhower from the bottom of their hearts." He did not say what the lesser part might do.

Demonstrations were now going on all the time. Group after group came to chant slogans and wave red flags outside the American Embassy's gates; they also squatted twelve deep in the roadway under the wall around the ambassador's house. They never failed to rise politely to their feet when Americans or other foreigners came picking their way through the crowds. But they were also inexorable in the pressure of their stylized chanting. "Ike, don't come." "Yankee, go home."

Vast mechanical voices filled the air around the besieged Diet, which the Socialists boycotted but where the Liberal-Democrats still forlornly sat, day after day. The demonstrators had filled the area with loud-speaker vans. They also marched round and round the Diet compound with their banners, and squatted as a solid mass of dogged resistance in the road. A special target was the Prime Minister's official house, directly across the street from the Diet, at the top of a steep hill running down to the American Embassy. Crowds swarmed outside Mr. Kishi's closed gates, clambered onto the roofs of his outhouses, and several times dropped into his courtyard and made sorties for his front door. After this had happened a number of times, the courtyard was pumped solid with policemen. Mr. Kishi's private home in the suburb of Shibuya, seven or eight miles across town, was even more closely besieged. The demonstrators crowded the narrow streets around it, filled every surrounding garden, and kept up a barrage of chanting and singing both day and night. Mr. Kishi's neighbors wished that almost anyone else were Prime Minister. The police added to the racket, roaring up and down continually on noisy motorbicycles and scattering huge police trucks about the surrounding roads. They presented a brisk appearance of being on the point of making a decisive move, but somehow they never did. Mr. Kishi himself seemed to be spending his days and nights dodging furtively from point to point, a zigzagging target constantly on the move. It was never very clear whether he was in the Diet, at his official residence, or concealed in his Shibuya home. Among his own Liberal-Democrats, a muttering began to grow that he ought to resign. There was, however, a notable lack of clarity as to what would happen if he did.

Equally devious in their wanderings about Tokyo became the big, chocolate-colored buses that took the children of American airmen to and from their various schools. The bus drivers were anxious not to cross the paths of demonstrating crowds, but the crowds became increasingly difficult to avoid as the numbers of the demonstrators steadily mounted. The American bases in the Tokyo region finally went on an almost permanent "condition green," meaning that the Americans should not venture out at all. The typhoon was blowing strongly now. Yet the crowds stayed polite, even friendly, to foreigners, including Americans. "Yankee, go home!" they cried—and grinned. Some, indeed, had never seen "Yankees" before; the organizers of the giant demonstrations were busily pulling in recruits even from remote country districts. American women were apt to be followed in Tokyo streets by wispy-bearded, rheumaticky farmers, as thin as sticks, in a state of manifest astonishment and ogle-eyed wonder: they had never before seen women with blonde hair. The recruits also included gaunt Buddhist priests, wearing saffron robes and banging rather hysterically at hand drums and gongs. But this motley multitude was exceedingly well organized. It marched with precision and was herded, as if by sheep dogs, by brisk and alert young men, who made it do their will by shouting through hand microphones and blowing shrilly on whistles. The young male students and the college girls brought to a high pitch of perfection a sort of snake dance in which they linked arms and pranced up and down and curvetted in and out along the streets, crying: "Washo! Washo!" Podgy Socialist Dietmen, wearing scarlet sashes and smoking cigarettes, looked on approvingly as these disciplined hosts, with their tall banners and their placards, swung past. And every television screen in Japan seemed to show nothing but marching Tokyo demonstrators.

Twenty thousand people went to Tokyo airport to challenge James Hagerty, the Press Secretary of President Eisenhower, who was flying in from Okinawa to see what sort of reception might await the President, and who planned to fly from Tokyo to Alaska to report to his chief. The crowd carried banners reading: "Hagerty Go to the Hell," "We Dislike Ike," and "Ike and U-2 Not to Japan." Right before Mr. Hagerty's plane landed, fighting broke out in various parts of the airport between the banner carriers and members of the Great Japan Patriotic party, who hit the demonstrators with Rising Sun flagpoles. Meanwhile, fifteen hundred students chose to squat across the only roadway out of the airport, 600 yards from the terminal building, and await Mr. Hagerty there. They did not believe that they had much chance of intercepting him; they expected that he would choose to elude them by using the Marine helicopter that had already passed over their heads, bearing the American ambassador to his meeting with the President's Press Secretary. But they were, nevertheless, determined to leave no road unblocked. If Mr. Hagerty did dodge them, he would find other demonstrators outside the Embassy.

The American ambassador was Douglas MacArthur II, the nephew of General MacArthur. A courageous and even pugnacious man, he saw the demonstrations as only an incident in a continuing struggle for the soul of Japan. He could not conceive that it could be in Japan's best interest to be neutral, especially at the behest of street crowds. As for the revised treaty with the United States which the demonstrators so passionately condemned, Mr. MacArthur could point out with perfect truth that it bound the United States to respect Japanese wishes, and not the other way around. The ambassador, however, underestimated the feeling of doubt about the worth of American words which the U-2 affair had aroused, and he overestimated the value of the support that the Japanese Liberal-Democrats appeared to have. People voted for them at election time rather than for Socialists, but were not otherwise well disposed to them.

MacArthur and Hagerty conferred as soon as the plane landed, and they decided to drive into Tokyo in the ambassador's official car, a black Cadillac, in order to see the route that President Eisenhower was due to travel nine days later with the Emperor of Japan seated beside him. Followed by two carloads of secret servicemen, the Cadillac drove off at high speed. It came up from the underpass on to the road leading out of the airport and braked sharply at sight of the great mass of students squatting in its way. The two other cars bumped to a halt behind it.

Other cars filled with Japanese and foreign reporters had followed in hot pursuit of Hagerty and MacArthur. In an instant, a colossal traffic jam locked them all into immobility. Newspapermen leaped from their stalled cars and ran forward to reach the halted Cadillac. Back at the airport terminal, the pilot of the ambassador's Marine helicopter was made aware that something had gone wrong; the helicopter rose into sight in the pale sky with a whirr and approached the melee like an inquisitive grasshopper. The large forces of Japanese policemen at the terminal continued, however, to devote all their energies to separating demonstrators from members of the Great Japan Patriotic party.

For a paralyzed instant, the students watched the Cadillac bear down upon them, and saw it swerve and brake. Then, with triumphant whoops, they threw themselves upon it. They beat upon its glossy surface with their fists and their banner poles, and succeeded in cracking its windshield. They laid hands on it

and rocked it to and fro in a quickening rhythm, chanting:
"Go-home-Ha-ga-tee!" Trapped inside, but with the doors
locked, Mr. MacArthur, Mr. Hagerty, and President Eisenhower's Appointments Secretary, Mr. Thomas Stephens, sat smoking cigarettes. Mr. Hagerty after a while boldly produced a tiny
camera and took pictures of students who had their faces
pressed against the windows. A demonstrators' sound truck,
which had given the students aid and comfort during their wait,
contained some Socialist party members. When the rhythmic
rocking of the ambassador's car seemed to be getting so intense
that the car was in danger of capsizing, one of them clambered
onto the roof of the Cadillac and brought the students under
control. They stopped rocking the Cadillac, and took instead to
singing the *Internationale*.

Yoshio Tanaka was quite right that the demonstrators lacked
the basic impulse towards violence. There was some hysteria,
but no anger. The secret servicemen managed after a while to
cordon themselves around the Cadillac, their backs to it so
that they faced the crowd, and gently pressed the students away
a little. One of the students inadvertently stood on the toe of
a secret serviceman; he immediately apologized. Henry Taylor,
the young American journalist who a few months later was
killed in the Congo, collided with a demonstrator as they both
rushed towards the Cadillac. Taylor had a button torn off his
coat, and a demonstrator politely spent ten minutes helping
Henry find it. American reporters and other foreigners who got
swallowed up in the vast crowd found Japanese obligingly clearing a path for them. Mr. Hagerty later said he believed that,
had the crowd been able to open the locked doors of the
Cadillac, they would have killed him. There seems to be no
real basis for this belief.

Several helicopters were now churning round in the sky directly above the debacle. The Marine helicopter several times
flew very low over the heads of the people, in a dangerous-
looking sideways drift, apparently while the pilot tried to esti-

mate his chances of landing alongside the Cadillac, or else of
lowering a rope to rescue the three occupants of the car. But in
coming so low it set up great storms of dust, and also irritated
the crowd with its loud roaring, so that in the end the demonstrators drove it off by throwing stones and broken bits of flagpole at it. Other helicopters, belonging to enterprising Japanese
newspapers and filled with photographers, also churned round
in slow circles overhead and added to the confusion.

The Japanese police made their appearance on the scene after
seventeen minutes had passed. Two thousand of them marched
the 600 yards from the terminal building in slow and stately
fashion. They advanced across the grass in a solid column, wearing white cotton gloves and bearing aloft yellow flags, resembling tourist-bus flags, carrying their squad numbers. They
began very slowly to make the demonstrators move aside so that
the Cadillac could inch forward until it had got nearer to a flat,
grass-covered space, which the police cleared and then blocked
off so that the Marine helicopter could land. All this took a
long time. Then, still protected by the secret servicemen, Mr.
MacArthur, Mr. Hagerty, and Mr. Stephens got out of the
Cadillac and headed for the helicopter that rested on the grass
50 feet away. They walked; they did not run. The students,
hoarse from continuous shouting, merely look on. They had
held the three Americans in detention for seventy minutes. In
a final bit of drama, a secret serviceman lost his balance as the
helicopter rose up, and tumbled six feet to the ground. He appeared unhurt.

Mr. Hagerty did not manage to meet Mr. Kishi, who was
kept from leaving his Shibuya home by dogged crowds. The
President's Press Secretary left Tokyo under cover of dusk the
following evening, and flew out of Japan from the American
air base at Tachikawa, where months before I had watched
demonstrators pull up the base fence and the Japanese police
patiently replant it. Before he left Tokyo, Mr. Hagerty observed that he didn't think "the Japanese people will permit

President Eisenhower to be treated the way we were." This implied an intention to let the Presidential visit proceed. Some had imagined that Hagerty would make his own rough treatment a reason for cancelling a project which looked dangerous and which had become embarrassing. Three former Japanese Prime Ministers urged that the visit should be postponed, and that Kishi should resign. Mr. Kishi's response was to let it be known that President Eisenhower would be protected not only by 25,000 policemen but also by 50,000 students guaranteed to be pro-American. It was also hinted from the Kishi camp that nothing could happen to President Eisenhower with Emperor Hirohito by his side.

Not much more than twenty-four hours before President Eisenhower was to land in Tokyo, a determined assault was made on the Prime Minister's official residence, across the street from the Diet. For the first time, policemen used their sticks with vigor on the Zengakuren students, throwing them out of Kishi's courtyard and then pursuing them down the steep hill towards the American Embassy. Shortly afterwards, the police were busy arresting right-wing fanatics who turned up at the Diet wearing black shirts. They had rammed their automobiles into the Zengakuren students grouped around the Diet's south gate; then the blackshirts had leaped out of the cars and begun clubbing heads.

While the police arrested the students' attackers, the students set to work on the wooden barricades and barbed wire with which the Diet was now encircled. They cut the wire with pliers, and smashed down the barricades. Any police who attempted to stop them were stoned. There were girls as well as men in the crowd of student demonstrators, and I asked one who reminded me of O-Sei, the girl I had met in Nara, what they thought they were doing. "Preserving democracy," she answered promptly. "It is very undemocratic of the police to prevent us from entering the Diet compound."

"What would you do if they let you inside?"

"Burn down the Diet, to show our contempt for bourgeois politics."

The crowd demonstrating outside the Diet was now so huge that it had ceased to be merely a student or even a Sohyo, labor union, affair. The students spearheaded the attacks, but in the crowd were also schoolteachers and even professors. One of the professors, though I did not know it at the time, was Professor Kamba, who months before had complained that the Zengakuren had captured his daughter's interests. He had changed his mind, decided his daughter and the Zengakuren were right, and had joined in the shouts against Kishi.

To replace the smashed wooden barricades, the police brought up heavy trucks and posted them in front of each of the Diet's seven gates. The students tied ropes to the trucks and began hauling them away, and the police turned hoses on the students who were doing this. Other students ripped down a baseball net that had been put up to catch rocks that were thrown into the Diet compound, and then charged through the gap they had made. The policemen guarding the spot fell back inside the compound, pursued by students. Then they re-formed, and countercharged. The students were forced back. One girl fell, and did not rise again. She wore a yellow jersey, and black slacks. It was Michiko Kamba. She had been trampled to death.

Wounded students and policemen were carried into the basement of the Diet. Others crawled about unattended. Ambulances screamed up and down between the Diet and nearby hospitals. The Diet courtyard was a littered battlefield. Fighting continued. The students had been driven back into the streets, but they went on throwing stones. Inside the Diet compound, people walking about would collapse suddenly, hit by a stone. Outside, truck loud-speakers were hoarsely bawling the *Internationale*.

The students were still trying to move the trucks. They managed to turn one over, and set fire to it. This seemed an excellent plan to them. They promptly set fire to the other six. The police hoses failed to put out the fires, or to quell the students. The students became black silhouettes, dancing and shouting "Washo!" around the flames. The glare lit up the night sky over the pale white Diet building. The police sent for more trucks. The students seized them as they arrived, and set fire to them also. After a while, ten, fifteen, seventeen trucks were burning all around the Diet.

Across the street, the Prime Minister was holding a Cabinet meeting. The flames of the seventeen burning police trucks luridly lit up the countenances of the seventeen Cabinet Ministers. The United States Government, said Mr. Kishi, had notified him that postponement of the President's trip could be requested by Japan up to the time the President left Manila. After that, it would be very difficult to postpone the trip. What did they advise? Mr. Hayato Ikeda, who was destined to succeed Mr. Kishi as Prime Minister, thought that putting off the visit would be "bowing to Communist pressure." The others were not so sure. The Director of Police cautiously pointed out that there was "a limit to the guarantees the police can give concerning the protection of the President." These words would have frightened a less assured man than Kishi. However, he promised to think the matter over. He was not given much time. Early next morning, he received a visit from an Imperial chamberlain. The chamberlains had decided that the Emperor must "not be put in a position where he might be involved in politics." This meant that Emperor Hirohito would not ride with President Eisenhower through the streets of Tokyo. But not until the afternoon did Mr. Kishi announce to the Cabinet that Japan was requesting postponement of the President's visit.

The demonstrators were, however, determined to continue their agitation against the security treaty with the United

States. Their numbers had now swollen to almost a quarter of
a million. Snake-dancing and waving banners, they choked the
streets. The police had no control over them, beyond prevent-
ing them from breaking into such places as the Diet, Kishi's
house, the American Embassy, and police headquarters near the
Imperial moat. But though the demonstrators continued to mass
outside those places, they no longer made any serious attempts
to enter them. They were content to chant: "Kishi must go!"
and "Kishi, kill yourself!" When an obscure mechanic with
right-wing sympathies suddenly produced a knife and, in the
still-littered courtyard of the Diet, stabbed an elderly Socialist
Dietman who was collecting signatures against the treaty, the
demonstrators did not become angrier; they seemed shocked
but sobered. One girl was dead already. The demonstrators
decorated the Diet gate where she had died with an enormous
wreath, and said Buddhist prayers for Michiko Kamba. This
was the day President Eisenhower was to have landed in Tokyo.
The President spent the day, instead, on Okinawa, closely
guarded by Marines against a comparative handful of Okinawans shouting for their land back and for an end to American bases. Most Okinawans did not see the President at all.

Mr. Kishi sat quietly at home watching baseball on television. The Chunichi Dragons beat the Tokyo Giants 3-1. At
midnight, when the security treaty automatically became law,
the Prime Minister nibbled a sandwich. The Japanese newspapers were calling for his resignation. They had condemned
him for passing the security treaty through the Diet, and for
clinging to his plan to have President Eisenhower visit Japan
despite the demonstrations. Now they said that by asking the
President to postpone his visit Kishi had lost face himself and
had made Japan lose face also, and ought to be held to account
for this.

But the typhoon had ceased to blow. Exhaustion had set in.
The demonstrators, their fury expended, melted away. In mild
weather, students and other people strolled in the streets around

the Diet. The young men went coatless, in white shirts, and the girls wore summer dresses. The streets were again passable, and the Diet no longer under siege. A solitary Diet guard stood at the gate where thousands had fought and fled, where Michiko Kamba had died. He made no attempt to keep people out. Very few seemed to want to enter.

XIV

TOKYO:

AFTER THE TYPHOON

*At their meetings nothing is heard but cries,
shouts and confusion.*
JAMES I ON HIS PARLIAMENT

I HAD GONE to a Tokyo Western-style hotel to meet a *gaijin*, and when I was ready to leave I found Sano-san, my driver, deep in conversation with a countrified-looking man, who seemed bewildered and whom he was reassuring.

"This is my mother's cousin, Mr. Katawara, from southern Kyushu," said Sano-san, as we bowed and exchanged name cards. "He is a delegate to the Liberal-Democratic convention."

The Liberal-Democrats I knew were meeting in Tokyo, to choose a new party president. Mr. Kishi was the party president, but his doom was sealed, and he was to be replaced. The new party president would also succeed Mr. Kishi as Prime Minister. The convention was, therefore, an important affair.

But Mr. Katawara did not seem at all to relish having been caught up in it. He gave the impression of a plain man who had been unwittingly involved in great affairs and now wished himself elsewhere. It was hot in Tokyo that summer, and very frequently he mopped his brow with a big handkerchief. Sano-san encouraged him to retell his story, and conveyed it to me in portions, as his mother's cousin narrated it.

"I belong to one of the factions of the party. As you know, there are eight. My faction bought me an air ticket to get here. But before I could board the plane, a *hakoshi* from another faction proposed I take the train instead. He said all meals

286

would be paid for and there would be plenty of sake. With all that has been going on up here, and everything in the melting pot as it were, what after all does it matter which faction pays one's fare? Besides, this *hakoshi* is a man I have an *on* to."

"What is a *hakoshi?*" I asked Sano-san, and he replied, grinning: "A delegate 'rustler'; he hijacks delegates from other factions for *his* faction."

"But hardly was I on the train," Mr. Katawara continued, "when another *hakoshi* got into the seat beside me, and urged me to break my journey at Atami. He said he didn't have to tell me what a pleasant place Atami was, and, of course, he would see to it that I didn't lose by it. 'Besides,' he said, 'the convention will easily get along without you in the early stages. Nothing really important happens for at least two days; and just so long as you are there for the final ballot for the party posts, you will have done your duty, so how about it?'"

"What happened at Atami?" Sano-san asked him.

"I had a night of love," said Mr. Katawara, with a broad smirk. "They don't exaggerate about the girls there. . . . But also, in the morning on the lacquer table with my breakfast there was an *o-chugen*, a midsummer gift, you know. A cake box that didn't have a cake in it; instead it was stuffed with yen notes.

"Well, that was all right. I pocketed it and off I went to catch the train, as arranged. But imagine my embarrassment when I found waiting for me, here at Tokyo station, a representative of my own faction, which had bought my air ticket in the first place! They had somehow got wind of my being on the train, and had come to reproach me. I had a red face, I can tell you. There was nothing I could say. I humbly agreed to do anything he asked, so he got me in a cab, and brought me here."

"And now," Sano-san concluded on behalf of his mother's cousin, "his own faction counts him *kanzume* once more: in the can for them. They have taken over the entire hotel, you know, for *their* delegates, so they reckon he is quite safe, and won't be lured away again."

"But why a Western-style hotel?"

"Ah, all the factions are booking Western-style hotels, this convention. They prefer proper walls to Japanese paper walls, which tend to leak secrets to eavesdroppers."

The convention itself was held in a large Toyko hall. It was decorated with large trees, gay with white and pink artificial blossoms, from whose branches hung large imitation dice, presumably to indicate the sporting nature of the event. In between the numerous speeches, to which the delegates listened while eating out of wooden lunch boxes balanced on their knees, the public-address system dispensed soothing music— "Autumn Leaves," played by the Kostelanetz orchestra, was one tune I recognized.

The eight factions were each supported by various industrial and commercial combinations, who were reported to have spent about four million dollars in all to obtain backing among the delegates for their candidates for party posts. Several of the factions were trying very hard to put together a stop-Ikeda ticket; but this was proving difficult, since Mr. Ikeda was reported to have the confidence of two banks, a major shipbuilder, a powerful mutual trust, one of Japan's most famous *zaibatsu* firms, and also such votes as Mr. Kishi himself was in a position to throw that way. Mr. Ikeda, therefore, won the party presidency on the second ballot by a handsome majority, to which one rival, by generously agreeing to withdraw from the race, contributed a block of votes said to have cost $280,000 to scrape together. Mr. Ikeda said, amid *banzais*, that it was only too true that he had actively desired the post of party president; he wished to apologize to the convention for his unworthy stubbornness and disgraceful persistence. But he promised to adopt a low posture henceforth. "I have always enjoyed golf, and geishas," said Mr. Ikeda frankly. "But these are far removed from the lives of the common people of Japan, and from now on I am going to live like a common man."

Then all the delegates drove from the hall—through 30,000 demonstrators who had been quickly reassembled, as it seemed from nowhere, to shout "Down with Ikeda!"—to Mr. Kishi's official residence across the street from the Diet. There were gaily striped tents on the lawn; all security precautions had been relaxed or even abandoned; and foaming beer was being served in large glass tankards. Mr. Kishi raised his glass to call for three cheers for Mr. Ikeda. Then he walked alone into his dining room, where a man called Taisuke Aramaki, one of the hangers-on of the party who belonged on the fringes with the *hakoshi* and so forth, was waiting for him, with a knife. Mr. Kishi turned to run, and Aramaki stabbed him in the buttock. Dripping with blood, Mr. Kishi was carried to a car and thence to the hospital.

The reason for the stabbing, though obscure, seemed to be connected with pledges about the succession to the Premiership which Mr. Kishi was alleged to have given not just to one, but to several, party members besides Mr. Ikeda. From his hospital bed, Mr. Kishi resigned, along with his entire cabinet. One of his first callers was the Socialist leader, Mr. Inejiro Asanuma, who went to express his sympathy, and also to tell him that the Socialists were in a mood to let bygones be bygones, and to cease their boycott of the Diet.

(2)

Jane and I attended the wedding of Yoshio Tanaka and Yumiko Showa. Yoshio was such an unpredictable young man that we did not know quite what to expect. The wedding was just as surprising as we had thought it might be, but not at all for the reasons we had imagined.

As his *nakodo*, or go-between, Yoshio chose the film producer.

He did not want to have a *nakodo* at all, regarding such a functionary as purely feudal. Yumiko said it was as well to keep on the right side of the film producer, and anyway they had to have a *nakodo*, for how else could they have a *miai?*

Yoshio said if there were going to be such things as a *miai* in his life, then the whole thing was off. The *miai* was not only feudal; it was a gross violation of human rights, and probably contrary to the Constitution.

Yumiko said if there were not a *miai*, or formal meeting of the couple with their respective parents, supervised by the *nakodo*, she would never be able to face her mother again. Her mother, she was aware, was an old-fashioned woman, and Yoshio probably had no time for her. All the same, she was her mother, and if they were married she would be Yoshio's mother-in-law. If her mother could not be humored to the extent of a *miai*, then the whole thing was indeed off, and she now knew what she had always suspected, that Yoshio was just an unfeeling Japanese man.

Yoshio, who in fact was rather fond of Yumiko's mother, and who also knew that his own mother would mourn for the rest of her life if there were not a *miai*—he did not care a fig what his father thought or felt—sullenly agreed. All the same, as a last gesture of defiance, he turned up at the *miai* drunk. The *miai* was held at a famous old Japanese restaurant in Tokyo. After everyone else had arrived, and bowed very low, and eyed each other warily, and relapsed into awkward silence, Yoshio strode into the room. Drunk. He was red-faced, his eyes rolled, and he had developed an awkward tendency to make large, violent, uncertain gestures that gravely imperiled the paper screen doors and walls. He explained, in an unnecessarily loud voice, that he had arrived drunk because a wife-to-be, instead of being lulled into a false sense of security by her fiancé's being constantly and artificially on his best behavior, ought to be allowed to see the very worst she could expect. "To put on humble airs and adopt a low posture," said Yoshio, "to try to pretend that one has no vices, is feudal. I am a modern man and you must take me for what I am. Frequently I drink."

He was disconcerted, yet heartened, to find that this bravado had quite the opposite effect from what he had expected. The film producer, who had privately concluded that although good-looking Yoshio was a bit of a prig, immediately warmed to him. Yumiko's mother said, timidly, that it would be very surprising if a Japanese man did not drink. Yoshio's mother said, daringly, that there were worse things than drink, and gave her husband a meaningful glance. Ignoring it, Mr. Tanaka looked on his son a little more approvingly than he had ever done before, his thoughts moving on the same track as the film producer's.

Yumiko said: "Very well, Yoshio; you have made your point. When you come home at night, drunk, I will not jump on you hysterically, asking where you have been or with whom. But I won't strip off your clothes, either, or put you tenderly to bed, as a well-disciplined Japanese wife is supposed to, for that would be feudal and, more important, it is the sort of thing that only spoils a husband. No. If you come home drunk, after midnight, I'll let you in; but if you fall on the floor and go to sleep there, I'll leave you and return to my own warm bed. Now, do sit down and stop waving your arms about. We have to discuss all the arrangements for the wedding."

Knowing nothing of all this, Jane and I were startled to learn that Yoshio had meekly agreed to a wedding with Shinto rites, and that he was willing to stand with bowed head and meekly clasped hands while the *nakodo* delivered the traditional speech. Yumiko stood as meekly at his side, wearing a wedding kimono, a great black wig gleaming with oil, and with her face painted the traditional dead white. Moreover, Yoshio's mother and father were both present, and not only them, but also the Hayamas, the Katamas, and others of our neighbors in Hata-

Yuguri. And, to our further surprise, they all seemed to be on good terms.

After the film producer in his role of *nakodo* had formally introduced Mr. and Mrs. Tanaka, Junior, to the guests, and had gone on to make some pretty broad wedding jokes in the traditional style, Yumiko slipped away, and presently returned a modern Japanese woman, in a smart Western going-away costume. They were going to the Inland Sea for their honeymoon.

"And now it is all over?" I said to Yoshio. "All those noisy demonstrations. And that girl's death— What was it all *for*, Yoshio?"

"It is not over," said Yoshio scornfully. "We still have a long way to go, in Japan. We are still fighting feudalism."

"Wanting to burn down the Diet because you can't get your way strikes me as just childish, not feudal."

"You don't understand the Japanese character. Kishi should not have forced the security treaty through the Diet. It was what we call the tyranny of the majority. By being so contemptuous of the Opposition, he made them lose face in an intolerable way. In Japan, face is very important. And it is not finished yet. Now the right wing has lost face. The feudal elements also find the situation intolerable. They will do something, you will see. That is what I meant when I said that in Japan we are still fighting feudalism."

"Ah, stop talking politics!" cried Yumiko. She came up to him, and put her arm in his. She looked up at him, smiling. "You see, I'm not a demure Japanese woman. I embrace you in public."

Yoshio looked down at her, and was suddenly all eagerness to start off on his honeymoon.

We had loaned them our car to take them to the railway station, with Sano-san to drive it. To make it a proper wedding party, Jane had conspired to have some old shoes tied to the rear bumper. We found Sano-san busily untying them, and angrily throwing them into the trunk.

"But you are spoiling our surprise by taking them off!" Jane cried.

"I will not drive a car with shoes tied behind it," said Sano-san, half-weeping. "I would rather die—or kill someone. It is too great a loss of face."

Yoshio knew what he was talking about when he said that face was all-important in Japan.

(3)

The right-wing extremists had not been nearly numerous enough to attempt to counter the great demonstrations around the Diet and against Kishi. There were about 11,000 of them, and they were deeply divided among themselves, some simply wanting to restore Emperor worship, and others, more Western-minded, wanting somehow to associate such a restoration with Hitler's swastika flag. But they all had sharp knives, and were quick to use them.

Inejiro Asanuma was fond of debating with his political opponents. During the demonstrations, he wanted to debate "American imperialism" with the American ambassador, Mr. MacArthur. After Hayato Ikeda replaced Mr. Kishi as Prime Minister of Japan, Asanuma longed to debate with Ikeda. He got his chance whan an interparty debate was arranged. It was to take place in the Hibiya Hall in Tokyo and to be watched and heard on several million television screens. The televiewers got much more than they bargained for.

The front seats in the hall were filled with teen-agers belonging to the Great Japan Patriotic party. While Asanuma spoke, they threw leaflets at him and shouted: "Shut up, Communist!" Mr. Asanuma, who weighed well over 200 pounds and looked rather like a *sumo* wrestler, ignored them and went on criticizing the security treaty with the United States, developing his argument very much along the lines of the conversations with Yoshio Tanaka that I have described in this book.

Suddenly, a slender seventeen-year-old youth called Otoya Yamaguchi appeared on the stage where Mr. Ikeda was sitting and Mr. Asanuma was speaking. He rushed forward as if he were in a football game, and hurtled himself against Mr. Asanuma's bulk. With both hands he gripped a samurai sword with a twelve-inch blade, and he *slid* it into Mr. Asanuma's abdomen. Then he pulled it out, took a fresh grip on it, and stabbed Asanuma again, this time in the chest. The television cameras caught and relayed it all.

The leader of the Great Japan Patriotic party, a man called Bin Akao who reportedly worships Adolf Hitler as well as the Japanese Emperor, carefully explained that the young man had lately been expelled from his party. However, he described Mr. Asanuma's killing as "a heaven-sent punishment." The youth told the police he had hoped to be able to kill Mr. Sanzo Nosaka, of the Japan Communist party, and Mr. Takeshi Kobayashi, of the Japan Teachers' Union, as well as Mr. Asanuma.

Mr. Asanuma's Socialist colleagues accused the conservatives of encouraging, or even hiring, murder thugs. Mr. Ikeda and the Liberal-Democrats denied the charge, and said the recent mass demonstrations had inspired this renewal of violence in Japan. My own view was that Yoshio had been right in prophesying that the price of face would continue to prove high.

In his detention cell in Tokyo, Otoya Yamaguchi used tooth powder mixed with water to paint on the wall the mystic words: "Seven lives for my country; 10,000 years for the Emperor." Then he turned his bed sheets into a rope and hanged himself from the light fixture. He had, it seemed, been conveniently lodged in the only detention cell in Japan with a light fixture strong enough for such a purpose.

From the left, there came a slap at the Emperor and his family. A Tokyo magazine published a short story that depicted an imaginary revolution of the future, in which the Imperial family were one by one taken out and executed in a public square. Whereupon, another seventeen-year-old youth who also had an association with the Great Japan Patriotic party went to work with *his* knife. He failed to find the writer of the story or the publisher of the magazine, but contented himself with wounding the magazine publisher's wife, and stabbing a house-maid to death.

As Ambassador MacArthur had said, the great demonstrations were only an incident in the struggle for Japan.

(4)

Sano-san drove us for the last time to the airport. He had for-given us for the wedding-shoes episode, and was full of anxious solicitude that *we* should not lose face in those last hours in Japan.

"You have your passports?"

"Check. What's more, they're new ones, and full of brand-new visas."

"Your alien registration cards, for turning over to emigration authorities?"

"Check."

"Your health forms, duly filled in?"

"Stop worrying, Sano-san. We have everything."

"I shall not be able to accompany you through customs and emigration, to make sure you are all right."

"You don't have to. We have our tickets, passports, every-thing. It's absolutely all right. We're just awfully sorry to be leaving Japan."

"Yes," said Sano-san, sympathetically. He could appreciate

that. To be a *gaijin* was bad enough. To be a *gaijin*, and to have to leave Japan and go and dwell in outer darkness, far from Japanese culture, was surely a dreadful fate. I could see that he genuinely felt sorry for us. And, as a matter of fact, we were feeling rather sorry for ourselves.

He came with us as far as he could, to the head of the stairs that led down to customs, emigration, the departing passengers' lounge, the waiting plane. And there, at the head of the stairs, we said our good-bys.

Customs inspection was purely nominal. Our bags were briskly ticketed, and taken away. On to emigration.

Health: check. Alien registration cards: check.

The emigration clerk, a spectacled youth with gaunt cheeks, wearing a peaked cap, peered closely at Jane's passport.

"But this is a new passport?"

"Yes; we required several new visas, so, for convenience, they gave us new passports."

"But the new passports do not state when you arrived in Japan."

"No; you will find that information in our alien registration cards."

"So I have already observed. Nevertheless, the date is not stated in your new passports. Do you have your old passports with you?"

"No; they are with our other belongings, which have already left Japan, by sea."

"In that case," said the spectacled youth, "I am afraid you will not become air-borne today. The matter will have to be investigated."

"What! But that's ridiculous! We have our air tickets. The plane is waiting. You cannot hold up all those other passengers —if you will only call up the Hata-Yuguri ward office and check with the alien registration people there—I never heard anything so ridiculous in my life—"

"Adopt a low posture!" Jane hissed in my ear.

"Unless," said the clerk, suavely, "you write out a full apology. If you will do that, the matter may be overlooked. Of course, I can make no promises."

"I won't write out an apology!" I cried. "Why, I've *never* had to write an apology, all the time I have been in Japan! I was too clever for—I mean, I just didn't have to, that's all. And to have to write an apology now, when we're on the very point of leaving! I won't do it. The loss of face would be too much.

"What," I asked him sullenly, "do you wish me to say?"

"I shall dictate, if you wish. Please commence: 'I wish to apologize humbly for my grave oversight in not being furnished with all correct documents necessary for my family and myself to leave Japan. I realize that this puts the emigration department to serious inconvenience, and I crave forgiveness for my stupidity, and ask that on this one occasion it be overlooked. . . .'

"I think that will do," said the emigration clerk, generously. "Yes, I am sure that will be perfectly all right."

He gave back our passports, our health cards, our air tickets. He bowed, very gravely, and out of habit I found myself bowing back.

"*Sayonara!*" he said.

(5)

The jet liner took off at a steep angle. We cut, slanting, through a cloud, and suddenly we were above it and in a breathtaking world.

The white cloud ceiling had become a gigantic floor, which stretched, smooth and level, far to the horizon. It looked as if we could have got out of the plane, and walked on it. And there, far away across that shining white flat surface, resembling a vast floor in a fantastic dream, the white cone of Mount Fuji shone above the cloud. It was the perfect component of this Dali dream. All it needed was a red *torii* gate beside it, standing on the cloud floor.

And then in the swift turnabout of the plane the sacred mountain was gone, and all of that marvelous country.

INDEX

i

INDEX

INDEX

ALEXANDER CAMPBELL was born in Edinburgh in 1912 and was educated at Edinburgh University. He worked as an editorial writer on a Scottish newspaper until 1937, when he moved to South Africa, where he eventually became the Johannesburg bureau chief for *Time* and *Life*. He was transferred to New Delhi in 1954. Following these assignments, he wrote *The Heart of Africa* (1954) and *The Heart of India* (1958). His present book on Japan is the result of a four-year tour of duty as Tokyo bureau chief for *Time* and *Life*. Shortly after completing *The Heart of Japan* he resigned from *Time* and *Life* to become Washington correspondent for *The Economist* (London). Mr. Campbell is married and is the father of three children.

August 1961

A NOTE ON THE TYPE

THIS BOOK is set in Electra, a Linotype face designed by the late W. A. Dwiggins (1880–1956). This face cannot be classified as either modern or old-style. It is not based on any historical model, nor does it echo any particular period or style. It avoids the extreme contrasts between thick and thin elements that mark most modern faces, and attempts to give a feeling of fluidity, power, and speed.

Composed, printed, and bound by
Kingsport Press, Inc., Kingsport, Tenn.
Paper manufactured by
S. D. Warren Company, Boston.
Typography and binding design based on originals by
W. A. DWIGGINS